GENDER AND JUSTICE IN MULTICULTURAL LIBERAL STATES

Gender and Justice in Multicultural Liberal States

MONIQUE DEVEAUX

OXFORD

UNIVERSITY PRESS

OXFORD
UNIVERSITY PRESS

Great Clarendon Street, Oxford OX2 6DP

Oxford University Press is a department of the University of Oxford.
It furthers the University's objective of excellence in research, scholarship,
and education by publishing worldwide in

Oxford New York

Auckland Cape Town Dar es Salaam Hong Kong Karachi
Kuala Lumpur Madrid Melbourne Mexico City Nairobi
New Delhi Shanghai Taipei Toronto

With offices in

Argentina Austria Brazil Chile Czech Republic France Greece
Guatemala Hungary Italy Japan Poland Portugal Singapore
South Korea Switzerland Thailand Turkey Ukraine Vietnam

Oxford is a registered trade mark of Oxford University Press
in the UK and in certain other countries

Published in the United States
by Oxford University Press Inc., New York

British Library Cataloguing in Publication Data

Data available

Library of Congress Cataloging in Publication Data

Deveaux, Monique.
Gender and justice in multicultural liberal states / Monique Deveaux.
p. cm.
Includes bibliographical references and index.
1. Women's rights. 2. Minorities—Civil rights. 3. Pluralism (Social sciences)
4. Multiculturalism. 5. Culture conflict. 6. Toleration. 7. Social justice.
8. Sex role. 9. Liberalism.
I. Title.
HQ1236.D48 2006
305.48—dc22   2006019917

Typeset by SPI Publisher Services, Pondicherry, India
Printed in Great Britain
on acid-free paper by
Biddles Ltd., King's Lynn, Norfolk

ISBN 978–0–19–928979–0

Contents

Acknowledgments

This book is centrally concerned with the tension between cultural group rights and protections on one hand, and gender equality and justice on the other. That these two kinds of 'equalities' might conflict was first made apparent to me in the early 1990s, when I worked for Canada's main feminist organization, the National Action Committee on the Status of Women (NAC). At that time, federal negotiations were under way to secure greater sovereignty for First Nations peoples. Some Native women's groups argued that their right to sexual equality might be undermined if First Nations peoples were to receive immunity from the Charter of Rights and Freedoms, as promised under the proposed accord. I was inspired by the efforts of the Native Women's Association of Canada, NAC, and other groups that dared to press the issue of sexual equality and protest women's political exclusion from constitutional negotiations in this heady political climate. However, I was also troubled that Aboriginal peoples' aspirations for self-government were pitted by circumstances against sexual equality rights, and reasoned at the time that there must be a way to get beyond this impasse of 'conflicting equalities'.

Later, after graduate studies, I returned to this problem and began to develop examples of other instances in which sexual equality protections stood in tension with cultural group rights. My earliest framings of the problem were belied by a study of the actual manifestation of these conflicts, particularly in Canada and South Africa. Eventually, I resolved to let the case illustrations guide me in the development of a normative framework that could help to mediate and resolve tensions between cultural and sexual justice. I am indebted to the many activists and academics who shared with me their analyses of the gender/culture tension in Canada, South Africa, and Britain, and whose perspectives helped to shape my interpretation of the problem. The opportunity to give portions of this preliminary work as talks in academic settings was a tremendous help. I thank the Political Science Departments at the University of Rochester, the University of Toronto, and the University of Victoria for their thoughtful responses to my work, and fellows (and audience members) at the Radcliffe Institute for Advanced Study, where I presented some of the core ideas for the book in a public lecture in early 2002. Participants at conferences at the University of Edinburgh, University of Nagoya, and especially University of British Columbia (on 'Sexual Justice/Cultural Justice') and the University of Nebraska (on 'Minorities Within

Minorities') helped me to question, and so to revise, many of my normative arguments.

For their astute comments on parts of the draft manuscript, either as talks, journal articles, or as chapters, I am grateful to Barbara Arneil, James Bohman, Denise Buell, Joseph Carens, James Johnson, Will Kymlicka, the late Susan Okin, Jeff Spinner-Halev, James Tully, Stephen White, and anonymous reviewers for *Political Studies* and *Political Theory*. For providing incisive comments and excellent suggestions for revising the book for publication, I thank Chandran Kukathas, Deen Chatterjee, and a third, anonymous, reviewer for Oxford University Press. To Avigail Eisenberg and Paul Voice, I owe a special debt, for reading and commenting extensively on the whole manuscript. Thanks are also due to Dominic Byatt at Oxford University Press for his support for the project and for being patient about its completion. Hilary Barraford edited an early version of the manuscript, making it much more readable; EunSu Chang provided invaluable help with research for Chapter 4, and generously took on the task of compiling the book's bibliography; and Sarah Hirsch and Ryan McNeely lent additional help in preparing the final manuscript.

For financial assistance that enabled the writing of this book, I thank the Radcliffe Institute for Advanced Study at Harvard University, for a wonderful fellowship year (2001–2); the National Endowment for the Humanities, for a summer research stipend which permitted me to devote time to writing in 2001; Williams College, for funding from the Class of 1945 World Fellowship, which made it possible to conduct interviews in Britain in 2001 and South Africa in early 2002, and for generously allowing me an extra semester's leave; and the Rockefeller Foundation, for a short but productive team research residency at Bellagio, Italy, in May 2003 on the subject of sexual and cultural justice.

Some parts of this book have appeared elsewhere in print. Thanks to Sage Publications for permission to incorporate parts of my article, 'A Deliberative Approach to Conflicts of Culture', *Political Theory*, 31/6 (2003), 780–807, into Chapters 4 and 7; to Blackwell Publishing, for giving permission to use my article, 'Conflicting Equalities? Cultural Group Rights and Sex Equality', *Political Studies*, 48/3 (2000), 522–39, some of which appears in Chapter 5; and to Routledge/Taylor and Francis, for granting permission to use my article, 'Liberal Constitutions and Traditional Cultures: The South African Customary Law Debate', *Citizenship Studies*, 7/2 (2003), 161–80, parts of which are included in Chapter 7.

Finally, for their moral support and encouragement during the writing of this book, I thank Avigail Eisenberg, Cathy Johnson, Tamara Metz, Cheryl Shanks, and especially Paul Voice.

1

Introduction

Much normative political theory of the 1980s and 1990s emphasized the importance of citizens' group-based cultural differences, and the need to recognize and formally accommodate cultural minority groups in liberal democratic states.[1] The current mood, by contrast, reflects a preoccupation with the *internal* differences of social and cultural collectivities, and with whether and how such differences should affect the status of their claims for greater accommodation. This altered focus is due in part to political theorists' embrace of a more fluid and complex understanding of cultural identities, a consequence, perhaps, of what has been called the 'Geertz-effect' in political theory.[2] Increasingly, cultural identity has come to be viewed as a dynamic and changing phenomenon, and cultural practices and arrangements are recognized as sites of contestation. This intensified attention to the internal differences of social and cultural communities may also reflect a growing awareness of the political character of cultural identities, and of cultural justice struggles generally, in plural liberal democracies. From disagreements within Native American communities over membership rules, to disputes among South Asian immigrants about norms and rules governing arranged marriages, these struggles increasingly reveal the strategic and contested nature of group identities, and the sometimes fractured solidarities of ethnic, linguistic, and religious minorities in multicultural liberal polities.

Wider recognition of the fact of disagreements and conflicts within minority cultural groups has in turn focused attention on the potential for mistreatment of vulnerable members of such communities.[3] This is the problem

---

[1] I use the term 'cultural groups' to cover a broad range of groups whose members share an identity based on ethnic, linguistic, racial, or religious characteristics, and for whom these aspects strongly shape the self- and ascriptive identification of individual members. Such collectivities are sometimes referred to as 'encompassing groups' or 'societal cultures' to indicate that they may shape not only the self-understandings of members but also their community contexts, opportunities, life choices, and so forth.

[2] David Scott, 'Culture in Political Theory', *Political Theory*, 31/1 (2003), 92–115, p. 111.

[3] The descriptor 'minority' refers here to the social and legal status of particular practices, not to whether they are practiced by few or many. This distinction is important because in some states, such as South Africa, 'minority' practices—for example, those concerning customary marriage—may actually be practiced by a majority of the population. I do not mean to suggest

of 'internal minorities', as Leslie Green has called it, or that of 'minorities within minorities.'[4] The more autonomy a group has over its practices and arrangements, and the more nonliberal the character of the group, the greater the risk that individuals may be subjected to rights violations.[5] National cultural and ethnic minorities who are accorded collective rights, and religious communities that enjoy special dispensation in order to accommodate their traditions and values, are among the prime subjects of concern here. Political theorists have pointed to the right of Orthodox Jews in Israel to maintain a system of personal law that prevents many women (but not men) from obtaining a divorce decree without their spouse's consent and the right of the Amish in the United States to remove their children from high school at age 15, as examples of how cultural rights can leave some group members susceptible to mistreatment. Immigrant groups whose cultural practices are largely unhampered by law are also sometimes accused of unjust customs, such as sex-segregated religious schooling that only prepares girls for traditional lives. Within both national minority and immigrant communities, the spectrum of vulnerable individuals is thus quite broad, and might include religious minorities within the group, gays and lesbians, individuals who resist particular conventions, and girls and women in general.

Against this political backdrop, calls by cultural minority groups for greater recognition and rights inevitably raise questions about the proper scope and limits of such accommodation. Posing the greatest challenge are those demonstrably nonliberal cultural groups that adhere to practices that reflect and reinforce traditional and, by liberal lights, discriminatory, cultural or religious norms, roles, and worldviews. Where the customs and arrangements of traditional cultural communities stand in tension with the broader liberal norms of the society in which they live, how should multicultural, liberal democratic states respond? Should the (intolerant) practices of nonliberal groups be tolerated—if so, on what grounds, and to what effect? These questions acquire a special urgency when the norms and practices of cultural groups clash with individual rights protections guaranteed under liberal

---

that only the practices of cultural minorities should be subjected to critical scrutiny and potential reform; however, to the extent that a debate has risen within political theory regarding the ambiguous legal status of practices of such minorities, my intention is to try to steer this response in a more democratic direction.

    [4] See Leslie Green, 'Internal Minorities and their Rights', in *Group Rights*, ed. Judith Baker (Toronto: University of Toronto Press, 1994), and *Minorities Within Minorities: Equality, Rights and Diversity*, eds. Avigail Eisenberg and Jeff Spinner-Halev (Cambridge: Cambridge University Press, 2005).

    [5] The term 'nonliberal' is usually used by political theorists to refer to groups or practices that restrict individual liberty in very pronounced ways, and so risk violating liberal norms. I use the term similarly in this book, but also include communities and customs that stipulate rigid social hierarchies or prescribe sharply differentiated gender roles for men and women.

constitutional law, but they also arise in connection with more everyday social customs and arrangements.

By most accounts, nowhere is the tension between policies of multi-cultural accommodation and liberal principles and protections more apparent than in the area of women's rights and roles. In particular, the concern that special group rights and provisions for cultural minorities might undercut the rights of women group members, or even jeopardize liberal sex equality guarantees more generally, has recently emerged as a daunting problem for proponents of multiculturalism. Religious groups and ethnic minority (especially immigrant) communities, and indigenous groups that discriminate against women in some way, are a particular focus of concern. In some cases, the cultural practices and arrangements of groups are protected by customary systems of law or by sanctioned religious systems of family and personal law (e.g. in India, South Africa, and Israel) that may conflict with a constitutional commitment to sexual equality. The road to group accommodation is increasingly a legal and political minefield, then, and it is far from clear how customs that stand in tension with individual rights legislation, such as sexual equality protections, can be permitted—or, still less, protected—without undermining the universality of such rights.

Perhaps the central paradigm framing most current political, and to a lesser extent, scholarly discussion of what I call 'conflicts of culture' is that of liberal toleration, which generates the question, 'What should the liberal state tolerate, and what should it prohibit?' This emphasis on toleration is, as I shall shortly argue, highly problematic in that it cuts short a fuller discussion of group claims about identity and self-governance; of the many possible processes for the evaluation and reform of cultural practices; and of the power relationships between minority groups and the state. In effect, the litmus test for the soundness of arguments for policies of cultural accommodation thus becomes whether such arguments unwittingly permit individual rights violations, including sex-based inequalities, or whether proponents of cultural recognition seek to grant collective rights at the expense of vulnerable members (such as women). The questions are fairly posed, and I ask a version of them myself in the coming chapters. However, it is important to see how they can also rely on a dangerously false dichotomy, namely, that between cultural groups and their rights on the one hand, and women and their rights on the other. Yet women make up at least half of the cultural communities in question, and some, as we know, defend precisely those practices and arrangements that make liberals uncomfortable, like arranged marriage and polygyny. This is why, in my view, it is not really an option to be 'pro-women' and against cultural rights. Although our preferences and commitments should not always be taken at face value—particularly in highly constrained circumstances—it is nonetheless unsatisfactory to merely set women's evaluative assessments aside where they stand in tension with liberal norms.

This book tries to move away from the paradigm of toleration, and to focus instead on how we might democratically mediate the tensions between the claims of cultural and religious minorities with respect to women's rights and roles, and the demands of liberal democratic states. Here my concern is tensions that arise as a direct result of claims for formal rights and protections for cultural or religious norms and arrangements, not the difficulties that arise when a member of a distinct group simply invokes a 'cultural defense' to excuse an action or to plead extenuating circumstances.[6] On the whole, political theorists writing on issues of cultural diversity have been slow to ask about the implications of cultural group rights and accommodation for gender equality, or for gender justice more broadly. As feminist thinkers have long noted, it is precisely because sex roles and arrangements are often seen as private, and so excluded from the realm of politics, that framing gender issues as problems of justice is so difficult; sex inequalities are in a sense unnoticeable because they are such a pervasive part of community life. Where liberal political theorists have directly addressed this issue, they have tended to leverage liberal norms as a litmus test for assessing the claims of cultural minorities, without good justification (or results). As I argue in Chapter 2, this approach is an overly blunt instrument for dealing with the challenges posed by cultural minority practices and arrangements; as such, it risks unjustly prohibiting practices that ought to be allowed, and at the same time, ignores forms of sexual injustice that escape the rights frame (such as restriction of girls' educational and occupational opportunities through cultural pressures). Human rights frameworks, which I discuss in Chapter 3, fare somewhat better in that they appeal to a broader range of human needs and possible forms of harm. However, human rights are far from dispositive when trying to resolve disputes over gendered cultural roles, practices, and arrangements, as cultural group rights are also often defended in the language of human rights.

It is not only liberal political theorists' responses to this problem that have fallen short. The relationship between cultural group accommodation and sex equality also presents a formidable challenge to deliberative democracy, as I argue in Chapter 4. A deliberative democratic approach to conflict resolution that purports to secure respect for cultural pluralism, as mine does, will require changes which traditional cultural collectivities may vehemently

---

[6] See especially Alison Renteln, *The Cultural Defense* (Oxford: Oxford University Press, 2004). Instances of the latter are growing in number and significance, and have been the subject of considerable recent scholarship.

reject, thereby rendering the prospect of moral consensus impossible. In particular, a deliberative democratic approach to resolving disputes about the value and status of cultural practices will require that female members of cultural groups have a voice in evaluating and deciding the fate of their communities' customs, both by including women in formal decision-making processes and developing new, more inclusive, forums for mediating cultural disputes.[7] To accomplish this greater enfranchisement of women in both formal and informal democratic spaces, we will need to examine the practical impediments to their empowerment in their communities, and the cultural barriers to their participation in public life.[8]

* * *

When cultural practices and arrangements that are protected by policies of multicultural accommodation stand in tension with constitutional guarantees of sex equality, or when social practices are internally contested within communities, difficult conflicts of culture emerge that usually involve the liberal state at some level. This conflict and its challenges are the subject of this book, which takes as its focus three main tasks. In the first place, I aim to reframe the disputes over so-called nonliberal cultural practices and arrangements, highlighting their intragroup and strategic, political character. Second, I offer an analysis of illustrative instances in which cultural group practices and individual rights protections have clashed in South Africa, Canada, and Britain, providing a contextualized discussion of this pervasive normative and political dilemma. And third, I develop an approach to mediating cultural conflicts over women's rights and roles which foregrounds the deliberative judgments of cultural group members themselves, as well as strategies of bargaining and compromise. This approach, which insists on norms of democratic legitimacy and political inclusion, is broadly situated within deliberative democracy theory. Crucially, however, it depends on a greatly expanded conception of 'the political', one that includes not simply formal political deliberation but also informal spaces of democratic activity and expression. It also accords particular attention to the need to empower

[7] Other political theorists have also stressed the importance of including female members of cultural groups in decisions about contested practices. See Susan Moller Okin, 'Is Multiculturalism Bad for Women?' and 'Reply', in *Is Multiculturalism Bad for Women?*, eds. Joshua Cohen et al. (Princeton, NJ: Princeton University Press, 1999); and Jeff Spinner-Halev, 'Feminism, Multiculturalism, Oppression, and the State', *Ethics*, 112 (2001), 84–113, p. 108.

[8] The cultural obstacles to women's participation in public life are not always obvious. For instance, Sawitri Saharso has written of the internalized psychological barriers to autonomous behavior or action, which are common among women 'raised in a culture that does not value autonomy.' See her 'Female Autonomy and Cultural Imperative: Two Hearts Beating Together', in *Citizenship in Diverse Societies*, eds. Will Kymlicka and Wayne Norman (Oxford: Oxford University Press, 2000), p. 228.

vulnerable members of cultural communities by shifting power away from those community leaders who try to silence and intimidate them, and expanding opportunities for critique, resistance, and reform.

My approach to mediating the phenomenon of cultural conflicts shares with other democratic theorists the intuition that the insights of deliberative democracy theory can and should be applied to problems of intercultural justice. Seyla Benhabib, Joseph Carens, Bhikhu Parekh, James Tully, and Iris Young have all argued for dialogical and deliberative approach as a response to cultural minorities' claims for recognition and accommodation, and as a means of grappling with specific conflicts of culture.[9] While sharing these authors' intuition that inclusive political deliberation must precede policy decisions about cultural conflicts, my perspective differs in important respects. As suggested above, unlike these thinkers, I argue that cultural conflicts involving cultural minorities are primarily political in character, and while they include normative dimensions, they do not necessarily entail deep disputes of moral value. This reframing of cultural disputes has implications for how liberal states should attempt to mediate such conflicts. Rather than exclusively foregrounding moral argumentation aimed at reaching normative consensus, I argue that *strategically* focused deliberation—in which participants seek negotiation and political compromise—is oftentimes a better solution to tensions between contested cultural practices and sex equality protections, both normatively and practically. The ensuing strategic agreements are often temporary, as they are contingent upon agents' shifting interests and assessments of practices, as well as upon social relations of power more broadly. Yet I argue that even these negotiated agreements and compromises can come to take on a settled normative quality, sometimes reinforcing thicker (and more durable) forms of moral assent. And finally, I contend that questions surrounding the legitimacy of contested cultural practices need not be resolved through formal political deliberation alone: certain types of informal democratic activity, such as forms of cultural resistance and reinvention, also speak to the validity of disputed customs, roles, and arrangements. Moreover, these informal sources of democratic expression can and should be introduced when citizens deliberate on the status and possible reform of contested cultural practices.

---

[9] Seyla Benhabib, *The Claims of Culture: Equality and Diversity in the Global Era* (Princeton, NJ: Princeton University Press, 2002); Joseph Carens, *Culture, Citizenship, and Community: A Contextual Exploration of Justice as Evenhandedness* (Oxford: Oxford University Press, 2000); Bhikhu Parekh, *Rethinking Multiculturalism: Cultural Diversity and Political Theory* (Cambridge, MA: Harvard University Press, 2000); James Tully, *Strange Multiplicity: Constitutionalism in an Age of Diversity* (Cambridge: Cambridge University Press, 1995); and Iris Young, *Inclusion and Democracy* (Oxford: Oxford University Press, 2000).

The task of reframing the problem of cultural conflicts in multicultural liberal states is, in my view, an urgent one. Conflicts between cultural rights and sex equality are often addressed as part of a broader dilemma of liberal toleration that asks 'Should the intolerant be tolerated?' Yet to understand conflicts between liberal democratic norms and the cultural practices of nonliberal minorities in these terms is deeply problematic. From the start, the toleration framework places the issue solely in the hands of the state, viewing cultural conflicts as primarily about shoring up the security and authority of the state, and only secondarily about delivering justice to minorities.[10] This state-centric view is rarely justified as such, but merely assumed, particularly by liberal theorists writing on cultural minority rights. As Rita Dhamoon has argued, this focus necessitates a view of culture in which only (ostensibly) discrete, highly bounded cultures are seen as worthy of notice, because only these can challenge the authority of the state. Such a move both ignores sources of cultural injustice suffered by groups who do not fit this description (such as gays and lesbians), and exaggerates the boundedness of cultural groups and their import-ance to political life in plural democratic states.[11]

In foregrounding the perspective and status of the state in this way, the liberal toleration paradigm also assumes that the main conflict is between the state and the cultural group in question. Yet as I argue, oftentimes the heart of the dispute lies within the cultural or religious community itself, even if it may first be brought to light—or compounded—by broader legal and social structures. Through its focus on the state–group schism, the toleration framework overlooks important democratic responses within cultural com-munities to their own contested cultural practices. As a result, the ways in which individuals resist, revise, and reinvent their social customs and tradi-tions drop from view. Yet these informal instances of democratic practice reveal much about the nature of the conflict: why a particular custom or arrangement is contested; how its practitioners attempt to change, or to resist its change; and who supports which version of a custom, and why. These responses can, moreover, also contribute to an evaluation of the validity or nonvalidity of contested customs and arrangements by helping to inform institutionalized forums of political deliberation. Such forums, often directed by cultural group members themselves, can become critical vehicles for determining the validity and future status of controversial cultural practices in liberal democratic states.

[10] For a parallel argument, see Barbara Arneil, 'Cultural Protections vs. Cultural Justice: Post-colonialism, Agonistic Justice and the Limitations of Liberal Theory', in *Sexual Justice/Cultural Justice: Critical Perspectives in Theory and Practice*, eds. Barbara Arneil, Monique Deveaux, Rita Dhamoon, and Avigail Eisenberg (forthcoming 2006, Routledge).

[11] See Rita Dhamoon, 'Shifting from Culture to Cultural: Critical Theorizing of Identity/Difference Politics', forthcoming, *Constellations* 13/3 (2006).

Not surprisingly, the state-centric liberal toleration framework, which I take up in Chapter 2, has generated inflexible responses to cultural practices ostensibly in conflict with liberal norms, ultimately yielding recommendations that states prohibit offending customs.[12] And indeed, some practices are clear candidates for restriction rather than deliberative resolution, such as infanticide, sati, and 'honor killings'.[13] Nor, in liberal democratic states, do these practices have defenders as such, although there is some dispute about the proper understanding of these customs and the best practical responses to them. Where harm or danger exists and subjects do not consent, decisions by liberal states to restrict or limit particular practices are mostly uncontroversial. Applying what I call a 'moral minimum' to an analysis of disputed practices will certainly support the prohibition of customs that result in serious physical harm, or which require outright coercion. Yet beyond these obvious cases, demands by traditional cultural groups for special accommodation may raise many more formidable challenges for government policymakers for which prohibition is not an adequate response. Nor will mere prohibition of certain customs—combined with appeals to liberal individual rights—automatically protect the internal minorities of cultural communities. Attempts to restrict controversial cultural practices through legal and coercive means can also fail to protect vulnerable members of such groups, such as women, by leaving certain individuals more exposed to private forms of oppression.[14] It is thus no surprise that the zero-tolerance response to problem of tensions between collective cultural claims and individual rights advanced by some liberal thinkers, such as Brian Barry, Will Kymlicka, and Susan Moller Okin,[15] has come under criticism.

A different response by liberal political theorists to tensions between gender equality and cultural protections urges a largely laissez-faire approach. In Chapter 2, I discuss the work of Chandran Kukathas, who opposes formal

---

[12] See for example Brian Barry, *Culture and Equality* (Cambridge, MA: Harvard University Press, 2001).

[13] So-called 'honor killings' involve the assassination of girls or women deemed to compromise a family's honor through sexual infidelity (real or suspected) or their refusal to marry a marriage partner chosen by the family. These killings are usually carried out by a male family member (father, brother, or even uncle or cousin). Cases of honor killings are reported annually in Britain, for example, in communities of Middle Eastern, North African, and (Muslim) South Asian descent.

[14] See the discussion by Jacob Levy, who also makes this point in *The Multiculturalism of Fear* (Oxford: Oxford University Press, 2000), pp. 53–62.

[15] See Kymlicka's *Multicultural Citizenship: A Liberal Theory of Minority Rights* (Oxford: Oxford University Press, 1995), and *Politics in the Vernacular: Nationalism, Multiculturalism, and Citizenship* (Oxford: Oxford University Press, 2001); Okin, 'Is Multiculturalism Bad for Women?'; and Okin, 'Feminism and Multiculturalism: Some Tensions', *Ethics*, 108 (1998), 661–84.

cultural rights. Kukathas nonetheless believes that in liberal societies, the state is not warranted to meddle in the affairs of citizens' cultural arrangements, since to do so would violate the rights of freedom of association and freedom of conscience.[16] Some cultural rights proponents also adopt a hands-off position: Jeff Spinner-Halev, for example, contends that as a matter of equal justice, the liberal state should not determine the internal arrangements and personal laws of religious groups. He is especially concerned about the injustice of imposing external reforms on oppressed groups, and argues that the liberal state's role should be limited to the practical construction and implementation of communities' personal laws, but should not include the selection or reform of those laws.[17] Yet granting cultural communities near-complete autonomy over the allocation of rights and benefits to group members overlooks the harm that may befall vulnerable group members (notably women), as well as the impact on prospects for societywide policies of gender equality.

Another liberal approach to conflicts of culture, which intersects with those sketched above, is the 'women's rights as human rights' paradigm, which appeals to human rights norms to justify protection from cultural and religious practices that harm or discriminate against women. Two normative liberal theories that employ a broadly human rights-based perspective are the philosopher Onora O'Neill's neo-Kantian perspective, which focuses on agents' consent and its requirements, and Martha Nussbaum's 'capabilities approach'.[18] As I discuss in Chapter 3, however, these perspectives are of limited use when it comes to hard cases of cultural conflict that involve socialization more than overt force. Nussbaum, with her Aristotelian-inflected liberalism, argues that customs common in traditional societies—such as arranged marriage and polygyny—should be prohibited because they undercut capabilities for human functioning.[19] Numerous problems arise, however, when an account of capabilities embedded in a conception of human flourishing is used to judge the validity and permissibility of contested practices across different cultures. Nussbaum's claim that a capabilities approach is 'sensitive to pluralism and cultural difference' is put into serious question given the liberal perfectionist framework that undergirds her theory.[20]

* * *

---

[16] See for example Chandran Kukathas, 'Are There Any Cultural Rights?', *Political Theory*, 20 (1995), 105–39.

[17] Spinner-Halev, 'Feminism, Multiculturalism, Oppression', esp. pp. 86 and 107–9.

[18] See especially Onora O'Neill, *Bounds of Justice* (Cambridge: Cambridge University Press, 2000), and Martha Nussbaum, *Women and Human Development: The Capabilities Approach* (Cambridge: Cambridge University Press, 2000).

[19] Nussbaum, *Women and Human Development*, esp. Ch. 4.　　[20] Ibid., p. 81.

As this brief overview of recent responses to the problem of cultural conflicts suggests, political theorists need to think much harder not only about *how* such conflicts might be resolved, but about how they should best be *understood* in the first place. This book is in the first instance an attempt to reframe tensions between cultural and sexual equality as problems of power and democracy, and specifically, as problems of democratic practice. The main questions posed in the book are *how should cultural disagreements and conflicts about women's status, roles, and arrangements be understood, and how should they be mediated or resolved in democratic societies?* However, once we look at specific cases of cultural conflicts, we quickly see that many additional questions need to be asked. Rather than asking what the liberal state ought to tolerate, I suggest that we pose questions that might help to reveal the social, cultural, and political meanings and purposes of practices: Why has a particular custom or arrangement come under fire now? Who is supporting it and who is opposing it? What are the relative power positions of the supporters and dissenters? What channels are available for dissent, and for reform? How has the state impacted the conflict, and are there ways in which the state (and semi- and nongovernmental organizations, or NGOs) can support the safe articulation of dissenters' criticisms and demands for reform?

In my view, these questions are best answered through contextual discussion of concrete instances of conflicting equalities. My point of departure in two of the country case studies (those of South Africa and Canada) is the tension that exists between constitutional protections for sex equality, on the one hand, and formal protections for cultural groups and recognition of a parallel system of religious or customary law, on the other. In a third example I explore, that of the issue of arranged and forced marriage among some South Asian communities in Britain, a conflict is ostensibly presented between the custom of arranged marriage and liberal norms of choice and autonomy. Although these examples may seem unique to the states in which they arise, these kinds of tensions are, arguably, likely to increase in scope and occurrence with efforts to expand cultural rights and protections in liberal democracies. Political theorists can help to illuminate the points of friction between cultural group norms and liberal democratic principles, and suggest some ways of mediating these. We can also draw attention to power struggles within communities, and reflect on the role of the state in either shoring up cultural power structures or, conversely, democratizing power more broadly.[21]

---

[21] For example, anthropologist Unni Wikan discusses Norwegian officials' reluctance to challenge the newly increased power of male immigrants over their families in their host society, in *Generous Betrayal: Politics of Culture in the New Europe* (Chicago and London: University of Chicago Press, 2002), p. 5.

CULTURAL CONFLICTS: POLITICAL NOT METAPHYSICAL?

In discussions of cultural practices that are, or appear to be, at odds with liberal norms, the liberal toleration framework emphasizes the 'otherness' of the custom or group in question. Sometimes this characterization is used to justify the prohibition of a practice. Equally, however, it can lend an unwarranted reverence to customs that are actually questioned, ignored, or rejected by group members, thereby exaggerating the importance of a custom within a cultural community's life. Discussing practices in abstraction from the social and political relationships that sustain them, as the toleration frame tends to do, also leads to a curious conflation and even distortion of customs. For example, customs such as 'clitoridectormy, polygamy, [and] the marriage of children' are run together in a list of dubious illiberal traditions that liberal societies ought vigilantly to guard against, or else condemn when practiced in nonliberal societies.[22] This abstracted view of social practices treats customs as more static than they really are, erasing the multiple meanings and forms that any given practice or cultural arrangement (like arranged marriage) may take. Moreover, such an approach to social traditions imputes a coherence and fixity to social *identities* that may not be warranted, and which social and cultural anthropologists increasingly reject as false. As Clifford Geertz writes:

The view of culture, *a* culture, this culture, as a consensus on fundamentals—shared conceptions, shared feelings, shared values—seems hardly viable in the face of so much dispersion and disassembly; it is the faults and fissures that seem to mark out the landscape of collective selfhood. Whatever it is that defines identity in border-less capitalism and the global village it is not deep-going agreements on deep-going matters, but something more like the recurrence of familiar divisions, persisting arguments, standing threats, the notion that whatever else may happen, the order of difference must be somehow maintained.[23]

The recognition that cultural traditions—like social and cultural identities—invariably take different and often conflicting forms, and have varied and contested interpretations at any given time, has recently begun to inform the way that political theorists think about social practices.[24] This recognition has not been much in evidence, however, in the writing of thinkers keen to portray dilemmas posed by certain cultural traditions and belief systems as

[22] Okin, 'Is Multiculturalism Bad for Women?', p. 14.

[23] Clifford Geertz, *Available Light: Anthropological Reflections on Philosophical Topics* (Princeton, NJ: Princeton University Press, 2000), p. 250.

[24] David Scott ('Culture in Political Theory') argues that political theorists who advocate cultural group recognition have tended to appropriate anthropologists' more recent conception of culture as porous and contested without submitting this account to critical questioning.

formidable but ultimately indefensible challenges to liberal rationalism. Samuel Huntington's clash of civilizations thesis, which predicts that 'the great
divisions among human kind and the dominating source of conflict ... will be
cultural ... [and not] primarily ideological or primarily economic',[25] is perhaps the most extreme example. Cultural relativists may reify social groups as
much as cultural absolutists, however: '"cultural relativists"' tendency to
describe differences in terms of simple opposition—Western versus non-
Western—without exploring how specific cultural practices are constituted
and justified "essentializes" culture itself.'[26] At the other end of the spectrum,
religious traditionalists sometimes emphasize the incommensurability of
their own belief systems with dominant liberal paradigms precisely to resist
demands for change from dissenters within their communities as well-
concerned outsiders. Leaders of national ethnic groups seeking some degree
of legal and political autonomy from the liberal state may also have a
strategic interest in presenting their social identities as continuous and
unchanging. As one anthropologist notes, 'Ironically, just as the older concept
of culture seems less appropriate for contemporary society, it is being
vigorously re-appropriated by indigenous peoples in search for sovereignty
and self-determination.'[27]

The oversimple contention that many nonliberal, non-Western cultural
practices are basically incompatible with, and pose a potential threat to, liberal
constitutional norms and ways of life is closely related to another assumption
that I challenge in this book. This is the claim that conflicts between a group's
cultural practices and particular liberal principles are essentially deep conflicts
of moral value between one (minority) culture and another (dominant)
culture. Both the 'deep values' understanding of the nature of cultural conflicts
and its attendant thesis of moral incommensurability are evident in writings
by both liberal political theorists and proponents of deliberative democracy.
Some scholars, however, are beginning to challenge these twin assumptions.
James Johnson, for example, argues that while proponents of cultural
accommodation may acknowledge the ways in which individuals construct
social meaning, they 'typically forget that neither we nor others make
meaning in a naive or disinterested way'; in so doing, 'they neglect the

---

[25] Samuel Huntington, 'The Clash of Civilizations', *Foreign Affairs* (Summer 1993), 22–49.

[26] Tracy Higgins, 'Anti-Essentialism, Relativism, and Human Rights', *Harvard Women's Law Journal*, 19 (1996), reprinted in *International Human Rights in Context: Law, Politics, Morals*, eds. Henry Steiner and Philip Alston (New York and Oxford: Oxford University Press, 2000), p. 407. Uma Narayan also makes this point in her essay, 'Essence of Culture and A Sense of History: A Feminist Critique, of Cultural Essentialism', *Hypatia*, 13/2 (1998), 80–100.

[27] Sally Engle Merry, 'Changing Rights, Changing Culture', in *Culture and Rights: Anthropological Perspectives*, eds. J. K. Cowan, M. B. Dembour, and R. Wilson (Cambridge: Cambridge University Press, 2001), p. 42.

inevitable politics of culture'.[28] Social anthropologist Unni Wikan rejects accounts of immigrant cultures in Europe that emphasize their otherness vis-à-vis the wider society. Indeed, given cultures' fluidity, the impact of social and political processes on cultural forms, and the vicissitudes of individual differences, Wikan argues that it no longer makes sense to speak of the 'transmission from one generation to another as the distinguishing mark of culture'.[29]

Following in this vein, a central argument of this book is that disputes about cultural roles and practices most often arise from disruptions to social power relationships and hierarchies, which often get played out as struggles over which identities, roles, arrangements, and practices ought to prevail and which ought not to. Cultural roles, identities, and customs may thus be the *occasion* for intragroup social and political confrontations without necessarily being the underlying *source* of conflict. But equally, the very definition of social and cultural identities is a contested process and may generate ongoing intragroup conflict, particularly during times of rapid political change. As Amélie Rorty reminds us, 'cultural descriptions are politically and ideologically laden'; moreover, she adds, '[t]he implicit cultural essentialism of a good deal of celebratory multiculturalism disguises the powerful intra-cultural politics of determining the right of authoritative description.'[30] Similarly, Johnson argues that the 'salience' of 'any social and political identity' is 'itself typically a strategic artifact', the result of actions by reasoning agents who can anticipate the consequences of particular presentations of identities— including influencing the actions of other actors.[31]

To claim that conflicts of culture are very often intracultural and political in nature is of course not to deny the extent to which external factors shape the internal debates about customs. Quite the contrary: such factors can escalate existing internal contestations of traditions as well as give rise to new ones. Decolonization, economic globalization, increased migration, and a host of other factors have contributed to the kinds of rapid social changes that in turn exert pressures on any number of traditional cultural practices, from the domestic division of labor to marriage customs and inheritance rules. Political demands for change from 'host' society (or majority) institutions can also exert pressures on members of cultural minority groups, which can

---

[28] James Johnson, 'Liberalism and the Politics of Cultural Authenticity', *Politics, Philosophy, and Economics*, 1/2 (2002), 213–36, pp. 217–18.

[29] Wikan, *Generous Betrayal*, p. 80.

[30] Amélie Rorty, 'The Hidden Politics of Cultural Identification', *Political Theory*, 22/1 (1994), 152–66, p. 158.

[31] James Johnson, 'Why Respect Culture?', *American Journal of Political Science*, 44/3 (2000), 405–18, p. 413.

issue in a defensive retreat into conservative cultural forms and identities—or, alternately, newly negotiated identities. While some community members will welcome such changes, others may have reason to deny that such an evolution is taking place, or to attempt to solidify practices into a more rigid form. The liberal state may also have the opposite effect on minority cultures: as Sarah Song has argued, we need to be 'attentive to how majority and minority cultures interact in hierarchy-reinforcing ways', and mindful of the fact that '[m]ajority norms and practices also pose obstacles to the pursuit of gender equality within minority cultures'.[32] Cultural conflicts about identities and practices may thus arise in response to new legal and political institutions that impact cultural arrangements in contentious ways. The self-definitions of group members will also change readily in response to such changes; as Rorty suggests, 'As a good deal of such characterization is dynamically and dialectically responsive to politically charged external stereotyping, intracultural self-definition often changes with extracultural perceptions (and vice-versa).'[33]

This rendering of cultural conflicts as primarily intracultural and strategic or political in character is one that I illustrate through discussions of such tensions in South Africa, Canada, and Britain, in Chapters 5 through 7. In cases where nonliberal cultural groups face a crisis over a particular contested custom, we often see that traditional leaders perceive their power base as under threat, either from within the community or as a result of some external change. These kinds of challenges in turn may give rise to a phenomenon in which 'powerful individuals and groups...monopolize the interpretation of cultural norms and manipulate them to their own advantage.'[34] New political frameworks—such as Canada's 1982 Charter of Rights and Freedoms or South Africa's 1996 Constitution—may also bring to light existing sources of friction between group factions. Vulnerable cultural group members sometimes seek the support of individual rights protections when their own leaders refuse to treat them fairly, as happened in the case of both black women in postapartheid South Africa and Native women in Canada during constitutional negotiations.

In arguing for an explicitly political and intracultural understanding of tensions between cultural rights and sex equality protections, I recognize that I am at odds with many democratic theorists writing about cultural

---

[32] Sarah Song, 'Majority Norms, Multiculturalism, and Gender Equality', *American Political Science Review*, 99/4 (2005), 473–489, p. 474.

[33] Rorty, 'The Hidden Politics of Cultural Identification', p. 158.

[34] Abdullahi Ahmed An-Na'im, 'Toward a Cross-Cultural Approach to Defining International Standards of Human Rights', in *Human Rights in Cross-Cultural Perspectives: A Quest for Consensus*, ed. A. A. An-Na'im (Philadelphia: University of Pennsylvania Press, 1992), pp. 27–8.

conflicts.³⁵ But if this picture of the character of cultural conflicts is right, then authentic instances of moral incommensurability between cultural groups in liberal democratic states are a comparatively rare phenomenon. This also suggests that cultural group protections (even for nonliberal minorities) may not be incompatible with individual rights protections, or at least are less frequently so than some multicultural proponents suggest. If practices evolve and change through the actions of cultural agents, and can be made to change through internal reform, then it is possible there are few cases where real incommensurability exists. Similarly, if cultural identities are shaped and negotiated in a nexus of social and political relationships, these too are malleable. Identities, like the particular terms and forms of customs, are negotiated partly in response to situations of asymmetrical power relations and roles; and if we can show the contexts in which identities have been shaped, we can perhaps expose the dogmatic rhetoric that seeks to fix identities and defend them on those terms. As one anthropologist observes, 'The important question about culture is, therefore, how cultural practices are introduced, appropriated, deployed, reintroduced and redefined in a social field of power over a historical period.'³⁶ Recognizing the political character of cultural conflicts makes it easier to identify the strategic purposes underlying group members' particular interpretations of cultural norms and practices. The conflicts themselves are also potentially rendered more tractable, I argue, as they are made amenable to negotiation and compromise-based solutions.

INTERNAL MINORITIES AND DEMOCRATIC AGENCY

The terms 'internal minorities' and 'minorities within minorities' are increasingly used to describe the position of vulnerable individuals or groups vis-à-vis more powerful members within cultural communities.³⁷ Whether we are talking about Aboriginal women subject to discriminatory membership rules, or Catholic gays and lesbians demanding accommodation in the Church, there is a sense in which such individuals do indeed constitute an internal

---

³⁵ For example, this view of cultural conflict as primarily political stands in contrast to the deeply moral characterization of cultural differences advanced by, for example, Charles Taylor, 'The Politics of Recognition', in *Multiculturalism and the 'Politics of Recognition'*, ed. Amy Gutmann (Princeton, NJ: Princeton University Press, 1992); Avigail Eisenberg, 'Diversity and Equality: Three Approaches to Cultural and Sexual Difference', *Journal of Political Philosophy*, 11/1 (2003), 41–64; and Spinner-Halev, 'Feminism, Multiculturalism, Oppression.'

³⁶ Merry, 'Changing Rights, Changing Culture', p. 46.

³⁷ See Green, 'Internal Minorities and their Rights', and Eisenberg and Spinner-Halev, eds., *Minorities Within Minorities*.

minority. At the same time, however, this description tends to portray vulnerable individuals too readily as wholly powerless and in need of protection; it down plays their agency and attributes to them a fixed position within a system of social power. Neither term captures the complexity of situations in which members of cultural or religious groups may find themselves—simultaneously vulnerable and yet possibly empowered in certain respects, even in very closed, hierarchical groups. Individual members of groups can and do challenge discriminatory rules or practices within their cultures, by protesting to group leaders or seeking political and legal support outside of the collective. These political expressions are often accompanied by less formal acts of resistance to cultural rules or restrictions, such as efforts by individuals to reshape social roles and customs, and to transform 'official' accounts of these, so as to better reflect individuals' own lived experience of social practices. Whether they are direct or indirect in character, these expressions signal real challenges to prevailing arrangements and hierarchies within cultural communities.

In describing vulnerable members of cultural groups as internal minorities, then, we should be careful not to obscure the very real forms of agency that such individuals can and do exercise. Democratic activity is not confined to formal political processes; it is also reflected in acts of cultural dissent, subversion, and reinvention in a range of social settings. Inchoate democratic activity can be identified in the homes, schools, places of worship, and religious training of traditional communities; in social practices around marriage, birth, and the initiation of young people into adulthood; and in the provision of community and social services (e.g. domestic abuse centers run for and by women from traditional cultures). These important forms of democratic expression are rendered invisible by oversimple distinctions drawn between social and family life on the one hand and public, political life on the other. We can counter this invisibility by asking how work, social activities, and domestic arrangements and practices function as spaces of cultural resistance and transformation. Redefining the scope of democratic activity also amplifies the *basis* for democratic legitimacy, as I argue in the coming chapters.

To stress the inchoate and informal aspects of democratic agency of persons in this way is not to deny that traditional leaders of many nonliberal groups wield tremendous power over their members, nor that they may have the power to suppress liberal reforms that would improve the lot of certain individuals in the group. Indeed, some such leaders reject the very applicability of individual rights protections with regards to their own community: this was the stance taken by the leadership of the Assembly of First Nations (AFN) in Canada with respect to Canada's Charter of Rights and Freedoms, for example. But while one axis of cultural conflict may well be that of ethnic or religious group leaders versus the state, the core dispute, as I will argue, often lies within the community itself. External pressures brought to bear by the state and other actors (by legal reform groups, advocates of women's equality, etc.) may, however, expose and exacerbate points of tension within cultural communities, as we shall see.

CULTURAL CONFLICTS IN CONTEXT

To establish my argument that conflicts of culture are best understood as political, not moral, it is useful to reflect on specific cases. Consider the following three examples of conflicts between cultural group practices and liberal norms that pivot on questions of sex roles and status, which I develop in Chapters 5 through 7:

(a) During negotiations for Aboriginal or Native self-determination in Canada in the early 1990s, Aboriginal leaders insisted that their communities should not be bound by the 1982 Charter of Rights and Freedoms, on the grounds that it stood in tension with Native social and legal norms and so could undercut the goal of Aboriginal self-government. Many Native women's groups opposed this tactic, worrying that it would leave women unprotected and vulnerable to the patriarchal attitudes and strategic interests of their leaders. Although they fully supported the goal of Aboriginal self-government, many Native women urged the Canadian government to ensure that any future political arrangement should not exempt Aboriginal peoples from the Charter.[38]

(b) In South Africa in 1998, the government initiated a process for reforming African customary marriage, an institution that accords many more benefits and rights to men than to women. In hearings sponsored by the South African Law Commission, traditional African chiefs and headmen argued that customary law should remain unchanged and free of legal monitoring by the state. A few years earlier, these chiefs had also sought to ensure that African customary law would not be subject to the new Bill of Rights. In response, many government officials, women's rights advocates, legal reform groups, and black women's associations countered that a radically reformed, egalitarian form of customary marriage should prevail.

[38] This example is the subject of my 'Conflicting Equalities? Cultural Group Rights and Sex Equality', *Political Studies*, 48/3 (2000), 522–39. The main Native groups at loggerheads were the AFN (the country's largest Aboriginal group) and the Native Women's Association of Canada.

(c) Arranged or customary marriage in South Asian immigrant communities in Britain has recently come under intense government and police scrutiny. Since early 2001, there have been calls to ban the practice after some well-publicized cases of *forced* marriage came to light (about 10% of customary marriages in the UK are thought to be forced). Traditionalists deny the prevalence of forced unions and want the practice to continue without any state interference, but many South Asian community groups welcome the prospect of increased monitoring and practical and legal support for those seeking to avoid or leave forced marriages.

These examples serve to underscore the political character of tensions between cultural group protections and individual rights, for several reasons. Each involves significant disagreement about a cultural practice in a context lacking shared understandings and attitudes about women's status and the validity of government oversight of traditional cultural practices. Additionally, the disputes possess a political character that is partly obscured by accounts of cultural disagreements as deep conflicts of moral value. Finally, each involves considerable *intracultural* conflict over the interpretation, meaning, and legitimacy of customs or forms of customs: communities themselves disagree about the purpose and proper form of social practices.[39]

The claim that disputes about the customs and arrangements of cultural minority groups within liberal democratic states are very often intracultural and political in character should not come as a surprise. The rapid social changes associated with processes of colonization, decolonization, and economic globalization—notably urban migration and the breakdown of traditional communities—inevitably contribute to crises of cultural legitimacy. As Abdulahi An-Na'im has argued, internal disputes over political legitimacy and the sources of cultural authority are profoundly shaped by the strategic interests that group members, particularly the elite, have in directing or controlling community decisions.[40] As the brief summaries of gendered cultural conflicts in South Africa, Canada, and Britain illustrate, disputes

---

[39] In connection with sex equality related reforms of customary law in South Africa, Victoria Bronstein has argued convincingly that these are primarily matters of 'intra-cultural conflicts between "internal" women and other members of the group.' See her 'Reconceptualizing the Customary Law Debate in South Africa', *South African Journal on Human Rights*, 14 (1998), 388–410, esp. p. 390.

[40] Abdullahi An-Na'im, 'Problems of Universal Cultural Legitimacy for Human Rights', (p. 36) and An-Na'im and Francis Deng, 'Introduction', (p. 1) both in *Human Rights in Africa: Cross-Cultural Perspectives*, eds. An-Na'im and Deng (Washington, DC: The Brookings Institution, 1990). See also Bonny Ibhawoh's discussion of 'the internal struggle for control over cultural sources and symbols' in 'Between Culture and Constitution: Evaluating the Cultural Legitimacy of Human Rights in the African State', *Human Rights Quarterly*, 22 (2000), 838–60, p. 850.

about the validity and potential reform of cultural practices often reveal struggles between factions of groups with different vested interests in the status or particular form of customs, and different degrees (and forms) of power. These observations about the character of cultural conflicts are especially relevant for disagreements about gender roles and arrangements.

The recasting of cultural conflicts as more intracultural and political than typically supposed gives us a preliminary glimpse into why a *deliberative* approach to resolving such disputes might be preferable to an approach that insists on liberal principles as trumps. If disputes about the status of cultural practices and arrangements are primarily internal, reflecting struggles over the purpose and proper form of practices, as well as over decision-making authority and power, then deliberative democratic processes can bring these differences to the fore and ideally permit the fair adjudication of members' claims. Deliberative democracy theory offers a more inclusive and egalitarian approach to political dialogue and decision-making, and can help us to think about how to deepen the democratic character of our political institutions more generally.[41] Suitably revised—in ways that I set out in Chapter 4—this theoretical approach can also suggest how conflicts over the meaning and status of contested cultural practices can be mediated and potentially resolved through processes of deliberation, negotiation, and compromise. Finally, deliberative democracy theory may also advise how we might render our institutions more responsive to conditions of social pluralism more generally.

CULTURE AND DEMOCRATIC LEGITIMACY

The approach to mediating cultural conflicts developed in this book begins with a claim about the requirements of democratic legitimacy in plural, liberal societies. Insofar as liberal states fail to centrally include cultural group members in deliberations about the future status and possible reform of their community's customs and arrangements, I argue, they ignore the demands of democratic legitimacy. In suspending this norm and assuming that fair decisions about cultural practices do not require (or indeed may preclude) the meaningful inclusion of cultural group members, some

---

[41] I also draw secondarily on some of the principles and goals of associative democracy. See Paul Hirst, *Associative Democracy* (Amherst, MA: University of Massachusetts Press, 1994 [first published by Polity Press, 1994]) and *Reinventing Democracy*, eds. Paul Hirst and Sunil Khilnani (Oxford: Blackwell, 1996).

juridical, rights-based liberal responses to cultural conflicts fail to support democratic principles and practices. These liberal approaches, which I take up in Chapter 2, may contribute to outcomes that are ill conceived and potentially counterproductive from a policy point of view. As my discussion of cultural conflicts in South Africa, Canada, and Britain will illustrate, proposals for the reform of cultural practices that are derived from the mere application of liberal principles (however laudable) risk misconstruing the actual or *lived* form of these practices; as such, they may generate proposals which, if implemented, might perpetuate, or even worsen, the many forms of oppression faced by vulnerable members of cultural groups, such as women. By contrast, cultural communities that have a central role in reevaluating their own customs and arrangements contribute to the legitimacy of the resulting proposals (for retaining, eliminating, or reforming practices), also, arguably, greatly increasing their practicability.

To ensure the legitimacy and practical viability of proposals for the evaluation and reform of cultural practices that appear to violate gender justice, we will need to deepen our democratic practices and foster broader inclusion of citizens in political deliberation and decision-making processes—particularly vulnerable members of already marginalized cultural and religious communities. Crucially, this shift goes beyond merely including diverse citizens in existing political institutions; it requires that we expand our understanding of what constitutes democratic political activity, and proliferate the spaces for such activity. Increasingly, democratic thinkers, such as proponents of associational democracy, 'third way' democracy, and agonistic democracy, argue that democratic life is no longer confined to formal political institutions, and that this shift should be supported and expanded. Mark Warren, for example, writes of a 'second transformation of democracy', characterized by the increasing expansion of democratic life outside formal representative politics—into social movements and other political activities that involve citizens more directly (e.g. associations, interest groups, referenda, and political chat rooms).[42] I concur with this observation, and try to apply these insights to my argument that intracultural conflicts ought to be resolved through democratic means, understood in light of an expanded view of the scope of democracy.

Unlike proponents of associational and third way democracy, however, I try to push the definition of democratic life still further. These thinkers believe that democracy's expansion follows from the increasing structural inability of

---

[42] Mark Warren, 'A Second Transformation of Democracy?', in *Democracy Transformed? Expanding Political Opportunities in Advanced Industrial Democracies*, eds. Bruce Cain, Russell Dalton, and Susan Scarrow (Oxford: Oxford University Press, 2003).

governments to govern effectively; democratic life thus spills over into civil society, where ordinary citizens can experience more direct and greater political influence.[43] But the new spaces of democracy implied by this analysis are still of a particular character: recognizably political, collectivist, marked by directed or strategic action. Far from being restricted to what many would recognize as political processes, democratic activity, I argue, is also to be found in a wide array of social practices and responses to cultural norms and restrictions. These include deliberate (yet often covert) attempts to subvert or resist customs and arrangements—or what James Scott calls 'everyday forms of resistance', using the 'weapons of the weak'—but also more organic ways in which agents shape and change their social and cultural environments.[44] By acknowledging the implications that work, domestic arrangements, and social activities and affiliations can have for citizens' equality and political standing, we redefine our understanding of democratic expression and contestation.

With this expanded conception of democratic activity in mind, I develop a deliberative democratic approach to evaluating and reforming cultural group practices which cause internal disputes or which conflict with the liberal constitutional state's formal (though not necessarily substantive) commitment to sex equality. This view foregrounds concrete dialogue among affected citizens as the most democratically legitimate and just means of determining the validity, future status, and best form of contested cultural practices. Admittedly, this approach depends on a conception of democratic legitimacy that may be at odds with the canonical views of certain traditional groups whose cultural practices are in question, particularly conservative religious communities that look to religious leaders and texts as their sources of moral authority and legitimacy. This is an important objection, one that I take up in Chapters 4 and 8. While not denying this tension, I argue that the ideal of democratic legitimacy is not strictly a liberal or Western conception, but rather that it has support among even so-called nonliberal communities.

The central normative claims I advance with respect to the deliberative democratic resolution of cultural conflicts are as follows. First, by fostering radically democratic and politically inclusive forums (both formal and informal) for deliberating about the implications and legal status of contested cultural practices, we express a substantive commitment to norms of democratic legitimacy and respect for cultural pluralism. Second, a deliberative framework for resolving conflicts of culture can help to successfully engage and amplify existing criticisms of particular cultural practices and

---

[43] Ibid., pp. 241–2.
[44] James C. Scott, *Weapons of the Weak: Everyday Forms of Peasant Resistance* (New Haven, CT: Yale University Press, 1985).

arrangements within communities by supporting their safe public articulation both within the community and in the larger society, and in turn expanding the scope of democratic activity and contestation. And third, practical dialogue and deliberative decision-making that includes cultural group members and representatives from the state and civil society can produce democratically legitimate solutions to cultural disputes that both protect and empower vulnerable group members, such as women. Crucially, however, democratic solutions are not necessarily liberal in content in the sense of privileging liberal norms of personal autonomy and individual rights. But democratic solutions do meet a critical test of procedural justice, I contend. Provided that open and democratic procedures of deliberation and decision-making are observed, and proposed policies will not permit practices that disenfranchise or undercut the ability of any members to deliberate in future, cultural practices that sit uneasily with liberal values may justly be affirmed.

2

Liberal Approaches to Conflicts of Culture

Political theorists have recently begun to consider whether liberal democratic states can accommodate nonliberal cultural groups without undercutting the norm of sex equality. Several prominent liberal political theorists, notably Brian Barry, Susan Moller Okin, and Will Kymlicka, have argued that the sorts of illiberal restrictions that some traditional cultures seek to impose on their members cannot be squared with liberal commitments to autonomy and individual rights, including the right of sex equality.[1] For these thinkers, practices and arrangements that serve to undermine women's equal dignity and equal access to opportunities are simply indefensible in a liberal polity. The claim that systematic sex inequalities are incompatible with core liberal principles may appear unproblematic enough, though it might surprise some liberal thinkers of the past who defended racial hierarchies and strict sex role differentiation. Yet as I argue, in favoring liberal over democratic responses to conflicts of culture, we fail to accord the respect owed to cultural minorities. In their haste to use the state's power to protect vulnerable group members, liberals also overlook strategies for resolving cultural disputes more democratically, and in ways that might actually empower internal minorities.

Alternative liberal responses to conflicts of culture argue against strong forms of state interference in the affairs of cultural and religious groups, and in the latter part of this chapter, I explore these. Philosopher Jorge Valadez defends a form of deliberative democracy that is explicitly grounded in liberal principles of autonomy and equality, and which stresses the need to protect individual civil liberties.[2] Although Valadez embraces a robust vision of deliberative democratic forums for disputes over culture, for him, liberal

---

[1] Okin, 'Is Multiculturalism Bad for Women?', and 'Reply'; Will Kymlicka, 'Liberal Complacencies', in *Is Multiculturalism Bad for Women?*, eds. Joshua Cohen, Martha Nussbaum, and Matthew Howard (Princeton, NJ: Princeton University Press, 1999); Kymlicka, *Multicultural Citizenship*, Chs. 3 and 5; and Barry, *Culture and Equality*.

[2] Jorge Valadez, *Deliberative Democracy, Political Legitimacy, and Self-Determination in Multicultural Societies* (Boulder, CO: Westview Press, 2001).

principles set limits to both the form and possible outcomes of such deliberations.[3]

Two especially influential arguments against state interference in the affairs of cultural and religious groups are those of Chandran Kukathas and Jeff Spinner-Halev. Where Kukathas has advanced a liberal argument against state restrictions on groups' illiberal practices, he does so on the grounds that these violate individuals' freedom association and freedom of conscience.[4] By contrast, Spinner-Halev supports cultural rights protections, but argues against state interference in the arrangements of illiberal minorities on the grounds that it violates groups' right to shape their own collective identities.[5] While Kukathas' and Spinner-Halev's approaches both accord extensive autonomy to cultural communities, they downplay the dangers to less powerful individuals and place too much faith in the right of exit. Laissez-faire approaches to rights conflicts, I argue, risk compounding the vulnerability of some individuals within cultural minority communities, and in so doing, may undercut the very legitimacy of groups' own political and decision-making structures.

THE LIBERAL DILEMMA OF TOLERATION

Cultural minority practices that fall in the gray area between serious harm and clear innocuousness—such as arranged marriage and sex-segregated religious-based education—present hard cases for pluralist liberals. Indeed, hard cases of cultural difference are nothing new for liberalism: from John Locke's discussion of whether the state should extend tolerance to Catholics, to John Stuart Mill's conflicted reflections on Mormons and their practice of polygamy, it is apparent that liberals have historically grappled with the limits of toleration. The question of whether the liberal state ought to accommodate specifically nonliberal cultural and religious minorities (or some of their practices) also has a long history, one to which classical liberals like Locke offered largely prudential responses. Contemporary liberals, by contrast, give explicitly normative reasons for permitting or prohibiting particular practices, yet like earlier liberals, they worry that accommodations for pluralism may work against a common civic identity or even risk causing political

---

[3] It is for this reason that I include Valadez in the present discussion of liberal thinkers' responses to cultural conflicts, as well as in Chapter 4, on deliberative democratic approaches to such conflicts.

[4] Chandran Kukathas, *The Liberal Archipelago: A Theory of Diversity and Freedom* (Oxford: Oxford University Press, 2003).

[5] Spinner-Halev, 'Feminism, Multiculturalism, Oppression', and his *Surviving Diversity: Religion and Democratic Citizenship* (Baltimore, MD: Johns Hopkins University Press, 1994).

instability. As a consequence, today's liberals generally argue that specifically *nonliberal* minorities should be accorded minimal tolerance but not substantive recognition in the form of language rights or other collective cultural protections.[6] Where tolerance is extended, liberal thinkers embrace the right of exit as a bulwark against the abuse and oppression of vulnerable group members.[7]

As noted in Chapter 1, current debates in political theory about which cultural practices liberal states ought to permit, and which it ought to prohibit, continue the historical discussion within liberalism about the proper limits of liberal tolerance. This contemporary discussion also incorporates the conceptual faults and biases of the earlier debate.[8] Specifically, the question that today's liberals pose—whether the state ought to allow or accommodate nonliberal social practices and arrangements (and if so, which)—echoes the classic liberal dilemma of toleration: namely, how can liberal societies tolerate the intolerant? This apparent conundrum presupposes, but without challenging, tremendous power inequalities between the liberal state and the offending yet subordinate cultural group: the state alone may determine the terms of toleration and accommodation. Although a robust public debate may precede the state's decision, it is unlikely to influence the actual legislation or policy that emerges. For example, in the case of the Muslim headscarf affair in France, French school and government officials worried that the wearing of the chador by French schoolgirls had largely become a public, political statement. Despite a range of public views on the matter, the French National Assembly voted in 2004 to ban the wearing of conspicuous religious markers in schools, thereby deeming such clothing and symbols beyond the scope of the toleration normally extended to religious practice.[9] As Spinner-Halev has argued, state-mandated reforms, such as the French law against wearing religious clothing in schools, fundamentally ignores the oppressed character of a minority group and members' consequent mistrust of the broader society and state; as a consequence, such reforms risk not only injustice but also failure.[10]

---

[6] This is the position Brian Barry defends, which I discuss below; see also Charles Larmore, *Patterns of Moral Complexity* (Cambridge: Cambridge University Press, 1987).

[7] See especially Kukathas, 'Are There Any Cultural Rights?', and *The Liberal Archipelago*.

[8] For a fuller discussion see Monique Deveaux, *Cultural Pluralism and Dilemmas of Justice* (Ithaca, NY: Cornell University Press, 2000), esp. Ch. 2.

[9] Anna Elisabetta Galeotti, 'Citizenship and Equality: The Place for Toleration', *Political Theory*, 21/4 (1993), 585–605, pp. 593–4; the French National Assembly voted on February 10, 2004 to adopt a law prohibiting the wearing of conspicuous religious signs in public schools.

[10] Spinner-Halev, 'Feminism, Multiculturalism, Oppression', pp. 85, 95, and 107.

Ironically, it is often in the name of protecting internal minorities—saving groups from themselves, as it were—that this heavy-handed approach to legislating against minority practices is advocated.[11] Liberals such as Joseph Raz explicitly invoke the language of toleration, citing concerns about the harm of internal minorities to justify state restrictions against illiberal minorities. But Raz, like other comprehensive liberals, also smuggles in a number of liberal perfectionist ideals in his defense of limits to toleration, arguably undercutting the liberal case for cultural rights:

The limits of toleration are in denying communities the right to repress their own members, in discouraging intolerant attitudes to outsiders, in insisting on making exit from the community a viable option for its members. Beyond that, liberal multiculturalism will also require all groups to allow their members access to adequate opportunities for self-expression and participation in the economic life of the country, and the cultivation of the attitudes and skills required for effective participation in the political culture of the community.[12]

The expansiveness of this list of requirements that cultural minority groups must adhere to in order to merit state toleration and accommodation seems to be at odds with Raz's account of the collective rights—indeed, the fundamental purpose—of cultural groups. In particular, his claims that religious and cultural communities should be permitted to educate their children in the culture of their groups, and that differential gender socializing is unobjectionable within limits, stands in tension with the claim that groups must afford their members the skills and opportunities to participate in the life of their communities as well as the wider society.[13] This tension, in my view, is emblematic of the difficulty of liberal toleration approaches to the issue of cultural accommodation.

JURIDICAL AND POLITICAL APPROACHES TO CONFLICTS OF CULTURE

The paradigm of toleration informs what we might call a liberal 'juridical', a priori approach to contested cultural practices, as opposed to the political

---

[11] See for example Leslie Green, 'Internal Minorities and their Rights'. Green focuses on the oppression of cultural group members by other members, and neglects the broader context of groups' (possible) oppression at the hand of the state, and their social and political inequality.

[12] Joseph Raz, 'Multiculturalism: A Liberal Perspective', *Ethics in the Public Domain: Essays in the Morality of Law and Politics* (Oxford: Clarendon Press, 1994), p. 175.

[13] Ibid., pp. 174–5.

approach I defend.[14] Barry, Kymlicka, and Okin, all of whom have urged renewed assertion of liberal principles of individual equality and personal autonomy in the face of nonliberal cultural practices, adopt such a juridical approach to conflicts of culture.[15] In practical terms, these thinkers support a strategy of reinforcing legislation that protects individual rights, including sex equality rights, and rejecting exemptions that permit cultural or religious groups to blatantly discriminate against their own members.[16] By contrast, a political approach to the problem of disputed customs and to the issue of internal minorities, such as I defend, stresses a more democratic resolution of conflicts, and foregrounds the contributions of cultural community members themselves in resolving disagreements over contested membership rules, social roles, and cultural practices or arrangements.

These two approaches—the juridical and the political—are by no means necessarily opposed. Politically inclusive deliberation will oftentimes yield proposals for legislative reform, for example. But to the extent that these positions signal different orientations to conflicts of culture, they can and should be disambiguated. My own view is that a political, and more deeply democratic, approach to disputes over controversial cultural practices is the most just and effective way to proceed. Cultural groups whose practices have been called into question (either by group members or by the liberal state) should play the central role in evaluating, debating, and if necessary proposing reforms of contested cultural practices.[17] In many cases, democratic forums for such debate and reform already exist within cultural minority communities; where they do not, the liberal state can facilitate the establishment of such forums, as well as include cultural group members prominently in government-initiated efforts to explore possible legislative remedies.[18]

---

[14] Here I am borrowing a distinction that Melissa Williams uses in distinguishing two dominant ways of defining justice toward groups in culturally plural societies. See her 'Justice Towards Groups: Political Not Juridical', *Political Theory*, 23/1 (1995), 67–91, esp. pp. 68–9.

[15] See especially Barry, *Culture and Equality* and Okin, 'Is Multiculturalism Bad for Women?'.

[16] Legal thinkers who concur with this approach argue that all citizens, including members of indigenous groups, should be protected by a common constitution framed around individual rights. Where groups are covered by additional legal frameworks that cede certain autonomous powers to a collective entity—such as the U.S. Indian Civil Rights Act (1968)—critics urge that amendments are essential in order to ensure nondiscrimination against vulnerable members within the group.

[17] See Monique Deveaux, 'A Deliberative Approach to Conflicts of Culture', *Political Theory*, 31/6 (2003), 780–807.

[18] For example, the *Task Force on Forced Marriages*, established by the British Home Office in 2000 with the purpose of looking into allegations of forced marriages within the practice of arranged marriage among certain immigrant groups in Britain, was composed largely of members of different sectors of South Asian and Middle Eastern communities.

If decisions about contested practices are made without genuine input from affected members, cultural group leaders can and should be held accountable through the courts—as, for example, in cases where Native women have protested the way that discriminatory Indian membership rules unjustly caused them to be disenfranchised from their bands.

Taken alone, the liberal juridical framework, when applied to the issue of contested cultural practices, is deeply problematic. In the first place, it tends to assume that cultural disputes reflect a fundamental moral incommensurability between group-oriented cultural minorities and individualist-oriented liberal society. This assertion further supposes that there is an essential conflict between collective, cultural rights, and individual rights—an assumption that derives from a distinct strain of modern natural law theory which views individual rights as more fundamental than (and prior to) any other form of rights.[19] Yet individual and group rights are at least conceptually compatible, and certain such rights are arguably legally interdependent (e.g. as suggested by the United Nations' 1992 *Declaration on the Rights of Persons belonging to National or Ethnic, Religious and Linguistic Minorities*). Some liberal thinkers have sought to challenge the idea of an essential conflict between group-based protections and individual rights and liberties[20]; sympathetic as they are to group rights, however, few have provided much in the way of a conceptual framework for mediating cultural conflicts through democratic processes.[21] As we see, the lack of a commitment within liberal political theory to more inclusive and democratic decision-making procedures, combined with liberalism's historical suspicion of group-based rights, make it difficult to fairly evaluate, or conceive of ways to reform, a range of contested cultural practices *democratically*.

---

[19] Liberal political theory's mistrust of group-based rights in general has its roots in seventeenth century liberalism, which stressed individual liberty and religious toleration. Later came John Stuart Mill's forceful critique of the ways in which social groups—specifically, culture and tradition—stifle individuals, preventing intellectual virtuosity and social progress. More recent liberals worry about the propensity for cultural and religious groups to exacerbate the problem of 'adaptive preferences', wherein individuals come unconsciously to adapt their expectations and ambitions to fit their restricted life circumstances and diminished options.

[20] See Carens, *Culture, Citizenship, and Community*; aforementioned work by Kymlicka as well as his earlier, *Liberalism, Community and Culture* (Oxford: Clarendon Press, 1989); and Parekh, *Rethinking Multiculturalism*.

[21] Those thinkers writing loosely within the liberal tradition who have given attention to the issue of adjudicating cultural conflicts include Avigail Eisenberg, 'Public Institutions and the Assessment of Cultural Identity', unpublished manuscript (2004); Carens, *Culture, Citizenship, and Community*; and Tully, *Strange Multiplicity*.

OKIN'S LIBERAL FEMINISM

Political theorist Susan Moller Okin is well known for her critique of unjust gender relations, including unjust family arrangements, in liberal societies.[22] Recently she has extended this critique to a discussion of sex roles and social customs among cultural minorities. In reference to the issue of how immigrant groups treat girls, Okin makes the general observation that 'In many of the cultural groups that now form significant minorities in the United States, Canada, and Europe, families place their daughters under significantly greater constraints than their sons.'[23] And commenting on religious group rights, Okin writes that

In the case of a more patriarchal minority culture in the context of a less patriarchal majority culture, no argument can be made on the basis of self-respect or freedom that the female members of the culture have a clear interest in its preservation. Indeed, they *might* be much better off if the culture into which they were born were either to become extinct (so that its members would become integrated into the less sexist surrounding culture) or, preferably, to be encouraged to alter itself so as to reinforce the equality of women—at least to the degree to which this value is upheld in the majority culture.[24]

While Okin may well be right that protection for nonliberal cultural groups cannot reasonably be defended using liberal appeals to individual self-respect or freedom, this does not make Okin's stronger claim ('they might be much better off...') true. Since this claim is comparative in nature, establishing it would require that the full range of constraints of culturally mainstream society on girls and women be explored. But by framing the issue of contested cultural practices as a conflict between the sexist and patriarchal practices of minority cultures on the one hand, and the values of more egalitarian, liberal societies on the other, Okin fails to bring into the equation the importance of sex inequalities within mainstream social relations and institutions.[25]

Okin's skeptical tone with respect to the claims of cultural and religious minorities for special group rights has been much maligned, and for this

---

[22] See Susan Moller Okin, *Justice, Gender, and the Family* (New York: Basic Books, 1989).

[23] Okin, ' "Mistresses of Their Own Destiny": Group Rights, Gender, and Realistic Rights of Exit', *Ethics*, 112 (2002), 205–30, esp. p. 220.

[24] Okin, 'Is Multiculturalism Bad for Women?', pp. 22–3. Also see her ' "Mistresses of Their Own Destiny" ', pp. 220–1.

[25] Anne Norton also notes Okin's apparent cultural double standard, whereby, unlike Western cultures, non-Western cultures are judged not 'according to their principles but according to their practices'. See Norton, 'Review Essay on Euben, Okin, and Nussbaum', *Political Theory*, 29/5 (2001), 736–49, p. 741.

reason it is worth looking especially closely at her argument. In her essay 'Is Multiculturalism Bad for Women?', Okin expresses serious misgivings about the recent trend in liberal democratic theory toward endorsing forms of group recognition and accommodation. In particular, she urges proponents of multiculturalism to think long and hard about the implications of special cultural rights for the fate of women within these groups. Okin also cautions us not to be fooled into accepting the reassurances of group elders, who often have a vested interest in perpetuating social power relations within their groups that subordinate women. While acknowledging that minority groups will continue to be bound by liberal democratic laws in the public sphere, Okin worries that discrimination and oppression in the private realm will go unnoticed and so unchecked. These inequalities, she believes, may be reinforced by policies that protect those traditional cultural minorities with established sexual hierarchies. Formal group rights in particular may make it all too easy for groups to engage in private forms of discrimination: 'It is by no means clear... from a feminist point of view, that minority group rights are "part of the solution". They may well exacerbate the problem [of sex inequality].'[26]

The argument Okin advances is in some respects a comprehensive liberal one, stressing the importance of norms of equality and protection for individual rights and personal autonomy. A good life, for Okin, is one that entails plenty of life options, and in which one exercises capacities for reflection and choice. Not surprisingly, Okin thus invokes the power of law and social policy in helping to stamp out sexual double standards, urging that liberal states not hesitate to employ legislative, social policy, and criminal law measures that could protect girls and women rendered vulnerable by their cultures. As far as more coercive forms of intervention (such as prohibition) are concerned, Okin's position is more equivocal. She also takes seriously the liberal virtue of toleration, and this leads her to endorse a consultative over juridical approach at times. This is perhaps best illustrated by her emphasis on the need to include the voices of disempowered members of cultural groups, especially women, in consultations about group rights; young women in particular, she urges, must be included in debates about disputed customs and practices.[27]

---

[26] Okin, 'Is Multiculturalism Bad for Women?', p. 22.

[27] Ibid., p. 24, and Okin, 'Reply', p. 117. See also Okin's 'Multiculturalism and Feminism: No Simple Question, No Simple Answers', in *Minorities Within Minorities*, eds. Avigail Eisenberg and Jeff Spinner-Halev (Cambridge University Press, 2005), pp. 74, 86, and 88. Elsewhere, Okin writes, 'Women who are struggling against culturally or religiously sanctioned violations of women's rights... need... to be carefully listened to; [and] to have the opportunities to engage in deliberation that can lead to the recognition of unmet needs and unrecognized rights and to the development of strategies for change'. See Okin, 'Feminism, Women's Human Rights, and Cultural Differences', *Hypatia*, 13/2 (1998), 32–52, p. 48.

But by Okin's own account, her support for what she calls the 'democratic solution' is qualified: while talk is sometimes good, 'in the case of patriarchal religions that can make no good claims of past oppression', she unreservedly favors the liberal over the democratic solution.[28] Chiefly, it appears Okin is concerned that it may not be possible in traditional or patriarchal settings to achieve genuinely inclusive and democratic negotiations about contested aspects of cultures, without inequality and domination.[29] At these times, she endorses a less reflective, more a priori approach to decisions about the permissibility of gendered cultural practices, reaching for liberal rights as trumps, and in general insisting on the key role of the state in reforming cultural and religious groups. For example, Okin has in the past contended that 'the liberal state ... should not only not give special rights or exemptions to cultural and religious groups that discriminate against or oppress women. It should also enforce individual rights against such groups when the opportunity arises and encourage all groups within its borders to cease such practices.'[30] Still, 'in the case of cultural or religious groups that have recently suffered, or still suffer, from oppression at the hands of colonial powers or of the larger society', Okin allows that liberal solutions may not be preferable to democratic solutions in cases of gender inequality.[31] These groups, she acknowledges, have good reason to mistrust the state's overtures of protection and may quite reasonably side with their group when the state attempts to intervene ostensibly on their behalf.

While Okin's cautionary message about the dangers that attend cultural rights is at times insightful, the specific examples she cites ('clitoridectomy, polygamy, the marriage of children, or marriages that are otherwise coerced'),[32] and her generally unqualified appeal to liberal norms, ultimately leave her vulnerable to charges of ethnocentrism. Among the responses published alongside Okin's landmark essay, Bhikhu Parekh remarks that Okin 'takes liberalism as self-evidently true' without offering a satisfactory

[28] Okin, 'Multiculturalism and Feminism', p. 87.

[29] See Okin's reply to my argument for a deliberative approach to conflicts of culture in her 'Multiculturalism and Feminism', esp. pp. 83–6, and her discussion of Nussbaum's capability theory as a response to women's inequality and oppression in 'Poverty, Well-Being, and Gender: What Counts, Who's Heard?', *Philosophy and Public Affairs*, 31/3 (2003), 280–316, esp. p. 310.

[30] Okin, '"Mistresses of Their Own Destiny"', pp. 229–30.

[31] Okin, 'Multiculturalism and Feminism', p. 87.

[32] Okin, 'Is Multiculturalism Bad for Women?', p. 14. The terms that Okin employs are also ideologically loaded: for example, 'clitoridectomy' usually refers to the complete removal of the clitoris, which is a comparatively rare procedure; by contrast, the terms 'female genital surgeries' or 'genital alterations' are increasingly taken by anthropologists and international NGOs to be more accurate (and less politically charged) descriptions of these procedures. For a discussion of this shift, see Richard Shweder, 'What About "Female Genital Mutilation?" And Why Understanding Culture Matters in the First Place', *Daedalus* (Fall 2000), 208–32.

defense of liberal norms and practices. Joseph Raz comments that 'she seems somewhat blind...to the fact that the same social arrangements can have different social meanings, and therefore differing moral significance, in the context of different cultures. This leads her to judge other cultures more harshly than her own...'[33] Indeed, several authors responding to Okin's essay rightly take exception to what they view as her tendency to generalize about other cultures without reflecting critically on Western societies (as she does in her earlier work). In reply, Okin has readily acknowledged that majority cultures must not ignore their own poor track record with respect to oppression and marginalization.[34] Ultimately, however, she remains unpersuaded by claims and counterexamples illustrating comparable inequalities in mainstream Western cultures or the purportedly empowering impact of traditional cultural practices for women. Yet even if Okin's skepticism on this matter is warranted, it is far from clear, as Raz notes, that liberal states should reject policies of multiculturalism on the basis of a handful of pernicious but comparatively rare practices.[35]

Perhaps the biggest difficulty with Okin's comprehensive liberal paradigm is that it sets ideals of individual and sexual equality and individual autonomy above all other political norms, without adequate justification. She fully recognizes that the values and norms endorsed by cultural minority communities may stand in tension with certain liberal principles, but treats such conflicts as indefensible, and certainly not as warranting accommodation. The possible legitimacy of these claims, even in the case of indigenous groups with aspirations for self-government, is not a matter Okin much dwells on. Lacking in her analysis, thus, is both an appreciation of the legitimacy of some claims for formal cultural autonomy, as well as a full understanding of the tremendous power imbalances between cultural and religious communities and the liberal state. This explains why Okin sometimes treats minority cultural practices as if they warranted special critical scrutiny, without asking whether corresponding reflection on mainstream social customs may also be warranted.[36] Underscoring the power of the liberal state, Okin writes:

[W]hy, on liberal premises and within a liberal society, should a cultural group be 'entitled to try to live by their ways' if these ways violate the individual rights of their

---

[33] Joseph Raz, 'How Perfect Should One Be? And Whose Culture Is?', in *Is Multiculturalism Bad for Women?*, eds. Joshua Cohen et al. (Princeton, NJ: Princeton University Press, 1999), p. 98.

[34] Okin, 'Reply', p. 121.

[35] Raz, 'How Perfect', p. 97.

[36] As Spinner-Halev notes, in her critique of the implications of cultural group rights, Okin also focuses her attention on immigrant and religious groups in the United States. However, most cultural rights proponents, including Kymlicka, do not advocate special rights for such groups. See Spinner-Halev, 'Feminism, Multiculturalism, Oppression', p. 87.

members? Why shouldn't the liberal state, instead, make it clear to members of such groups, preferably by education but where necessary by punishment, that such practices are not to be tolerated?[37]

Finally, Okin proposes that liberal states declare as invalid many religious and cultural groups' systems of leadership and internal decision-making processes. Those traditional structures of leadership in religious and cultural communities that appear patriarchal or in other ways unrepresentative are quite simply unjust. This may well be true. But the suggestion that the liberal state ought simply to dismantle (or prohibit) what are complex and in some cases long-standing forms of leadership or self-government (as in the case of indigenous peoples) on the grounds that these are not recognizably egalitarian opens the door to political oppression, and certainly flies in the face of liberal commitments to toleration and freedom of association.[38] Okin asserts that patriarchal-style traditional leaders should be barred from deliberations with the state or else 'not represented in the deliberations more than their own numbers in the population warrant'.[39] While reform of cultural and religious groups' internal power structures may well be warranted and urged by internal minorities, whether and how it is to be changed must surely be a subject for extensive deliberation (which nonstate or semigovernmental agencies might be better placed to moderate, as I discuss in Chapter 4). Moreover, such a proposal is unlikely to ensure the broad inclusion of women's voices that Okin seeks; instead, it is more likely to lead those religious and cultural groups that are under scrutiny to resist cooperation and close ranks. This may then leave the state few options other than more forceful kinds of solutions, and in turn will do nothing to help empower vulnerable members within such groups, such as women.

KYMLICKA'S AUTONOMY-BASED LIBERALISM

Like Okin, Kymlicka defends a form of liberalism at the core of which lies ideals of individual autonomy and equality; he thinks such a 'comprehensive liberalism'[40] is defensible even in culturally plural liberal societies, such as Canada and the United States. Unlike Okin, however, Kymlicka is not in the

---

[37] Okin, 'Feminism and Multiculturalism: Some Tensions', p. 676.

[38] See especially Kukathas, *The Liberal Archipelago*.

[39] Okin, 'Multiculturalism and Feminism', p. 83.

[40] I use this term in the sense first used by John Rawls, who contrasts comprehensive liberalism with a more minimal form, that of political liberalism.

least ambivalent about endorsing group-based rights and protections for national minorities and certain recent immigrant groups. Indeed, he has long argued that liberal states should extend group rights and special arrangements to disadvantaged cultural communities—especially national minorities and some 'polyethnic' or immigrant groups—as a matter of liberal justice. Absent such special forms of accommodation, members of some cultural minorities cannot enjoy the opportunities afforded by liberal society, and equality and individual freedom more generally. This is because such opportunities and freedoms are determined in large part by one's access to a 'societal culture' which Kymlicka defines as 'a set of institutions, covering both public and private life, with a common language, which has historically developed over time on a given territory, which provides people with a wide range of choices about how to lead their lives'.[41] National minority groups do not readily have access to a thriving societal culture so defined, and so may need special rights to help ensure the survival of their communities, or else to facilitate their integration into broader social, political, and economic structures, as in the case of many immigrant groups.[42]

Where does Kymlicka's version of autonomy-based, comprehensive liberalism draw the lines of liberal tolerance, and how does it propose to deal with hard cases of cultural conflict, such as those concerning contested sex roles?[43] Kymlicka defends existing policies of multiculturalism in such states as Canada and Australia and believes that protections for cultural minorities should generally be made more extensive than they are at present. However, he attaches the proviso that cultural rights and protections must be ones that are likely to contribute to greater equality *between* minority groups and the rest of society; special rights are not justified if either their aim or effect is to sustain or create inequalities *within* cultural groups.[44] Kymlicka's liberal defense of cultural rights thus precludes special accommodation for groups that seek to significantly restrict the freedom and equality of their members. As Kymlicka reasons, 'a liberal view requires *freedom within* the minority group, and *equality between* the minority and majority groups'.[45]

For Kymlicka, even more so than for Okin, minority cultural practices are not simply to be prohibited by state edict—except those activities that involve clear violations of human rights, such as 'slavery or genocide or mass torture

---

[41] Will Kymlicka, 'Do We Need a Liberal Theory of Minority Rights?: Reply to Carens, Young, Parekh and Forst', *Constellations*, 4/1 (1997), p. 75. He first develops this argument in his *Liberalism, Community, and Culture*, especially Ch. 8.

[42] Kymlicka, 'Do We Need a Liberal Theory of Minority Rights?', p. 76.

[43] Also see the discussion in Deveaux, *Cultural Pluralism*, pp. 127–37.

[44] Kymlicka, *Multicultural Citizenship*, esp. p. 152.   [45] Ibid.

and expulsions'.[46] Rather, Kymlicka urges a politics of engagement, whereby liberals outside of the culture should speak out against recognized injustices and 'lend their support to any efforts the group makes to liberalize their culture'.[47] Kymlicka's strategy of liberalizing illiberal cultures has recently been echoed by Jacob Levy, who similarly warns of the dangers of merely prohibiting offending practices in culturally plural societies:

Direct state intervention is called for when the rights of women in minority cultures are violated; but for changes in patriarchal norms, a different approach is necessary. That approach commonly requires some policies of multicultural accommodation in order to allow women access to the rights of citizenship and while remaining members of their cultural communities. A rejection of multicultural policies might sometimes hasten the 'extinction' of illiberal cultures. Often, though, it means leaving women (and other victims of the culture's illiberalism) stranded, cutting them off from the rights and resources which might allow them to liberalize their culture from within.[48]

Levy's cautions about the negative effects of coercive responses to illiberal practices, particularly outright prohibition, are insights to which I return in subsequent chapters.

Equally critical, and signaling a clear difference with Okin's position, Kymlicka allows that national ethnic communities could opt out of federal or national rights frameworks entirely. This is consistent with his support for limited forms of self-government, in cases that warrant it—namely, those of certain national minorities. Where some degree of cultural autonomy has been won, and there exists a fundamental conflict between the social and legal principles of a national minority group (e.g. among Native or First Nations peoples in Canada) and specific liberal constitutional norms, it may be necessary to permit a group to be exempted from 'federal bills of rights and judicial review'.[49] Kymlicka sees such exemptions as an important option for cultural accommodation and coexistence in multination states, specifically for national minorities. However, this would clearly pave the way for possible rights violations against cultural group members, thereby running up against Kymlicka's stipulated (comprehensive liberal) conditions for policies of multicultural accommodation.

Given its commitment to core liberal principles of individual autonomy and equality, it is unlikely that Kymlicka's argument for cultural group rights could concede to accommodation for nonliberal customs and arrangements of traditional cultural minorities. In *Multicultural Citizenship*, Kymlicka recommends that liberal states adopt a strategy of liberalization vis-à-vis

---

[46] Ibid., p. 169.   [47] Ibid., p. 168.
[48] Levy, *The Multiculturalism of Fear*, p. 61.
[49] Kymlicka, *Multicultural Citizenship*, p. 168.

nonliberal groups, but allows that the practices in question may still warrant minimal toleration even if they do not deserve formal state support. Kymlicka also draws much reassurance from the existence of criminal and constitutional laws that set limits on permissible practices and arrangements, 'within the constraints of liberal-democratic values'.[50] But this seems to dodge, rather than face squarely, questions about practices that are not strictly prohibited by criminal law or in flagrant violation of a state's bill of rights. It is hard to avoid the conclusion that there exists a serious discrepancy between Kymlicka's stalwart defense of the liberal norms of autonomy and equality which ground his argument for multiculturalism, on the one hand, and his defense of collective cultural rights and protections, on the other. Only those cultural minorities with a reasonably liberal profile can count on formal accommodation by the liberal state.

In response to the criticism that his liberal theory of cultural rights sits uneasily with the values and arrangements of nonliberal cultural minorities, Kymlicka has offered two main replies. First, he has argued that his critics miscalculate or exaggerate the number of cultural minority groups in liberal democracies whose norms or practices directly challenge liberal principles: 'most members of most groups accept liberal democratic norms, whether they are immigrants or national minorities'.[51] Kymlicka however recognizes that there are exceptions, and cites such groups as Hasidic Jews or the Amish as examples. Yet this response is far from persuasive: Kymlicka says little, for example, about immigrants to Europe, North America, Australia and New Zealand from East Asia, North Africa, and the Indian subcontinent, some of whose practices and social arrangements are at odds with the liberal ideals of autonomy, individual choice, and equality that he stresses. Second and more importantly, Kymlicka has emphasized that applying minimal liberal criteria to cultural groups seeking special rights and accommodation is not simply a matter of asserting the hegemony of liberalism: 'liberals cannot assume that they are entitled to impose their principles', and moreover, 'some illiberal groups should be tolerated'.[52] Additionally, liberal states certainly should not seek to restrict particular practices or arrangements without considerable dialogue with the illiberal group in question: 'Relations between majority and minority groups should be determined by peaceful negotiation, not force'.[53] But there is, Kymlicka insists, a place for state-imposed restrictions regulating how group members may be treated; indeed, he sees such limits as critical to

---

[50] Kymlicka, *Politics in the Vernacular*, p. 176.

[51] Kymlicka, 'Do We Need a Liberal Theory of Minority Rights?', p. 81.

[52] Ibid., p. 84.

[53] Will Kymlicka, 'Two Models of Pluralism and Tolerance', *Analyse & Kritik*, 13 (1992), p. 52.

the overall success of multiculturalism, which he understands as aiming at the *integration* of cultural groups into the wider society under 'better and fairer terms of integration'.[54]

In one sense, then, Kymlicka's liberal multiculturalist framework seems to strike a compromise between liberal principles and the demand for cultural recognition or accommodation. Yet at the same time, he insists that we would do well to maintain a firm and transparent commitment to the value of personal autonomy in culturally plural societies, thereby delimiting the scope of practices deemed permissible on his liberal view.[55] This norm is not open to question or interpretation (as it is for certain other liberals, such as Jorge Valadez); nor does Kymlicka conceptualize autonomy and equality merely as normative requirements of public and political institutions, which would pose fewer restrictions on traditional groups. Rather, he has argued that these norms are also binding in the private sphere. According to Kymlicka, liberalism requires a strong conception of personal autonomy in public and private life; he faults John Rawls for supposing otherwise: 'The mere fact of *social plurality*, disconnected from any assumption of *individual autonomy*, cannot by itself defend the full range of liberal freedoms.'[56] Kymlicka's autonomy-based, comprehensive liberalism thus leads him to take a dim view of practices that restrict the range of options that agents enjoy, or diminish their freedom to make independent decisions about their lives. And significantly, this includes private, not merely public practices.[57]

It is here that the limits of Kymlicka's liberal approach to conflicts of culture begin to come into view, especially with respect to contested sex roles and arrangements. Kymlicka's comprehensive liberalism is partly indebted to a Millian-inspired model of human flourishing, one which foregrounds the importance of different life options and choices for individuals. Ironically, as we have seen, this commitment to freedom remains central to Kymlicka's liberal defense of policies of multiculturalism and group rights, even, presumably, for nonliberal minorities. But this autonomy-based conception of liberalism is at odds with the communal character of indigenous peoples, and the traditionalism of some immigrant groups, whose cultures often emphasize the need to shape and direct the choices of community members. Cultural

---

[54] Kymlicka, *Politics in the Vernacular*, p. 169.

[55] For Kymlicka's statement of the importance of autonomy to liberalism, see *Multicultural Citizenship*, esp. pp. 154–62, and 'Two Models of Pluralism and Tolerance', pp. 52–3.

[56] Kymlicka, *Multicultural Citizenship*, p. 163.

[57] In response to Okin's concerns about the implications of multiculturalism for women, Kymlicka has said that he means to include private and social arrangements within the scope of liberal objections to internal restrictions that some minority groups seek to impose on their members. See Kymlicka, 'Liberal Complacencies'.

conflicts concerning gender roles and arrangements are thus not easily resolvable on Kymlicka's model, except through the application of laws corresponding to liberal principles of sex equality and personal liberty.

Any conception of liberalism that insists that citizens must have available a wide range of life choices may find itself at odds with the claims of communities that seek to socialize their children into distinct and restrictive life roles, and to shape the choices of adult members. This is a difficult issue for liberals and democrats alike, one to which I return in Chapter 6, in my discussion of arranged marriage. The dilemma is especially accentuated in the case of religious minorities whose identities are bound up with a rejection of secular lifestyles and who may deeply resent state encroachments into their communities' affairs. For these groups, cultural recognition may require more considerable structures of community autonomy, in which they can assert their religious identities. Indeed, as more hard cases of cultural conflict begin to emerge in plural liberal states, we may be forced to conclude, along with Tariq Modood, that 'there is a theoretical incompatibility between multiculturalism and radical secularism'.[58] For comprehensive liberal proponents of cultural rights like Kymlicka, however, the dilemma remains as follows: if what cultures do is precisely to shape the lives of their members in myriad ways, on what grounds can certain forms of socialization be deemed permissible and others not, in the absence of extensive democratic deliberation?

BARRY'S LIBERALISM OF INDIVIDUAL RIGHTS

In *Culture and Equality*, Brian Barry defends traditional liberal principles against the claims of cultural minorities for special rights, protections, and exemptions.[59] Barry takes particular exception to the use of liberal principles to justify collective cultural rights, as evinced by the work of so-called liberal

---

[58] Tariq Modood, 'Anti-Essentialism, Multiculturalism, and the "Recognition" of Religious Groups', *The Journal of Political Philosophy*, 6/4 (1998), p. 397. Martin Chanock also argues that the profoundly secular character of liberal constitutionalism creates special challenges for group rights claims with a religious or cultural basis: 'Neither the discourses nor the institutions of Western constitutionalism appear to permit a relocaton of religion into the public and coercive realm'. See his '"Culture" and Human Rights: Orientalising, Occidentalising And Authenticity', in *Beyond Rights Talk and Culture Talk*, ed. Mahmood Mamdani (New York: St. Martin's Press, 2000), p. 17.

[59] For his full defense of liberal principles, see also Brian Barry, *Theories of Justice* (Cambridge, MA: Harvard University Press, 1989) and especially *Justice as Impartiality* (Cambridge, MA: Harvard University Press, 1995).

proponents of multiculturalism like Kymlicka. In Barry's view, efforts to discredit liberalism as inadequate to the demands of culturally plural societies, and to revise liberal theory accordingly, are gravely mistaken. However, he does not deny that social and economic inequalities in many cases track racial, ethnic, and (less frequently) religious differences in plural liberal societies. But Barry insists that these inequalities are due to structural patterns of pervasive social and economic disadvantage, rather than (as multiculturalists insist) disregard for groups' distinctive cultural identities. The solution is therefore to try to ensure that liberal states do a better job of securing equal rights and treatment for all, in part through the introduction of social and economic (positive) rights.

Barry is thus thoroughly skeptical of the multiculturalist agenda in political theory, and tries to demonstrate that much of the normative argumentation underpinning proposals for greater accommodation of cultural minorities in liberal democracies is fundamentally flawed. Many, if not most, of the specific proposals advanced by contemporary political theorists for special rights, exemptions, and other arrangements for cultural minorities are ill-defended and potentially disastrous from the vantage point of politics. Others are just plain silly, Barry claims: for example, Iris Young, he argues, ultimately advances a 'perverse thesis about the assimilationist impulse behind liberalism'. References to the Politically Correct Thought Police and the Commissioners of Political Correctness abound, reinforcing Barry's view that the demand for cultural group rights is a political strategy fuelled by a handful of wrong-headed intellectuals.[60]

Barry's polemical articulation and defense of traditional liberal principles is certainly sobering. He unpacks and holds up to critical scrutiny much of the rhetoric of recent political theory that endorses cultural pluralism, sometimes in quite useful ways. Moreover, Barry is, in my view, right to suggest that political conflicts over power, interest, and resources oftentimes lie at the heart of many claims for special cultural accommodation. Ultimately, however, Barry's claims that 'a politics of multiculturalism undermines a politics of redistribution' and that 'pursuit of the multiculturalist agenda makes the achievement of broadly based egalitarian policies more difficult' by 'diverting political effort away from universalistic goals' rely on a false dichotomy: redistribution versus recognition.[61] The very social and economic disadvantages and inequalities that Barry claims are misattributed to cultural and

---

[60] Barry, *Culture and Equality*, pp. 69, 271, and 328.

[61] Ibid. 8 and 325. Nancy Fraser coined this distinction but maintains that she does not view them as fundamentally opposed (far from it). See Fraser, 'From Redistribution to Recognition? Dilemmas of Justice in a "Postsocialist" Age', in her *Justice Interruptus: Critical Reflections on the 'Postsocialist' Condition* (New York and London: Routledge, 1997).

group identity by proponents of multiculturalism are, in many cases, inextricably bound up with issues of cultural injustice. This is particularly so for national minorities, from linguistic minorities like the Welsh and Québécois, to indigenous peoples in a number of democratic states. Yet Barry largely ignores the ongoing social and cultural effects of internal colonialism and racism, except insofar as they can be viewed through the lens of social and economic inequalities.

Beyond this conflation of recognition and redistribution, Barry's argument ultimately points to oversimple strategies of prohibition, without much community consultation or deliberation. For example, one of the cases he discusses at some length, the religious slaughter of animals for kosher and halal meat, is, for Barry, an issue that can and should be solved through (a priori) juridical reason alone:

Assuming that killing animals without prior stunning falls below the prevailing standards for the humane treatment of animals, the point is that those who are not prepared to eat meat from animals killed in any other way cannot eat meat without violating these minimum standards. It is not the law but the facts . . . of neurophysiology that make this so. The law may condone the additional suffering of animals killed without prior stunning, but if it does we should be clear that what it is doing is accommodating the tastes of a subset of carnivores, not observing the demands of religious freedom.[62]

Needless to say, this reply to observant Jews and Muslims in states where the issue of the slaughtering of animals according to religious custom has arisen is unlikely to build trust and cooperation between minority communities and the state. Barry concludes that laws permitting halal and kosher killing methods do not actually protect freedom of religion—since Muslims and Jews could always eat nonhalal or nonkosher meat, or become vegetarians— nor are these practices required by a commitment to freedom of conscience. The method by which he arrives at this conclusion is a striking illustration of the poverty of liberal a priori approaches to cultural disputes, however, for the views, experiences, self-understandings, and responses of Muslims and Jews play very little role in Barry's methodology. The application of this kind of juridical, nonconsultative, nondeliberative strategy is likely to exacerbate group–state tensions and underscore minority groups' status as supplicants to the state and second-class citizens. It is also unlikely that this approach would bring a halt to the practices in question, since minority groups may well deny the legitimacy of laws restricting their customs and so actively attempt to thwart them.

* * *

---

[62] Barry, *Culture and Equality*, pp. 45–6.

Okin and Barry, and to a lesser extent Kymlicka, wrongly view cultural disputes as necessarily revealing incommensurable moral values in liberal multicultural societies; it is thus no surprise that they see cultural conflicts as necessitating a reaffirmation of our commitments to individual liberal rights. But the thought that states can justly determine the permissibility of minority cultural practices largely by gauging their compatibility with individual rights and freedoms does not do justice to the requirements of norms of democratic legitimacy and respect for cultural pluralism. Moreover, it is not only the justice of state-directed initiatives that is in question, but also, as we see, their efficacy.

Alternative liberal approaches to cultural conflicts, and multiculturalism more generally, advocate a more laissez-faire response to the dilemmas posed by nonliberal groups. These range from views like that of Valadez, who defends multiculturalism on liberal grounds but suggests that cultural groups ought to be able to interpret and apply liberal norms and principles in their own ways, to Spinner-Halev's argument that oppressed groups in plural liberal societies ought to be granted presumptive autonomy and permitted to maintain illiberal practices, and finally to Kukathas' view that principles of freedom of conscience and freedom of association render unjust any restrictions on cultural groups, including those whose customs actually harm members.

'HANDS-OFF' LIBERAL APPROACHES: VALADEZ, KUKATHAS, AND SPINNER-HALEV

Like the other liberal thinkers discussed so far in this chapter, Valadez argues that even in plural liberal societies, there should be no equivocation regarding the state's commitments to core liberal principles of equality, autonomy, and civil and political rights more generally.[63] However, Valadez believes that autonomy is also valuable in its collective form, that is, insofar as it applies to 'ethnocultural groups'.[64] Moreover, according to Valadez, individual rights are 'communally mediated', thereby giving rise to legitimate group or collective rights. This means that cultural collectivities ought, under certain circumstances, to shape and define their own social practices and arrangements with minimal restraints:

---

[63] Valadez, *Deliberative Democracy,* p. 143.   [64] Ibid., p. 17.

As long as cultural groups respect the right of exit and the external judicial review of their implementation of liberal democratic rights, it is acceptable for them to imprint their own interpretation on civil, political, and entitlement rights by establishing alternative forms of property ownership, implementing their own forms of justice, establishing special requirements for entrance into or residence in tribal territories, determining educational policies, employing consensual procedures for making political decisions, and so forth. Cultural groups should be free to implement these policies even when they differ significantly from those used by the majority society.[65]

Can Valadez's proposal that ethnic and cultural minority groups be left to interpret liberal norms as they see fit be squared with a staunch commitment to individual political and civil rights? While the familiar individual autonomy rights that Valadez defends appear wholly uncontroversial, certain of these rights, including that of religious freedom, do in fact clash with the aspirations of some national minorities (which he otherwise wants to support): consider, for example, the Pueblo Indians' restrictions on freedom of religion, supported by the Supreme Court's decision in the Julia Martínez case. Other rights, such as that of sexual equality, will quickly run afoul of the customs and systems of governance and personal law defended by some national groups and even immigrant communities in liberal democracies. For instance, in postapartheid South Africa, the defenders of systems of customary law and traditional leadership generally reject gender equality. These examples should not lead us to conclude that civil and political rights should be trumped by cultural autonomy—far from it—but rather remind us that the mere assertion of such individual entitlements does not magically dissolve conflicts between these rights and existing practices. Nor does a defense of such rights obviate the need for democratic processes to mediate such tensions in plural liberal societies.

Valadez is right that there is more room for fluidity in the interpretation and application of liberal principles in multicultural societies than currently exists, and that a deliberative democratic framework for mediating intercultural conflicts can readily incorporate different views of content and application of principles (as I argue in Chapter 4). Nevertheless, it follows from the central role accorded to liberal individual autonomy in Valadez's defense of multiculturalism that there must be many more limits to nonliberal group-based cultural practices than he supposes—a fact which tends to undermine the laissez-faire aspect of his argument for cultural accommodation. Given Valadez's fundamental commitment to deliberative democracy, it is perhaps surprising that his discussion is ultimately vulnerable to similar criticisms as are a priori and juridical liberal views. In conceiving of a model of intercultural

[65] Ibid., pp. 18–19.

dialogue and dispute resolution, Valadez begins from the belief that 'deliberative democracy is particularly suited for multicultural societies because of
the existence of deep and enduring differences in conceptions of the good in
these societies'.[66] At times, thus, he seems to recognize that in plural societies,
even core liberal rights may apply differently to certain cultural communities;
but on the question of whether cultural groups must implement rights in
ways that 'conform to liberal interpretations', Valadez acknowledges that this
is 'difficult to determine in some cases'. This leads to seemingly inconsistent
recommendations: certain actions are simply unacceptable (mutilation; denying women political rights), but curiously, groups exercising membership
restrictions—including, if necessary, excluding certain women members and
so removing their political rights—ought not to be ruled out.[67]

These pronouncements are less ad hoc than they might at first seem. As for
Kymlicka, so for Valadez, the best defense of multiculturalism is ultimately
that it supports individual autonomy and flourishing by fostering 'preservation of cultural contexts which make life-options meaningful and within
which self-identity and collective responsibilities are established'.[68] A commitment to autonomy in turn 'makes it possible to articulate the political,
cultural, and economic institutional structures which are necessary for individuals to flourish in self-governing political communities'.[69] In theory, then,
Valadez's approach to multiculturalism, and to cultural conflicts, offers
minority groups more autonomy insofar as they should be able to interpret
liberal norms and principles differently. It is Valadez's entirely plausible
marriage of deliberative democracy and liberal principles that makes this
possible. But when it comes to actual inter- and especially intracultural
conflicts—the latter of which Valadez does not much discuss—the basic
tension between a priori commitments to liberal principles and particular
cultural practices and beliefs that challenge these commitments, remains.

Despite this, Valadez places tremendous stock in the importance of intercultural understanding, and practices aimed at increasing it, as a means of
fostering greater deliberative and political equality between minority and
majority communities.[70] Such intercultural understanding is presumably
expected to help mediate entrenched intercultural conflicts, a claim that
seems not unreasonable provided some deliberative resolution is pursued.
Some idea of how less severe cultural conflicts might be mediated according
to Valadez's approach is also suggested by his extensive discussion of civic
voluntary associations, which he views as 'mediating institutions' that can
help identify politically overlooked problems, serve as means for community

---

[66] Ibid., p. 6. [67] Ibid., p. 18. [68] Ibid., p. 17.
[69] Ibid., p. 142. [70] Ibid., p. 88.

self-empowerment, and help to forge social solidarity more generally.[71] Quite possibly, some such civic organizations could play a role in the evaluation and reform of cultural practices and arrangements.[72] But for hard cases of cultural conflict, such as those that concern questions of gender socialization and sexual inequality, it is difficult to see how Valadez's argument for multiculturalism would not in the end restrict more than it allows.

Even more so than Valadez, Kukathas believes that cultural and religious groups ought to be free to interpret—or indeed, ignore—liberal norms as they see fit. Kukathas presents a vision of liberal, multicultural society in which free association and toleration of diversity are of central importance. But rather than developing this thought into an argument for group-based cultural rights and protections, he views these principles as underscoring the commitment to an individualist standpoint more generally: individuals have fundamental value, quite apart from the groups that they may or may not be a part of.[73] Associations (groups, etc.) are critical to individuals—'society, in the end, is a kind of union of associations'[74]—but they are eminently mutable, as are, increasingly, the political boundaries that demarcate most kinds of groups.

Kukathas' view of groups and associations as essentially fluid, even if they are not always voluntary, contributes to his rejection of the case for group rights. For the state to accord formal group rights to minorities would be to treat groups as insular, closed entities, and will tend to entrench minorities (or majorities).[75] But more importantly, since on Kukathas' view what needs protection is the *individual*'s right to form, associate, or join groups (or not), or to disassociate from groups, it would be wrong-headed of the liberal state to artificially reinforce the power of groups. By granting cultural groups special powers and formal collective rights, the state oversteps its proper purview and may also risk undercutting the rights of individuals to freely associate. Much like Okin and Barry, who express misgivings about group-based protections, Kukathas emphatically 'rejects the assumption of a closed society, and rejects the idea of recognizing group rights or according

---

[71] Ibid., pp. 19, 84, and *passim*.

[72] Valadez writes, 'By providing citizens with a forum for the collective articulation and public expression of community problems and concerns, civic associations can inform governments of issues they have inadvertently or intentionally failed to address. The independent and grassroots character of civic associations enable them to introduce a variety of otherwise excluded perspectives into public discourse and, if necessary, challenge the government's position on issues of concern to substate communities. By broadening the range of voices on public issues, they heighten civic awareness of the diversity of needs and perspectives that should be taken into account in arriving at communally adequate solutions to social problems'. Ibid., p. 348. I explore the role of both ethnocultural group associations and civic voluntary organizations in mediating conflicts of culture in Chapters 5 and 8.

[73] Kukathas, *The Liberal Archipelago*, p. 90.   [74] Ibid., p. 84.   [75] Ibid., p. 89.

minorities political representation'.[76] Beyond this, Kukathas argues that it is simply not the state's proper purpose to pursue either 'cultural integration, or cultural engineering'.[77]

Yet so important to Kukathas are the principles of toleration of diversity and respect for freedom of association and conscience that he rejects suggestions (by Kymlicka, Okin, and Barry and others) that the liberal state ought to restrict groups *in any way*—even those groups that are themselves opposed to these principles in the sense of practicing internal discrimination against certain members, such as women, gays and lesbians, and nonbelievers. As Kukathas writes, 'a free society should tolerate all kinds of associations, including those which do not themselves seem to value freedom or abide by the principle of toleration, and which seem to embrace practices which are intolerable'.[78] An important consequence of this is that the state's authority with respect to associations would actually diminish, at the same time that the different authorities associated with groups would come to enjoy greater jurisdictional authority and independence (though not, Kukathas hastens to add, *sovereignty*, given the overlapping and interdependent nature of society, and globalization). This is all well and good, for in Kukathas' view, 'a society is a liberal society to the extent it is willing to tolerate the multiplication of authorities, including authorities which seek to disentangle themselves more thoroughly from the wider society—provided they are prepared to bear the costs this invariably involves.'[79] The flip side of this jurisdictional independence is that groups cannot expect any protections or support from the state, but they can reasonably expect noninterference (except where members' overlapping affiliations may rightfully bring other jurisdictional authorities into play).

A serious consequence of the relative jurisdictional independence which Kukathas supports is the danger that 'internal minorities' may suffer greater oppression than if cultural and religious groups were granted conditional rights, subject to, for example, Kymlicka's proviso that groups not oppress their own members. But this is par for the course, according to Kukathas: groups are legitimate insofar as members choose to stay put (or rather, choose not to leave), and this gives them the authority to govern their communities according to their own beliefs.[80] Kukathas fully acknowledges that under this arrangement, associations 'may indeed be quite illiberal', but insists that, nevertheless, 'the outside community has no right to intervene to prevent those members acting within their rights'.[81] In practice, Kukathas envisages that a multicultural society committed to toleration and freedom of

---

[76] Ibid., p. 5. [77] Ibid., p. 15. [78] Ibid., p. 17–18.
[79] Ibid., p. 27. [80] Ibid., p. 95. [81] Ibid., p. 96.

association and conscience could well lead to permitting such practices such as enforced arranged marriage, unschooled and illiterate children, refusal of standard medical treatment, and even practices 'which inflict cruel and "unusual" punishment'.[82] These are, however, acceptable costs in a free, multicultural society:

> The tolerationist position . . . must concede that, in principle, it is possible that under a regime of toleration some associations will condone or uphold practises which are harmful to children—and to others in those groups who are weak or vulnerable. What it relies upon to temper this is the pressures of civil association more generally, which induce a measure of conformity to the standards of the wider society.[83]

While in certain respects Kukathas' position may seem rash, it has been echoed by some proponents of multicultural group rights who are similarly worried about the propensity of liberal states to oppress minority communities under the guise of protecting internal minorities. Most notably, Spinner-Halev has argued that 'avoiding the injustice of imposing reforms on oppressed groups is often more important than avoiding the injustice of discrimination against women'.[84] Like Kukathas, Spinner-Halev seeks to protect cultural and religious groups' autonomy, which, unlike Kukathas, he believes will usually necessitate special cultural protections. To offer these protections on a strictly conditional basis, or to insist on reforming aspects of a religion or culture that conflict with liberal norms, is to fail to acknowledge the history of oppression suffered by minority groups as well as groups' right to shape their own identity. In Spinner-Halev's estimation, therefore, 'the injustice of allowing for individual rights and equality to be undermined must be balanced against the injustice of imposing reform on oppressed groups'.[85]

Using the example of religious groups' personal laws, Spinner-Halev makes a case for limiting the role of the state in formalizing, supporting, or prohibiting such laws.[86] This is a matter for groups themselves to decide. Spinner-Halev's 'democracy proposal', as he calls it, in principle 'increases the collective autonomy of the community, by giving all its members the power to decide upon its personal laws', but importantly, it does not require wide community participation in decision-making or reform processes ('the community itself will decide who establishes its rules').[87] Nor need it require political engagement with the majoritarian society: indeed, Spinner-Halev worries that participation in democratic political life tends to breed a degree

---

[82] Kukathas, *The Liberal Archipelago*, p. 134. [83] Ibid., p. 147.
[84] Spinner-Halev, 'Feminism, Multiculturalism, Oppression', p. 86.
[85] Ibid., p. 105. [86] Ibid., p. 108. [87] Ibid., p. 109.

of social and cultural homogeneity.[88] Rather, so long as group representatives are seen as legitimate and 'democratically accountable'—a standard he does not elaborate on—the actual internal process of reforming customs or laws may be fairly exclusive, albeit at least internal to the group.[89] Importantly, Spinner-Halev recognizes that if groups themselves have sole authority over the issue of which personal laws to implement and which of these to reform (and how), then there may be a corresponding diminution of personal autonomy for many group members[90]—particularly so for girls or women, as Spinner-Halev readily admits. Nor will the fact that his approach allows more organic forms of internal reform to occur necessarily make it more likely that religious personal laws will be made more sexually egalitarian (that is, it could go the other way).

Both Kukathas' and Spinner-Halev's hands-off positions, arising from very different premises, would seem vulnerable to the charge that they do not adequately protect internal minorities. Spinner-Halev sets the limits of group autonomy at the point of 'serious physical harm', and leans heavily on the right of exit to ensure that the mistreatment of internal minorities does not become excessive.[91] But these limits beg more questions: should a forced traditional marriage which involves no physical harm be permitted? On Spinner-Halev's view, the answer would appear to be yes; as he writes, 'while (personal laws) can and do harm women, the harm is not all encompassing'.[92] Similarly, the right of exit is hardly the bulwark against mistreatment that Spinner-Halev expects. While acknowledging the difficulty of leaving one's group, in many instances, he insists that it is not unreasonable to expect oppressed members to take the step of exiting: in the case of Native peoples, 'badly treated women (or men) can leave their tribe.... If women were refused education and subjected to humiliation, many would undoubtedly flee'.[93] But Spinner-Halev's optimism overlooks the very ways in which restrictions and ill treatment can condition women to fear their intimates and leaders alike, and so to adapt to their circumstances rather exit.

In response to obvious concerns about the prospect that his laissez-faire position may increase internal group oppression, Kukathas invokes several arguments, some more compelling than others. The most persuasive of these is his argument that in a liberal multicultural society, multiple authorities exist which can and do put pressure on communities whose practices seem

---

[88] Thus 'democracy tends to weaken group-based differences, not strengthen them'—the reason being that 'to have this sort of conversation, certain cultural similarities are needed and cultural references need to be shared'. See Spinner-Halev, 'Difference and Diversity in an Egalitarian Democracy', *The Journal of Political Philosophy*, 3/3 (1995), pp. 268–9.

[89] Spinner-Halev, 'Feminism, Multiculturalism, Oppression', pp. 109 and 108.

[90] Ibid., p. 109.   [91] Ibid., p. 98 and 106.   [92] Ibid., p. 107.   [93] Ibid., p. 106.

unjust or harmful. Here Kukathas offers a nonstate centered view of the public sphere as a realm marked by 'a *convergence* of moral practices', and which is 'not coextensive with the state'.[94] As a result, even in liberal democratic societies, we can assume that there is a plurality of norms governing different communities: 'there are... many (overlapping) public realms representing settlements where different practices have converged on particular standards to govern social interaction'.[95] There is no single moral authority or set of moral standards in a plural society; indeed, 'groups with "intolerable" practices would have the option of withdrawing from the wider moral community'.[96] While this latter suggestion raises concerns (which I discuss below), the recognition that there are plural standards of moral conduct in multicultural societies is an important insight. It is also the case, as Kukathas suggests, that persuasion, rather than force, is to be preferred as a means of fostering change from the outside[97]—although in my view, it is debatable just how effective this is in the absence of initiatives coming from inside cultural groups.

Related to this conceptualization of the public sphere, Kukathas reminds us that if multiple jurisdictional authorities are acknowledged, it is possible that individual members of cultural collectivities could raise legal challenges—based on their memberships in other associations or the larger state—against their groups, protesting their unjust treatment.[98] Indeed, pressure could be brought to bear from many different corners, depending on the multiple memberships of the individuals concerned, and the resources available to them. Through divided authority, 'liberty would be preserved to the extent that people would leave groups whose ways—or authorities—they could not abide, but those who preferred to live in such ways... were not forced to mend them to conform to the preferences of dissenters'.[99]

These safeguards—the right of exit and the right to appeal to different authorities to challenge one's unjust treatment—are some of the mechanisms that Kukathas relies on to support potential objections to his cultural freedom approach. But as Ayelet Shachar points out in connection with the right of exit, this puts a tremendous burden on those who suffer abuse to take on the system that oppresses them.[100] Why put the onus on individuals, rather than

---

[94] Kukathas, *The Liberal Archipelago*, p. 134.   [95] Ibid., p. 134.   [96] Ibid., p. 134.

[97] Ibid., p. 136–7. In light of his emphasis on persuasion, it is strange, then, that Kukathas is so leery of reform, claiming that being permitted only to practice a pale version of a custom is simply not the same (Ibid., p. 138).

[98] Ibid., p. 144.   [99] Ibid., p. 211.

[100] Ayelet Shachar, 'On Citizenship and Multicultural Vulnerability', *Political Theory*, 28 (2000), 64–89, p. 65.

introducing protections for those who suffer discrimination and abuse? Kukathas is right that we should tread very gingerly here, for outside interference is very often the source of injustice, sometimes in the form of continued colonial oppression.[101] It *is* within the scope of the liberal state's authority (at different levels) to protect the freedom of diverse associations and groups, according to Kukathas, but this does not apparently extend to state protections for cultural dissenters: 'the conscientious beliefs of the majority or the dominant also have weight', and state interference undercuts this.[102] But how is it, exactly, that extending certain protections to individuals that are structurally vulnerable to abuse and discrimination undermines the freedom of other group members? It is not so much a matter of seeking, naively, to make freedom of association or dissociation 'costless', as Kukathas suggests,[103] but rather of ensuring that there are some minimal protections in place that make it possible to say 'no' to aspects of a culture without paying for it with one's life. Kukathas might protest that taking steps to make people's exit options meaningful, or to ban discrimination practiced by a given group, is outside the proper purview of the state. The role of the state, in his view, is not to promote equality, for '[d]iversity is too complex for group equality to be reached without significantly altering the structure of diversity'; rather, '[i]ts role is to serve as an umpire'.[104] Yet extending support to less powerful group members and fostering forums in which their voices can be heard is surely a far cry from promoting substantive equality, as I argue in subsequent chapters.

Kukathas' defense of his laissez-faire approach depends in large part on his claim that group membership, while not necessarily voluntary, is nonetheless free in the sense that members could ultimately choose to leave. But there are good reasons not to use implied consent as the litmus test for the permissibility of practices. On the one hand, some cultural roles and arrangements do not throw up easy evidence of consent, so the notion that group members agree to customs may seem inapplicable or inappropriate. There is also the problem of adaptive preferences, particularly significant in the case of girls and women socialized to accept second-class status. On the other hand, *merely* securing consent may leave vulnerable individuals worse off or unprotected: when members of cultural minorities seemingly agree to customs that unduly restrict their own freedom or that of other members, even without evidence of extreme manipulation or coercion, there may still be cause for concern. Stark power imbalances within communities can make a farce of

---

[101] See especially Spinner-Halev, 'Feminism, Multiculturalism, Oppression'.
[102] Kukathas, *The Liberal Archipelago*, p. 116.
[103] Ibid., p. 112.   [104] Ibid., pp. 235 and 212.

such consent. In imputing consent to the reluctance of some cultural or religious group members to exit the community, we risk overlooking more subtle forms of coercion and so may fail to give much-needed support to cultural dissenters. According to Kukathas, disgruntled members and would-be reformers may opt *not* to leave the group for any number of reasons—some people do not mind constraints on their freedom, or make strategic calculations that it is better to stay—but the critical thing is that *they are not unfree to do so.*[105] However, this assertion begs questions, as Leslie Green notes:

[T]he bare existence of a right of exit does not establish that particular groups are free associations. The exit model is too much in the grip of an economic view of human nature, according to which well informed consumers enter and leave the market with low transaction costs. But the forms of group life that matter most to us are not at all like that: Group membership has noninstrumental value, entry is automatic or even ascriptive, the groups structure whole lives, and the transaction costs of change are huge. The notion that the dissatisfied might simply leave is, in such circumstances, fatuous.[106]

As Green continues, 'most people do not believe that failure to exit means that they have agreed to obey', because of the sheer difficulty or even impossibility of exiting, in many circumstances.[107] But even if we infer some kind of tacit consent to membership from the fact of nonexit, and were to overlook the extent to which cultural and religious groups are not really 'free' in Kukathas' sense, there is a further problem: as Green writes, 'it is not plausible to suppose that agreement has unlimited power. Agreements create, vary, and extinguish rights and duties only because there are good reasons to endorse the power-conferring rule that they may do so. But the underlying reasons do not go so far as to validate *every* purported exercise of the power in question'.[108]

Kukathas, then, has not really established that individuals always have the (minimal) autonomy and resources necessary to make the right of exit meaningful. Although Kukathas does not actually tout the value of autonomy, it is hard to deny that, as Green points out, 'individual autonomy is the value that grounds rights of exit'.[109] Yet here Kukathas trades on a slippery distinction between freedom and autonomy; he argues that one does not need to be autonomous or to make autonomous choices in order to be free.[110] Quite apart from the many questions this distinction begs, it ultimately prevents Kukathas from developing a more persuasive argument to the effect that individuals actually enjoy sufficient basic personal autonomy to exercise exit

[105] Ibid., p. 109.   [106] Leslie Green, 'Rights of Exit', *Legal Theory*, 4/2 (1998), 168–85, p. 175.
[107] Ibid., p. 172.   [108] Ibid., p. 175.   [109] Ibid., p. 167.
[110] Kukathas, *The Liberal Archipelago*, p. 113.

rights. Kukathas is rightly concerned that the liberal ideal of the free-chooser will wrongly become the standard for multicultural accommodation. To this end, he rightly asks us to recognize that individuals may wield agency in even the most traditional of cultures or religions. In the hypothetical case of Fatima, a Muslim mother and wife of a Malay fisherman in Peninsular Malaysia, he writes that 'she has not "chosen" it [her life]; she has simply not rejected it. She has acquiesced in a life she has been raised to lead; but she has not embraced it. Being free, she may reject it if she so chooses; but she may not choose at all and remain free'.[111] Kukathas describes Fatima's freedom as the freedom of liberty of conscience: she 'may live a life she has not rejected and is not forced to live a life she cannot accept'.[112] This seems to me the right characterization, for reasons that will be developed more fully later, in my discussion of arranged marriage (Chapter 6): one need not actively *choose* a particular kind of life in order to be considered, in some basic sense, free (or at least, not unfree). But this is not an adequate answer to more important challenges. Specifically, Kukathas needs to show how it is that the exit rights of all group members, including highly vulnerable, at-risk individuals, are meaningful, in order for this right to do the work he attributes to it (i.e. providing a safeguard against oppression).

For Kukathas to demonstrate that the right of exit functions as he says it does would require several things. In particular, Kukathas would need, first, to show that the strong socialization of members does not preclude exit. Evidence to support this claim will surely differ from group to group; but at least for some, '[e]ven to contemplate leaving requires enough cognitive and emotional distance to understand and envision a new future. Achieving that is a great challenge and it explains why rejecting one's family of origin, abandoning one's religion, or coming out of the closet are typically wrenching and life-transforming experiences'.[113] The socialization of girls and women presents special challenges. This is of course especially the case with children, who have no recourse against abuse by their parents, but it is equally true of women in some cultures. Okin and Shachar have both written convincingly of the different circumstances and contexts that women face which may make exit a particularly difficult, if not impossible, option. Without an understanding of the power relations within a group, and the particular cultural role played by women, the right of exit is, for many, a mere abstraction.[114] Women and girls face many more restrictions than boys and men in light of their different socialization, as Okin notes. Moreover, within some minority

---

[111] Ibid., p. 113.   [112] Ibid.   [113] Green, 'Rights of Exit', p. 172.
[114] Ayelet Shachar, *Multicultural Jurisdictions: Cultural Differences and Women's Rights* (Cambridge: Cambridge University Press, 2001), pp. 41 and 68–70.

cultures, girls have less access to education, resources, and opportunities that build up self-esteem and a sense of independence, which can undermine possibilities for exiting the group.[115] For Okin, stark differences in socialization are evidence of sexual discrimination, and warrant the rejection of group rights claims, as well as, quite possibly, state intervention in the affairs of the community in question.[116] Like Kukathas, I disagree sharply with Okin's conclusion, which seems much too invasive and intolerant. When the state intervenes by implementing laws based on a priori liberal principles, rather than pursuing a consultative approach foregrounding the deliberations of cultural group members themselves, internal minorities may remain disenfranchised and disempowered. That Okin's ultimate conclusion misses the mark does not, however, detract from her important insight that the right of exit is not a reliable safeguard against extreme oppression; as she puts it, 'What kind of a choice is one between total submission and total alienation from the person she understands herself to be?'[117]

Aside from the question of socialization and the constraints it engenders, there is the issue of the resources and opportunities for exit, as well as the consequences of leaving one's cultural community. In extreme cases, there are individuals who either cannot hope to exit their group alive, or without risking grave losses (custody of children; property and inheritance rights; one's livelihood; friends and relations). If circumstances are sufficiently extreme in terms of coercion or probable consequences of exit (such as in the case of honor killings), we would not want to say that the right of exit is genuinely enjoyed by all. Less dramatically but equally importantly, it would need to be the case that there is a safe haven of sorts for those fleeing their group. This is partly a matter of resources: the existence of shelters for women escaping abusive traditional marriages, a reasonable expectation of police protection, and resources to help them live outside of their marriages and possibly their communities. But there is also an institutional piece to this that may require significant changes on the part of the liberal state itself. As Jacob Levy argues, '[i]f the liberal polity is to offer freedom and refuge, it must genuinely differentiate itself from the communities being exited from. If the state's laws mirror the internal rules of the religious and cultural communities, then it can hardly claim to offer a viable alternative to them.'[118]

While Kukathas offers a compelling vision of cultural freedom, then, he wrongly portrays cultural and religious groups as fundamentally free

---

[115] Okin, '"Mistresses of Their Own Destiny"', esp. pp. 218–20.   [116] Ibid., p. 229.
[117] Ibid.
[118] Jacob Levy, 'Sexual Orientation, Exit and Refuge', in *Minorities Within Minorities*, eds. Avigail Eisenberg and Jeff Spinner-Halev (Cambridge: Cambridge University Press, 2005), p. 184.

associations, and overestimates the protective effect of the right of exit. As a consequence, he too readily overlooks the grievous harm that may befall vulnerable, at-risk members of cultural minorities. Although he is right that 'the threat of oppression is as likely to come from outside the minority community as it is from within', he has not shown that the potential violation of the majority's rights and freedom—in the form of intervention by external authorities—is necessarily greater than the harms suffered by vulnerable, at-risk members.[119] The potential for state interference that is itself ill-conceived or harmful is however real, and Kukathas supplies ample evidence of past state actions that were worse than the problems they were intended to remedy.[120] But to conclude from this that there is little legitimate or practicable role for outsiders (chiefly, but not exclusively, the state) in supporting or extending protection to internal minorities is unwarranted.

One alternative to heavy-handed forms of state intervention in the affairs of cultural and religious communities is look to innovative and inclusive forms of dispute resolution that can engage diverse stake-holders and empower silenced members of groups. For Kukathas, however, this constitutes a form of interference that is incompatible with liberal commitments to freedom of association and freedom of conscience. For similar reasons, he also rejects dialogue-based solutions as reinforcing a bias against certain groups that may not be able fully to articulate the meaning or good of their practices in such forums.[121] As I argue in the coming chapters, however, a deliberative approach to conflicts of culture could in fact be designed so as to minimize overt state interference and to foreground the authority of *all* group members. Moreover, such an approach might prove to be less of an imposition on groups (and so on freedom of association) than the legal challenges that Kukathas urges cultural dissenters to pursue against their communities, as members of other associations and the broader society. Finally, mediating conflicts of culture through a deliberative democratic process is also compatible with nonliberal outcomes, and so in this sense affirms the cultural freedom that Kukathas defends.

---

[119] Kukathas, *The Liberal Archipelago*, pp. 135–6; see also p. 112.

[120] Ibid. 135–6; Kukathas cautions that he does not mean to suggest that the state, or 'political societies', are 'uniquely oppressive; local communities or religious communities can be no less so'. Ibid., p. 192.

[121] Ibid., p. 138.

3

Women's Rights as Human Rights

In the last chapter, I argued that liberal responses to conflicts of culture are problematic for both normative and practical reasons, and that we should, wherever possible, eschew a priori and juridical approaches to cultural conflicts when it comes to evaluating and reforming harmful or sexually discriminatory cultural practices. For many, the dangers of internal colonialism and cultural or political oppression at the hands of the state speak against state-centric responses to cultural conflicts. Yet some critics of heavy-handed domestic responses to cultural and religious practices, including, sometimes, group members themselves, have increasingly looked to international institutions to challenge (or to defend) discriminatory practices and traditions, pursuing transnational legal and political solutions. Although international responses may also be perceived as unwanted intervention, appeals to human rights discourse and human rights instruments can play an important role in three circumstances: when national legislative or judicial frameworks oppress cultural minority groups, by prohibiting even nonharmful cultural practices and arrangements through legislation and/or criminal laws; conversely, when states give carte blanche to groups and fail to offer protections for 'minorities within minorities'; or finally, when the state denies cultural dissenters opportunities to contest and modify group practices, especially through legal means.

In this chapter, I ask whether the human rights framework is an effective resource for evaluating, and if necessary, reforming, gendered cultural practices. I explore this question first by means of an analysis of the movement for women's rights as human rights, and of the major international instruments for pressing women's human rights. Following this, I discuss the normative power of a human rights strategy for addressing the problem of internal minorities, particularly women, by taking up two philosophical arguments for securing women's rights and protecting them from harm. I look first at what I call the 'possible consent' argument advanced by Kantian philosopher Onora O'Neill. And second, I discuss Martha Nussbaum's capability theory, which asks what core capabilities and resources individuals (and specifically women) need for full human functioning. Lastly, I suggest how the human rights paradigm might be best utilized, and also how it might be rethought, to better address the issue of contested cultural and religious practices. Here, I join various immanent critics who note the limits of human rights frameworks, and argue that the practices surrounding the elaboration and rearticulation of human rights, as well as their application, must be made more deeply democratic and politically inclusive, particularly of women.

WHY LOOK TO HUMAN RIGHTS?

When liberal democratic states attempt to limit, reform, or prohibit cultural practices and arrangements of ethnic and religious groups, their actions may be perceived as unwanted intrusions, or even oppression. Not surprisingly, such intervention often backfires and even strengthens the custom in question: witness, for example, the renewed commitment to the wearing of the headscarf or chador in some North African communities in France and Turkey, where authorities have banned it from public schools and universities, respectively. Although in some cases, state bodies make efforts to consult with the community in question, too often these overtures have a token quality to them and do not help to build lasting political trust. A minority community's confidence in state-led reforms of their cultural arrangements is diminished still further when racism is pervasive in the broader social, economic, and political institutions.[1]

Whereas the liberal state's efforts to transform cultural or religious practices may be seen as repressive by some cultural communities—and may actually be so—human rights are thought by many to 'stand outside of, and above, politics, where politics is understood as the play of group preferences or state policy'.[2] Although I argue in this chapter that human rights law does *not* in fact stand above politics, it does nevertheless have certain advantages

---

[1] In Britain, the media backlash against the phenomenon of forced marriages included xenophobic attacks on the custom of arranged marriage generally and the family arrangements of South Asian Britons. Recently, in the wake of the London transport system bombings of July 7, 2005, there have been over 100 reported attacks on Muslim Britons (including one fatality), and some conservative journalists and commentators openly questioned whether policies to curb immigration and multiculturalism ought to be introduced. In Holland, following the assassination of the filmmaker Theo Van Gogh, racist and xenophobic incidents have also increased dramatically.

[2] Austin Sarat and Thomas Kearns, 'The Unsettled Status of Human Rights: An Introduction', in *Human Rights: Concepts, Contests, and Contingencies*, eds. A. Sarat and T. Kearns (Ann Arbor, MI: University of Michigan Press, 2001), p. 9.

over state-sponsored actions and processes. First, as mentioned above, certain international or transnational bodies may be less associated with state power than one's own government and so can set the stage for a less antagonistic consideration of calls for cultural reform or protections. Second, human rights law can target the actions of *states* that fail to treat some of their citizens with dignity, as in the case of states that continue to treat indigenous or Native peoples in a discriminatory manner. This is a large part of what makes human rights both powerful and yet highly contested. As Hilary Charlesworth notes:

The very basis of human rights law is controversial because it imposes restraints on governmental action in the name of individual or minority autonomy. Both authoritarian *and* democratically elected governments are subject to the constraints of human rights law. In this sense, human rights law is counter-majoritarian in that it provides protection for individuals, groups, and minorities so that, in certain defined contexts, their interests are not always sacrificed to those of the government or political majority of the day.[3]

States can also be called to account, through the use of human rights instruments, for their passive acceptance of practices that violate women's rights:

Traditionally, human rights law has been used to show government responsibility for abuse and to demand government redress. However, advocates for women's human rights have made a clear case that governments, while not directly responsible for private–agent abuse, can be seen as condoning it—through inadequate prosecution of wife abuse, sexual harassment, rape, etc.—and thus be held accountable.[4]

Third, human rights language has wide currency and can be taken up by cultural insiders and outsiders alike. Activists working on behalf of NGOs can invoke particular human rights in order to protest cultural or religious practices and arrangements that seriously harm or discriminate against persons. For example, at the 1993 World Conference on Human Rights in Vienna, activists presented delegates with a petition signed by half a million women, calling on them 'to recognize that rape as a tactic of war, transporting women for sexual slavery, and dowry deaths were all forms of torture and therefore violations of human rights'.[5] Carried out by private citizens but also

[3] Hilary Charlesworth, 'The Challenges of Human Rights Law for Religious Traditions', in *Religion and International Law*, eds. Mark Janis and Carolyn Evans (Boston, London, and The Hague: Martinus Nijhoff Publishers, 1999), p. 403.

[4] Elisabeth Friedman, 'Women's Human Rights: The Emergence of a Movement', in *Women's Rights, Human Rights: International Feminist Perspectives*, eds. Julie Peters and Andrea Wolper (New York and London: Routledge, 1995), p. 21.

[5] Temma Kaplan, 'Women's Rights as Human Rights: Grassroots Women Redefine Citizenship in a Global Context,' in *Women's Rights and Human Rights: International Historical Perspectives*, eds. Patricia Grimshaw, Katie Holmes, and Marilyn Lake (New York: Palgrave, 2001), p. 299.

sometimes representatives of the state (especially the military), these actions are sometimes defended by appeal to cultural or religious traditions (as in the case of dowry deaths), and ignored by the state. Human rights mechanisms can serve as an international ombudsman of sorts in these instances, applying necessary moral pressure on governments. For example, a key goal of women's human rights activists from the 1990s onward has been to try to get states to recognize and take responsibility for their role in condoning or failing to prevent domestic violence by private individuals (by failing to protect women, adequately punish perpetrators, etc.). While these efforts have met only with mixed success, the fact that human rights treaties can at least in principle bring the actions of both state actors and private agents (and communities) under scrutiny is an important benefit of the human rights framework.

There is a further reason why a human rights paradigm may prove a useful one for addressing customs, practices, and arrangements that discriminate against women. This concerns the paradoxical and multifaceted effects of globalization. Some of globalization's worst consequences are so grave and pervasive that they absolutely require a transnational political response, using the language of human rights and engaging citizens from multiple countries. Globalization has deepened women's poverty in many parts of the world, in many instances reducing their control over the type and conditions of work, and over the circumstances of their family life and place of abode. As the power of transnational capital has grown, the power of individual citizens to make decisions about important aspects of daily life has shrunk; women workers are often the most readily exploited, often working under informal and illegal conditions (e.g. textile and garment workers in both the global north and south). Women's ability to feed their families is also increasingly jeopardized by globalization: women produce 60 percent of the world's food, typically with minimal resources, and the commercialization of agriculture in the wake of globalization is threatening subsistence farming as well as compromising food security.[6]

Yet globalization has also, paradoxically, laid the basis for a more unified response to the harms suffered by women in the name of culture and religion.[7] It has done so by making it possible to see that many of the customs that states, NGOs, and individuals seek to challenge are ones that transcend state boundaries—for example, systems of customary or family and personal

[6] Vandana Shiva, 'Food Rights, Free Trade, and Fascism', in *Globalizing Rights: the Oxford Amnesty Lectures 1999*, ed. Matthew Gibney (Oxford: Oxford University Press, 2003), p. 107.

[7] See Brooke Ackerly's work on transnational feminism—for example, her 'Women's Human Rights Activists as Cross-Cultural Theorists', *International Journal of Feminist Politics*, 3/3 (2001), 1–36.

law that discriminate against women, and the widespread phenomenon of male violence against women. As a consequence, some of the movements and organizations dedicated to reforming or eradicating such practices are also, by necessity, transnational, such as the influential group Women Living Under Muslim Laws (WLUML), or the Catholic reform organization Women's Ordination Worldwide. It is possible that coordinating these efforts for reform on a regional or even global level might be more effective than local or even national efforts, provided the processes and institutions for this exist or can be developed. A good example of this is the virtual coup that women's rights activists from around the world effected at the Vienna World Conference on Human Rights in 1993, where they demanded that delegates recognize women's rights as human rights, and successfully secured a commitment to try to end violence against women. The end result of this intervention was the 1993 *United Nations Declaration on the Elimination of Violence Against Women*.[8] Similar efforts to construct a transnational feminist agenda occurred subsequently at the Bejing World Conference on Women in 1995.

A further effect of globalization relevant to the present discussion is the expansion and growing importance of the human rights framework in the political life of democratic and democratizing states. At the same time, globalization has begun to erode the authority of the traditional political entities, most notably the state. Perhaps the single most important upshot of this has been the opening up of potential spaces for transnational democratic processes and institutions (which have yet to be realized). As Jan Scholte writes, 'globalization has undercut liberal democracy through the state and created the need for supplementary—and in the long run perhaps even wholly different—democratic mechanisms.'[9] One possibility is that a more democratic human rights platform than currently exists, one that truly incorporates the voices of marginalized persons in formulating and debating rights, might emerge as a critical mechanism of global governance. In the meantime, women's activists, like environmental and antiglobalization activists, are looking more and more to human rights instruments to defend their rights, often as a way to pressure their own governments to introduce legislation to protect women. As Radhika Coomaraswamy, the Special Rapporteur on Violence Against Women for the United Nations Human Rights Commission, writes: 'Women transcending national boundaries in search of international protection is part of parallel developments in other areas of

---

[8] For good accounts of this activism, see Kaplan, 'Women's Rights as Human Rights' and Ursula O'Hare, 'Realizing Human Rights for Women', *Human Rights Quarterly*, 21/2 (1999), 364–402, esp. p. 365.

[9] Jan Aart Scholte, 'Globalization and (Un)Democracy', in his *Globalization: A Critical Introduction* (New York: St. Martin's Press, 2000), p. 261.

human rights. The dynamic growth of human rights law in the past two decades has challenged the hegemony of the nation-state and the sanctity of sovereign borders.'[10] There is also growing anthropological evidence of the spread of human rights discourse even among traditional and remote cultural groups, who make strategic use of rights talk to frame their grievances and press their justice claims.[11]

WOMEN'S RIGHTS AS HUMAN RIGHTS

Before evaluating the effectiveness of the human rights paradigm for addressing gendered cultural conflicts, it is useful to give an overview of the main conventions and declarations pertaining to women's rights. Most of the key human rights instruments in fact include provisions prohibiting sex discrimination, including the United Nations Charter (1945), the Universal Declaration of Human Rights (1948), the European Convention on Human Rights (1950), the European Convention on Human Rights and Fundamental Freedoms (1950), the International Covenant on Civil and Political Rights (1966), the International Covenant on Economic, Social, and Cultural Rights (1966), the American Convention on Human Rights (1969), the Declaration on the Elimination of All Forms of Intolerance and of Discrimination Based on Religion or Belief (1981), and the African Charter on Human and People's Rights (1987), also known as the Banjul Charter. With discrimination on the basis of gender formally prohibited in multiple documents, it is perhaps surprising that women's rights advocates considered these inadequate, and so pressed (and continue to press) for more comprehensive protection of women's rights within the human rights arsenal. Women's activists have consistently argued, however, that merely protecting women's rights alongside a host of other potentially *competing* rights—such as national minorities' rights to self-determination and religious freedom—causes women's rights to be trumped. Just as critically, mainstream human rights instruments may

[10] Radhika Coomaraswamy, 'Reinventing International Law: Women's Rights as Human Rights in the International Community', in *Debating Human Rights: Critical Essays from the United States and Asia*, ed. Peter Van Ness (London and New York: Routledge, 1999), p. 175.

[11] For example, indigenous women in the remote New Territories of Hong Kong used human rights language to protest sexually discriminatory, customary inheritance laws in the 1990s. According to scholars studying this female inheritance movement, human rights discourse was introduced deliberately and strategically by Hong Kong feminists who had exposure to these ideas. For a full discussion, see Sally Engle Merry and Rachel Stern, 'The Female Inheritance Movement in Hong Kong: Theorizing the Local/Global Interface', *Current Anthropology*, 46/3 (2005), 387–409.

guarantee women civil and political freedoms, but they have traditionally ignored important sources of women's oppression in the private sphere. For international human rights treaties to be effective, then, a dramatic conceptual shift was necessary so as to include the family and private realm as legitimate targets of human rights legislation.[12]

The major breakthrough for transnational feminist activists was the adoption of the UN Declaration on the Elimination of All Forms of Discrimination Against Women in 1967, and ultimately the Convention on the Elimination of All Forms of Discrimination Against Women (CEDAW) in 1979 (subsequently entered into force in 1981). Not only is CEDAW more comprehensive with respect to women's rights than previous conventions and declarations, but it insists on going beyond the familiar public/private distinction in order to identify and look at women's needs in a variety of areas. Shaheen Ali describes the key advances of CEDAW:

The definition of discrimination against women put forward in CEDAW is important as it transcends the traditional public/private dichotomy by calling for the international recognition of women's human rights both inside and outside the familiar sphere (article 1). The framers of this Convention realized that customs and practices as well as formal legislation often perpetuate discrimination against women (article 2). Article 5 of the Convention . . . addresses this issue by committing [signatory] state parties . . . to modify 'the social and cultural patterns of conduct of men and women' in order to eliminate prejudices and practices based on notions of inferiority and superiority of either sex. Other substantive provisions demand that state parties grant women complete equality in every field of life, be it nationality, family matters, contracts, right to property, etc.[13]

A major feminist criticism of traditional human rights law has been that it ignores the private, familial realm, which is for many women the main source of inequality, exploitation, and violence.[14] Some of the formal civil and political rights that women ostensibly enjoy are undercut by the restrictions, ill treatment, and oppression they experience in the private realm.[15] CEDAW, by contrast, enumerates harms against women in both public and private life, and includes not only civil and political rights but also social rights and

[12] See for example O'Hare, 'Realizing Human Rights for Women', p. 402.

[13] Shaheen Sardar Ali, 'Women's rights, CEDAW and International Human Rights Debates: Toward Empowerment?', in *Rethinking Empowerment: Gender and Development in a Global/ Local World*, eds. Jane Parpart, Shirin Rai, and Kathleen Staudt (London and New York: Routledge, 2002), p. 63.

[14] See for example Coomaraswamy, 'Reinventing International Law', pp. 170–1; Berta Esperanza Hernández-Truyol, 'Human Rights Through a Gendered Lens: Emergence, Evolution, Revolution', in *Women and International Human Rights Law*, Vol. 1, eds. Kelly Askin and Dorean Koenig (Transnational Publishers, Inc, 1999), pp. 32–4; and Friedman, 'Women's Human Rights', pp. 20–1.

[15] Hernández-Truyol, 'Human Rights Through a Gendered Lens', pp. 34–5.

rights of sexual and reproductive health. The introduction to CEDAW states that the Convention 'aims at enlarging our understanding of the concept of human rights, as it gives formal recognition to the influence of culture and tradition on restricting women's enjoyment of their fundamental rights. These forces take shape in stereotypes, customs and norms which give rise to the multitude of legal, political, and economic constraints on the advancement of women'; the preamble states that 'a change in the traditional role of men as well as the role of women in society and in the family is needed to achieve full equality between men and women.'

The comprehensiveness of CEDAW and its endorsement by a large number (154) of states[16] combine to make it the most important instrument within international law for promoting women's rights. And indeed, many successes have been claimed in its name: 'gains in women's employment, salary increases, access to schools, scholarships, and even "special measures", and quotas, stipulating the percentage of women who must be put forward in party lists, can be attributed to CEDAW.'[17] Certainly the symbolic significance of the Convention as an international set of standards for the treatment and entitlements of women should not be underestimated. But as with most international treaties and conventions stipulating human rights, it has built-in limitations. Of these, the most obvious is the purely voluntary nature of the agreement. State parties undertake to report, usually every four years, on their progress as regards the goals of the Convention, and these reports are subsequently reviewed by a committee established for this purpose.[18] However, there are no specific target goals (other than meeting the provisions of the Convention) or penalties for states that have made no strides toward women's equality; nor can states complain that the Convention has been violated by other states.[19] And as Ali notes, the modus operandi of CEDAW, which emphasizes dialogue and 'progressive implementation', means that 'there is little immediate pressure to implement and conform to the requirements of the Convention'.[20] Finally, the reporting procedure that is the main instrument of CEDAW 'is perhaps the least effective method devised by international law to enforce human rights standards', since '[i]ts success or failure depends heavily

[16] The United States Congress, notoriously, has refused to ratify CEDAW to date, although President Carter signed the Convention in 1980.

[17] Kaplan, 'Women's Rights as Human Rights', p. 303.

[18] CEDAW established a Committee on the Elimination of All Forms of Discrimination Against Women, made up of twenty-three members elected by the state parties.

[19] In contrast, as Ali notes, states can complain about other states using the Convention on the Elimination of All Forms of Racial Discrimination, 'on which CEDAW is closely modelled'. Only recently have individual women been granted the right to petition CEDAW. Ali, 'Women's Rights', pp. 64 and 75 (ff. 3).

[20] Ibid., p. 64.

on the goodwill of state parties', both in terms of voluntary reporting and compliance with the Convention.[21]

Beyond the formal, structural limitations of CEDAW, there are other reasons why the Convention has not been a particularly effective instrument for combating gendered forms of injustice. It is not uncommon for states to invoke national, religious, and cultural differences to defend practices that appear to discriminate against women, yet critically, CEDAW does not 'expressly... rule out any culture-based justifications for gender discrimination'.[22] Article 2 condemns 'discrimination against women in all its forms', and urges state parties 'to take all appropriate measures, including legislation, to modify or abolish existing laws, regulations, customs and practices which constitute discrimination against women'.[23] Article 5a asks state parties to 'take all appropriate measures' to 'modify the social and cultural patterns of conduct of men and women, with a view to achieving the elimination of prejudices and customary and all other practices which are based on the idea of the inferiority or the superiority of either of the sexes or on stereotyped roles for men and women'.[24] But the general nature of these provisions means that it is unrealistic to expect them to exert much pressure on states to reform sexually discriminatory practices.

Despite the relative weakness of these CEDAW articles referring to the social and cultural sources of sex discrimination, more states signed the convention with formal reservations than any other UN treaty to date. This fact cannot help but compromise the power and effectiveness of the Convention. Not only did a large proportion of the original state parties enter reservations, but so did subsequent state parties, with the effect that by 1989, when 100 states had signed, fully 41 of these 'had entered substantive reservations'.[25] In particular, a large number of Muslim countries have signed CEDAW with serious reservations, stating that some of the treaty's provisions conflict

---

[21] Ali, 'Women's Rights', p. 64.

[22] Ann Elizabeth Mayer, 'A "Benign" Apartheid: How Gender Apartheid Has Been Rationalized', *UCLA Journal of International Law and Foreign Affairs*, 5 (2000), 237–338, p. 271.

[23] United Nations General Assembly, *Convention on the Elimination of All Forms of Discrimination Against Women*, Article 2f.

[24] Ibid., Article 5a.

[25] Belinda Clark, 'The Vienna Convention Reservations Regime and the Convention on Discrimination Against Women', *The American Journal of International Law*, 85/2 (1991), 281–321, p. 282. Clark notes that of these 41 states' reservations, 19 'made a reservation only with respect to the provision dealing with dispute settlement'. Clark usefully compares this with the International Convention on the Elimination of All Forms of Racial Discrimination, which by 1989 had 128 signatories, of which 39 made reservations; fully 35 of these reservations, however, concern dispute settlement protocol, in contrast to less than half of the reservations lodged against CEDAW (p. 282 ff.11, and p. 283).

with Muslim personal and family law and traditional sex roles for men and women. Elisabeth Mayer explains one typical strategy:

Appeals to Islam may be used in combination with appeals to the complementarity thesis, with claims being made that countries are obliged to treat women in ways that recognize women's different nature and the different roles that women should play.... For example, Morocco included language in its reservation to Article 16 of CEDAW giving men and women equality in the family, saying: 'Equality of this kind is considered incompatible with the Islamic Shariah, which guarantees to each of the spouses rights and responsibilities within a framework of equilibrium and complementarity in order to preserve the sacred bond of matrimony.'[26]

Non-Muslim countries, however, also lodged reservations, citing the incompatability of certain CEDAW articles with their national traditional customs and practices in general (e.g. Malawi) or with specific arrangements, such as 'New Zealand's reservations regarding the Cook Islands' chiefly inheritance system' and Brazil's reservations regarding 'parts of the provisions on matrimonial property and family law'.[27] Women's groups and certain state parties have raised numerous concerns over the years regarding the number and kind of reservations to CEDAW, but ultimately to no avail.[28]

The issue of reservations or qualifications to states' signatures to CEDAW and the lack of compliance measures built into the Convention are evidence in the minds of some observers that CEDAW is seen as 'somehow separate and distinct from other multilateral treaties—even other UN human rights instruments'.[29] This suggestion has prompted a protracted debate within the United Nations on the question of whether all treaties ought to have the same standing. According to Belinda Clark:

Some states held that CEDAW should be afforded a lesser status than other treaties because its subject matter was culturally sensitive. The proposition was rarely articulated in precisely these terms, but it is a necessary implication of some of the responses to the Secretary-General, the arguments in the debates, and some of the reservations themselves, which refer to the Convention as a statement of intent or other document of rhetoric, rather than as the establishment or codification of international legal norms.[30]

---

[26] Mayer, 'A "Benign" Apartheid', pp. 270–1.

[27] Clark, 'The Vienna Convention Reservations Regime', p. 300.

[28] Clark notes that beginning in 1986, the CEDAW Committee formally raised the issue of states' reservations, but in time this was (falsely) 'spinned' by some state parties as an anti-Islamic attack; '[t]he fact that objections had also been made to reservations that did not relate to Islamic law or emanate from Muslim countries did not temper the criticism', nor did the fact that '[l]eading Third World supporters of CEDAW such as Kenya, Mexico and Nicaragua numbered among the states concerned by the derogatory nature of some of the reservations'. Ibid., p. 284.

[29] Ibid., p. 285.   [30] Ibid., p. 286.

These attempts to demote women's rights instruments do not necessarily have deep roots in states' religious beliefs, however: as Ann Elizabeth Mayer points out, the refusal to sign human rights conventions on ostensibly principled grounds 'may merely be a convenient pretext for denying freedoms that the government wishes to curtail for reasons of self-interest', whatever these may be.[31] Since reasons grounded in appeals to religious and cultural self-determination have enjoyed a not insignificant currency in human rights politics, this may be a rational strategy.

So far, I have focused on various institutional and political challenges in this discussion of instruments for promoting women's human rights. But there are also reasons of a more normative nature that suggest why a human rights framework is limited as a method with which to evaluate and precipitate the reform of sexually discriminatory cultural practices. One reason concerns the tension between women's human rights and the rights of national self-determination and freedom of religion. Not surprisingly, these latter rights are seen as nonnegotiable human rights by many states (and some national ethnic and religious minorities); where they conflict with provisions in international law protecting women's rights, especially the right to sexual equality, they are thought by many to have trumping power. The belief that a commitment to women's universal human rights may threaten the inalienable right of a people to self-determination and religious freedom—for instance, by conflicting with systems of personal and family law, traditional customs and roles, forth—is made clear by the nature of many of the formal reservations to CEDAW. As Hilary Charlesworth comments, 'in the context of women's rights, major religious traditions have regarded human rights as a sort of Trojan Horse, with a belly full of subversive values'.[32] Religious and traditional customs are the most frequently cited source of reservations to CEDAW provisions, as well as the reason why some states still refuse to sign or ratify the Convention (including the United States, for fear that it would need to pass some Equal Rights Amendment-style legislation in order to comply with the treaty).[33]

---

[31] Ann Elizabeth Mayer, 'Current Muslim Thinking on Human Rights', in *Human Rights in Africa: Cross-Cultural Perspectives*, eds. Abdullahi An Na'im and Francis Deng (Washington, DC: The Brookings Institute, 1990), pp. 136–7.

[32] Charlesworth, 'The Challenges of Human Rights Law', p. 409.

[33] This tension between women's rights and rights of cultural self-determination and religious freedom does not only arise in connection with CEDAW, since many other treaties also directly bear on the issue of sex roles and women's rights. For instance, at various conferences in the 1990s, such as the 1994 UN Conference on Population and Development (held at Cairo) and the 1995 World Summit on Social Development (in Copenhagen), both the Catholic and Islamic delegations were able to delay decisions on women's reproductive and sexual health issues through obstructive tactics, and also to weaken the final texts by lodging reservations. Ibid., p. 407.

Although human rights are sometimes thought to be mutually compatible and to form a seamless whole, then, there are real tensions between certain kinds of rights and the different *subjects* of rights. Just how women's human rights should be balanced against the right to culture, freedom of religion, and the right to self-determination is a matter of intense political and philosophical debate and disagreement. Taken alone, UN instruments do not present a clear or unified position on the matter, however, as Ali notes:

[I]t may be argued that the Religious Declaration of 1981, in conjunction with article 18 of the Universal Declaration of Human Rights and articles 18, 26 and 27 of the International Convention of Civil and Political Rights (ICCPR) create an invisible hierarchy of human rights by placing freedom of religion at a higher level than right to equality irrespective of sex and gender. It follows therefore that if the freedom to manifest and practise one's religion or belief led to discrimination against women, such discrimination could be upheld on the basis of these conventions. Thus, despite its holistic approach toward questions of women's empowerment through human rights, CEDAW fails to provide a clear methodology to resolve conflicting rights.[34]

At the same time as the right to culture and religious freedom are underscored in international treaties, there exists a curious tendency to downplay the actual impact of these rights on the different subjects of human rights and their communities, and the consequences for other kinds of rights that may be compromised or violated in the process. In particular, we see the lack of any real engagement with the content of religion and religious rights, and religion's impact on individuals and communities.[35] This is no mere oversight, but rather, goes hand in hand with the tendency within international law to treat religions and cultures as static and unchangeable, and to ignore the numerous internal challenges to religious traditions. Yet without engaging with the *content* of religions and fact of dissension, human rights laws protecting the right of religion can paradoxically hide or even protect de facto rights violations. This is particularly so in the area of women's equality rights. As law scholar Madhavi Sunder warns, 'in case after case in both international and national law, law is siding with fundamentalists over modernizers within religious and cultural communities'.[36]

The conservative tendency of international law with respect to religion is reinforced by the lack of mechanisms and processes within international law

---

[34] Ali, 'Women's Rights', p. 65.

[35] As Charlesworth writes, 'the engagement of human rights law and religion has been by and large at a procedural level, concerned with freedom of religion as an aspect of freedom of speech and thought. Even this limited engagement has been controversial, because some religious traditions cannot accept the idea of freedom to choose a religion'. Charlesworth, 'The Challenges of Human Rights Law,' p. 405.

[36] Madhavi Sunder, 'Piercing the Veil', *Yale Law Journal*, 112 (2003), 1399–1472, p. 1406.

for persons to challenge religious law and custom. Like a growing number of activists and scholars concerned about women's rights, Sunder believes that the human rights paradigm needs to be rethought on a deeper level in order to do justice to the complex interplay of religion in both public and private life, family and personal law, social and economic freedoms, and civil and political rights. If human rights instruments fail to recognize the relationship between these domains, women will continue to be left unprotected and disempowered in different cultural and political contexts. In the final part of this chapter, I examine some ways in which the theory and practice of international human rights might be rethought and reformed, drawing on work by immanent critics of human rights theory and practice. Next, however, I turn to a discussion of two of the most compelling contemporary normative theories that could potentially underpin a human rights approach to mediating conflicts over gendered cultural and religious practices and arrangements. Although the authors in question—O'Neill and Nussbaum— do not always draw out the human rights implications of their arguments, these are readily apparent, and both thinkers consider their approaches to be compatible with a human rights paradigm.[37]

'POSSIBLE CONSENT': O'NEILL'S KANTIAN MORAL UNIVERSALISM

Much recent writing in neo-Kantian moral and political philosophy and ethics points to the need for side constraints of noncoercion and nondeception in determining the justice of our social and cultural arrangements.[38] Like Okin's and Kymlicka's comprehensive liberalism, this broadly neo-Kantian perspective states that most rational persons would agree to arrangements and practices which safeguard their individual freedom and choice, or at the

---

[37] Nussbaum has gone on record as saying that the 'human rights view is underspecified, containing quite a few different views about what the basis of a rights claim is, who has the duties, and so forth'; however, she considers 'the capabilities approach ... [as] one species of a human rights view, which takes definite positions on these issues...,' Martha Nussbaum, 'On Hearing Women's Voices: A Reply to Susan Okin,' *Philosophy & Public Affairs*, 32/2 (2004), 193–205, p. 196. O'Neill, similarly, believes that human rights are of obvious political importance, but that we ought to specify more explicitly what it is that rights stand in for, and who the duty-bearers are with respect to these. See for example her 'Women's Rights: Whose Obligations?', in *Bounds of Justice*, p. 98.

[38] See Thomas Hill Jr., *Autonomy and Self-Respect* (Cambridge: Cambridge University Press, 1991); and Onora O'Neill, *Constructions of Reason: Explorations of Kant's Practical Philosophy* (Cambridge: Cambridge University Press, 1989), *Towards Justice and Virtue* (Cambridge: Cambridge University Press, 1996), and *Bounds of Justice*.

very least would not coerce them in unacceptable and arbitrary ways. If a person does not enjoy the capacities, conditions, or freedoms needed to refuse certain practices or arrangements, or cannot do so without fear of serious reprisal, it is spurious to claim that his or her meaningful consent has been (or could be) secured.[39] This is the position advanced by O'Neill, who argues that cultural arrangements that girls and women cannot refuse or reject without fear of reprisal, or because of insufficient options, are coercive and unjust.[40] O'Neill's Kantian approach to cultural conflicts thus directs our attention to the conditions under which agents adhere to particular customs and asks whether genuine consent to these is possible. But unlike the liberal approaches surveyed in the last chapter, her view does not so much posit the universal applicability of specific liberal norms (like autonomy) so much as it suggests that acceptable practices should not embody norms or incorporate conditions that are clearly *not* universalizable[41]—that is, which many people simply could not act upon without fear of harm, or else could not reject out of fear of reprisal. Accordingly, O'Neill sees the moral legitimacy of principles and practices as bound up with the *possible* agreement of all rational moral agents. Framed in this way, her position has some affinity with the a priori liberal position discussed in the last chapter, in the sense that it purports to be able to establish the legitimacy or illegitimacy of practices in a principled and somewhat formal or abstract way. However, since the focus of attention here is whether consent and refusal are *actually possible*, O'Neill's approach is grounded more

---

[39] O'Neill, 'Justice, Gender and International Boundaries', in *Bounds of Justice*.

[40] See Onora O'Neill, *Constructions of Reason*; 'Practices of Toleration', in *Democracy and the Mass Media*, ed. Judith Lichtenberg (Cambridge: Cambridge University Press, 1990); 'Justice, Gender, and International Boundaries', in *The Quality of Life*, eds. Martha Nussbaum and Amartya Sen (Oxford: Clarendon Press, 1992); and *Bounds of Justice*.

[41] Universalism is a broad term whose usage is as varied as it is prolific across political philosophy and ethical theory. The description 'universal' is variously taken to mean 'widely practiced' or 'widely accepted' as well as 'universally valid' in moral terms. Moral philosophers write of particular norms and principles and the maxims expressed by certain actions as 'universalizable', which, following Kant, is usually meant to denote that all rational persons could adopt and act upon particular principles or maxims. Outside circles of committed Kantians, however, it is often unclear whether a norm is deemed universal on the grounds that it could potentially be accepted by all rational agents, or whether a norm is merely presumed to be universal in the sense of indicating wide, *actual* agreement to the principle. The version of moral or ethical universalism I refer to here combines a claim of ethical consistency—or 'the idea that the rights or important interests of all persons ought to be protected or promoted equally and impartially'—with the thought that minimally just political principles are ones that agents could agree to be bound by. See Alan Gewirth, 'Common Morality and the Community of Rights', in *Prospects for a Common Morality*, ed. Gene Outka and John Reeder (Princeton, NJ: Princeton University Press, 1993), p. 32. For a discussion of the tendency to conflate actual consent with universalizability, see Samuel Fleischacker, *Integrity and Moral Relativism* (Leiden, Netherlands: E. J. Brill, 1992), Ch. 8.

in practical reason and could (in my view) readily be incorporated into deliberative models of politics.

The 'possible consent' perspective contends that the legitimacy of a particular custom or cultural convention derives in part from its broad acceptability to moral agents who are rational, capable, and in important respects, *free*. An agreement-based test to determine the acceptability of cultural practices and customs has some obvious strengths, especially with respect to customs defended on the basis of apparent—but, as it turns out, not real—consent. In cases where individuals cannot readily be seen to give genuine consent, it is helpful to be able to recognize the presence or absence of features and capacities that could lend evidence to claims of subjects' consent.[42] Some examples include cases of female genital surgeries performed on young girls, who may face extreme emotional and physical coercion, and child brides in arranged marriages, who are much too young to meaningfully consent to the match. Even the consent of an adult woman to arrangements like polygyny[43] might be questioned if she has few or no financial options for support, or fears violent reprisal at the hands of her husband.

According to O'Neill, determining the validity of a practice is thus not just a matter of scrutinizing the justice or injustice of particular institutions from a distance, but rather asking about the conditions under which consent is presumed to be given.[44] With respect to women in certain traditional cultures, we might consider women's capacities to reject particular treatment or renegotiate their circumstances. The human rights approach that would follow from O'Neill's possible consent perspective therefore differs from the classical paradigm in a few important respects. In the first place, it demands a human rights framework that goes beyond merely formal rights, responsibilities, and freedoms and asks about the lived reality behind formal rights and freedoms. O'Neill's perspective also requires that we ask who or what (the state?, the international community?, transnational organizations?) has which duties or responsibilities to support the exercise of basic rights—for example, by supplying housing or food or education. Finally, the possible consent view would also reject an over-sharp dichotomy between public and private life—though not dispense with the distinction entirely—on the grounds that it prevents us from inquiring about how exploitation or oppression in the private and social realms undercuts agents' capacities for autonomy.

For these reasons, it seems likely that the possible consent approach could also help illuminate human rights violations perpetrated in the name of culture and religion. Particularly important in this regard is O'Neill's

---

[42] Ibid., p. 318.

[43] The form of polygamy wherein a man takes more than one wife.

[44] O'Neill, 'Justice, Gender and International Boundaries,' p. 318.

argument that harmful and coercive practices may nonetheless *appear* legitimate insofar as individuals are often not in a position to actively resist particular customs or conventions. Other community members may collude in their silence, moreover, in the name of protecting an institution or preventing external interference by the state. Nor is it only coercion that might be at play; economic deprivation and social powerlessness can leave individuals without an effective voice with which to challenge or protest their circumstances. By asking about agents' capabilities and opportunities to refuse unwanted social arrangements and customs, we commit ourselves to investigating the circumstances surrounding (purported) instances of individual consent.[45] Among the specific human rights that this approach might support, therefore, are the right to education (often denied to girls and women), the right to choose or refuse a prospective marriage partner, and the right to plan (or refuse) childbearing.

These rights, and the circumstances that support them, may seem a simple endorsement of familiar individual liberal rights, and not a significant departure from the liberal a priori view discussed in the last chapter. But while the rights ultimately endorsed are similar, there are important differences. First, the possible consent view focuses much more on the duties and responsibilities—of individuals, states, and the international community—that attend rights than do contemporary liberal rights approaches. Any human rights list supported by O'Neill's argument would therefore say which entities are accountable for supporting different contexts of agency:

If women's rights are not redundant in our world, we need to ask what it would be to take them seriously. I have argued that taking them seriously is pre-eminently a matter of taking the obligations which are their counterparts seriously.... What matters for women is that the allocation of those obligations to provide goods and services should itself take account of the real resources and responsibilities, of the real capabilities and vulnerabilities, of those who are to bear the obligations. As long as some people, and today it is often (but by no means always) women, and especially poor women in poor economies, have fewer resources and carry higher burdens of others' dependence, as long as they are vulnerable in ways in which others are not, a case may be made for allocations of obligations which fall more on those who have more resources or carry lower burdens of others' dependence and consequently have greater capabilities.[46]

Second, as the above passage suggests, the question of which bodies have responsibilities to help secure people's various capabilities is not, on O'Neill's account of justice, bound by national borders. Rather, both global human rights instruments and strategies for 'transnational economic justice' follow

---

[45] Ibid.   [46] O'Neill, *Bounds of Justice*, pp. 110–11.

logically from the Kantian possible consent view[47]; as O'Neill comments, 'how can those who argue for principles of justice of universal scope, or for human rights, endorse structures that entail that the rights people actually have depend on where they are, or more precisely on which place recognizes them as citizen rather than as alien?'[48] This global view of the requirements of justice contrasts with some contemporary liberal contractarian views, which generally place responsibility for protecting individual rights and liberties squarely on the sovereign liberal state. O'Neill's approach also rightly places more emphasis on social and economic rights (both national and trans-national) generally than do some competing liberal views.

Lastly, O'Neill's possible consent approach does not risk automatically discounting traditional societies as does the a priori liberal view, for it does not privilege an *idealized* form of autonomy—that is, autonomy as complete personal independence and self-sufficiency. Rather, it alerts us to the ways in which individuals may be systematically disempowered and so prevented from acquiring even minimal capacities or opportunities to make important decisions and changes in their lives.[49] The central principles embodied in this approach—the thought that one agent ought not to have so much power over another that they can prevent their free use of reason, and freedom of choice and action; and the belief that people *ought* to be capable of reason, decide, and act for themselves—are ones that support and even require extensive human rights, including (national and transnational) social and economic rights. But these global human rights are, as we saw earlier, notoriously difficult to implement, for they are ultimately voluntary in nature, lacking in both compliance mechanisms and significant sanctions. This is especially so with regard to women's human rights. Thus, although O'Neill means for her approach to ground rights and obligations that have real political pur-chase, it may be that the possible consent view is better understood as a principled critique of domestic, regional, and global social and economic policies that perpetuate gross inequalities and exploitation.

Precisely *because* the possible consent view sees serious power imbalances as undercutting free agreement, however, there are reasons to think that this approach is of limited use in hard cases of cultural conflict involving social-ization rather than outright force. When what needs to be decided is the validity of minority cultural practices that do not overtly violate the

---

[47] See O'Neill, *Bounds of Justice*, especially Ch. 6, Ch. 7, and Ch. 9.

[48] Ibid., p. 170.

[49] For example, Saharso writes of the suicide in the Netherlands in 1988 of a Dutch Hindustani woman who had suffered from systematic, culturally sanctioned beatings by her husband, which prompted her family to ask that he be charged with incitement to suicide. See her 'Female Autonomy and Cultural Imperative,' p. 225.

autonomy of agents, but instead shape and constrict individuals' possible choices, preferences, and lifestyles, the possible consent view may simply be too heavy-handed. In particular, the rejection of power differentials built into this approach might make it difficult to defend cultural arrangements that are not perfectly egalitarian. As O'Neill writes:

The ways in which injury, violence, coercion, deception and the like can be used to undermine external freedom is not only by undermining individual capacities for action blow by blow, threat by threat, lie by lie, but also through sustaining cultures of intimidation, insecurity, deference, and evasiveness. What constitutes injury, or threat, or effective deception always depends on the relative power of those agents and agencies who act unjustly and the relative lack of power, and consequently enhanced vulnerability, of those who suffer injustice.[50]

The difficulty here is that social roles and practices are typically imposed or enacted in contexts of limited choice, in which case agents' abilities to refuse or accept such arrangements will always be compromised to some extent. O'Neill's perspective specifically signals this as problematic and, from the point of view of Kantian justice, wrong. But while sometimes a limited context of choice is a sign that harm or coercion is present, arguably it may equally be the case that people are making the best choices they can within the context of traditional societies.

Unlike comprehensive liberalism, the possible consent view does not fall into the trap of defending restrictions on cultural minority practices on the basis of an idealized form of autonomy. However, like other liberal approaches, O'Neill's view fails to fundamentally interrogate the norms of individual consent and personal autonomy from the vantage point of cultural differences, or try to apply these ideals to problems regarding disputed cultural or religious practices or arrangements. Like human rights discourse generally, the possible consent view emphasizes universalizable needs and rights, irrespective of cultural context. While the wide applicability of the possible consent view is implicit in O'Neill's defense of it, the conception itself is not worked out with cultural differences in mind, and so may be less widely valid than she thinks. By contrast, the capabilities approach, as developed by Martha Nussbaum, claims to offer a theory of social justice that is broadly applicable across, and sensitive to, different social and cultural settings.[51]

---

[50] O'Neill, *Bounds of Justice*, p. 139.

[51] The capabilities approach is closely linked with the human functioning approach, as developed by the economist and philosopher Amartya Sen, together with Martha Nussbaum.

NUSSBAUM'S CAPABILITIES APPROACH

Nussbaum's capabilities approach begins with the claim that social justice requires that people's basic human capabilities be fostered and supported.[52] Although Nussbaum contends that 'capabilities...have a very close relationship to human rights', she views her approach as clarifying much of the underlying confusion that plagues rights talk, and also as focusing attention where it belongs—that is, on people's actual capacities and opportunities.[53] Capabilities are, moreover much more complex than rights, standing in for more complex and varied functions and capacities, and presenting more opportunities for action; as a consequence, '[i]n some areas ... the best way of thinking about rights is to see them as *combined capabilities*'.[54] Below, I ask whether or not the capabilities approach improves upon existing human rights approaches with respect to the protection and empowerment of women, especially vis-à-vis their cultural and religious practices.

Central to Nussbaum's capability theory is the 'idea of a *threshold level of each capability*, beneath which it is held that truly human functioning is not available to citizens'.[55] To develop and sustain their basic or core human capabilities people need particular kinds of social resources and opportunities, which governments, insofar as it is within their power, ought to supply. Nor is this just a matter of individuals choosing a coherent life plan for which they need all-purpose primary social goods, in Rawls' sense; rather, Nussbaum specifies a list of ten 'central human functional capabilities' that contribute significantly to one's capacity to lead a life of well-being, and without which 'truly human functioning' is not possible.[56] The core capabilities include abilities relating to life, health, bodily integrity, and freedom from various forms of violence; the ability to use one's intellectual faculties and emotional senses; practical reason, or the ability to 'form a conception of the good and to engage in critical reflection about the planning of one's life'; the ability freely to choose with whom to affiliate; and the 'social bases of self-respect and non-humiliation', which include freedom from discrimination.[57] These capabilities, ground Nussbaum's claim that the capabilities approach is 'truly universal' in scope and ambition—a claim I shortly dispute.

---

[52] This discussion draws broadly from my review of Nussbaum's *Women and Human Development* in 'Political Morality and Culture: What Difference Do Differences Make?,' *Social Theory and Practice*, 28/3 (2002), 503–18, esp. pp. 513–16.

[53] Nussbaum, *Women and Human Development*, pp. 97 and 99.   [54] Ibid., p. 98.

[55] Ibid., p. 6.   [56] Ibid., pp. 78 and 6.   [57] Ibid., pp. 78–9.

For Nussbaum, these capabilities in turn require certain concrete social conditions for their realization and development: the capability for affiliation is dependent on 'having the social bases of self-respect and non-humiliation'; the capability for practical reason requires 'protection for the liberty of conscience', and so forth.[58] As such, the capabilities approach to social justice reformulates the Kantian principle that we ought to treat 'each person as an end' as a 'principle of each person's capability' so as to require that every individual's capacities be developed. The list becomes politically meaningful when joined with a social and political commitment to the 'principle of each person's capability', by which every individual person's capabilities are to be counted seriously. Clearly, however, most states do not yet fully support all of these capabilities for all of their citizens, and for this reason Nussbaum proposes that we use the capabilities list as a kind of normative lever to press governments to deliver the social supports necessary to develop and sustain core human capabilities.[59] Nussbaum in fact intends for her capabilities approach to shape the policies of the world's governments: 'the primary role for the capabilities account remains that of providing political principles that can underlie national constitutions', and 'the approach is recommended as a good idea to politicians in India or any other nation who want to make it the basis of national or local policy.'[60]

Nussbaum sees her capabilities approach as being particularly useful for getting at the issue of women's oppression, and to this end, she asks 'What social conditions, arrangements, and practices foster gender justice, and which do not?' Like O'Neill, Nussbaum is very wary of traditional cultures, for in her view, women's capabilities for human functioning are undercut by customs typical of traditional societies, such as arranged marriage and polygyny.[61] The central reason for this, as for O'Neill, concerns the ways in which these traditional arrangements remove women's choices and capacities for choice and so jeopardize their agency. However, anticipating the charge that the capabilities approach privileges a particular view of flourishing in which autonomy is central, Nussbaum stresses that the list is 'a partial and not a comprehensive conception of the good',[62] and moreover that it is 'emphatically, a list of *separate components*', such that a 'larger amount' of one good cannot be expected to replace another good.[63] These claims are crucial to Nussbaum's contention that the capabilities approach can accommodate circumstances of social and cultural

---

[58] Ibid., pp. 78–80.   [59] Ibid., p. 12.   [60] Ibid., pp. 104–5.
[61] Ibid., pp. 94, 109, 230, and Ch. 4; also see her *Sex and Social Justice* (Oxford: Oxford University Press, 1999).
[62] *Women and Human Development*, p. 96.   [63] Ibid., p. 81.

pluralism—that it is universally applicable.[64] By Nussbaum's own account, then, the list of core capabilities, therefore, must not simply reinscribe culturally specific, Western understandings of flourishing and well-being. But is this the case?

The basis of Nussbaum's assertion that the capabilities approach is compatible with wide social and cultural diversity is her claim that the list of capabilities she provides does not constitute a comprehensive conception of the good. But the thick Aristotelianism evident in Nussbaum's list of goods and capabilities makes this claim suspect at best. In particular, her list of capabilities would seem to favor a life of autonomy, choice, and reflection. Susan Okin makes a similar observation:

[Nussbaum's] highly intellectualized conception of a fully human life and some of the capacities central to living it seem to derive far more from an Aristotelian ideal than from any deep or broad familiarity with the lives of women in the less-developed world. As for the more sophisticated, even fanciful, items on her list, they seem to draw more from the life of a highly educated, artistically inclined, self-consciously and voluntarily religious Western woman than from the lives of the women to whom she spoke in India.[65]

Perhaps the most immediate problem is that the lives endorsed by Nussbaum's list of capabilities necessarily imply strong criticisms of traditional settings and arrangements, in ways that are not necessarily helpful to women. Specifically, the list's emphasis on choice and autonomy suggests that nothing short of a fully liberal egalitarian framework for the sexes can supply the requirements of social justice.[66] Not surprisingly, one practice that fails the threshold of the capabilities test is the traditional marriage: insofar as such marriages remove or make impossible the development of important capabilities through various restrictions, they ought not to be tolerated.[67] As Nussbaum writes, 'marriages in which capabilities to exit, to work, and so on, are permanently surrendered by contract should not be permitted, although of course partners may always choose not to exercise those capabilities'.[68] Not only traditional marriages, but

---

[64] Nussbaum writes that the capability approach 'yields a form of universalism that is sensitive to pluralism and cultural difference.' Ibid., p. 8.

[65] Susan Okin, 'Poverty, Well-Being, and Gender', p. 296.

[66] Anne Phillips also comes to this conclusion in her discussion of Nussbaum's capabilities approach: '[Nussbaum's] endorsement of a liberal understanding of autonomy begs too many questions; and in combining a classically liberal emphasis on choice with a feminist understanding of unjust social power, she is driven into a curiously illiberal liberalism'. See Phillips' 'Feminism and Liberalism Revisited: Has Martha Nussbaum Got it Right?', *Constellations*, 8/2 (2001), 249–66, p. 250.

[67] Nussbaum, *Women and Human Development*, p. 94.   [68] Ibid., p. 94.

also polygynous marriages, would likely compromise one's core capabilities for choice and autonomy, since the latter often render women financially vulnerable and so weaken their decision-making power.

Just as highly traditional, restrictive marriages warrant intervention, so do a number of other practices and arrangements that erode women's core capabilities. Customs that permanently diminish women's capacities for full human functioning top the list of objectionable practices; nor is the wrongness of these practices mitigated by a person's apparent consent (due in part to the phenomenon of adaptive preferences, discussed below). Here the Aristotelianism of Nussbaum's approach comes into full view: in the case of female circumcision/female genital mutilation (FGM), not only is the presumed consent of young girls invalid (as it would be for liberals generally), but so it is also for grown women, since such genital surgery would apparently cause her to permanently give up a capability central to her human flourishing (the capacity for sexual pleasure).[69] Nussbaum indirectly addresses this issue when she asks '[w]hat should we say when adults, apparently without coercion, want to sign away a major capability in a permanent way?'; she answers that '[f]requently, though certainly not always, we will judge that interference is justified to protect the capability'.[70] This paternalism seems unproblematic when applied to cases where important physical capabilities are to be surrendered in contexts of evident coercion; it is much more problematic, however, when applied to traditional roles and arrangements, which are more often marked by culture pressure, and not force per se (e.g. arranged marriage).

In response to the concern that the capabilities list is biased toward certain kinds of lives, Nussbaum maintains that her liberal-Aristotelian account of flourishing is applicable to persons of diverse cultures and societies, and can be used to make '*comparisons of life quality*' between them.[71] People can use the core capabilities to choose very different kinds of lives, in Nussbaum's view. Here the distinction she draws between human capabilities on the one hand and the *actual functionings* of persons on the other becomes important: whereas a list of actual *functionings*—that is, the particular ends to which capabilities are put—would be too prescriptive, a list of capabilities is not. This is because capabilities are simply a measure of someone's capacity to live a life of choice and well-being, however defined. Nussbaum claims that this

---

[69] See Nussbaum, *Sex and Social Justice*, Ch. 4. In her discussion of FGM, Nussbaum concludes that 'we should continue to keep FGM on the list of unacceptable practices that violate women's human rights, and we should be ashamed of ourselves if we do not use whatever privilege and power has come our way to make it disappear forever' (*Sex and Social Justice*, p. 129).

[70] Nussbaum, *Women and Human Development*, p. 93.   [71] Ibid., p. 6.

important proviso makes the capabilities approach more inclusive of cultural and religious diversity than the earlier 'functionings approach' favored by Amartya Sen.[72] To require that states work to secure their citizens' basic capabilities is not, therefore, to privilege especially 'liberal' lives, in her view; a person may choose not to exercise one of her central human capabilities, or choose a nonlist good, and fashion her life accordingly (without necessarily risking a substandard life).[73] There is nothing in this conception, she claims, to preclude individuals choosing traditional lives—provided that they already enjoy a threshold level of the core capabilities (which also entails an adequate range of choices).

These qualifications only take us so far. The normative thickness of Nussbaum's conception of the good comes into sharp relief when she discusses roles and arrangements that bind women in many traditional societies, and which she asserts are largely incompatible with her list of capabilities. Capabilities theory, combined with a Kantian conception of respect for persons as ends in themselves, will require that people 'take a stand against some very common ways of treating women—as childlike, as incompetent in matters of property and contract, as mere adjuncts of a family line, as reproducers and care givers rather than as having their own lives to live'.[74] But what of cases where women seem to accept or even embrace these subordinate roles? Nussbaum acknowledges the prospect that some women, especially those in traditional societies, might not choose or want certain of the basic capabilities enumerated in the list—namely, those that conflict with their customary roles. Ultimately, however, she dismisses this possibility as a rather disingenuous explanation for women's subordination, through her discussion of the problem of adaptive preferences. Covering the familiar objections to choices that appear suspicious from a rationalist liberal perspective, Nussbaum concludes that the apparent choices of women in restrictive cultures are mostly the result of adaptive preferences, and are in any case constrained choices. Not only does this imply that problematic choices are not real or authentic ones, but also that under the right circumstances, women's preferences would naturally change to better reflect the core human capabilities.[75] But whether they will change in accordance with Nussbaum's predictions is surely an open question.

---

[72] Nussbaum does not engage Sen's most recent work, which focuses on what he calls people's 'capabilities for freedom'—which is apparently closer to her own approach. See his *Development as Freedom* (New York: Random House, 1999).

[73] *Women and Human Development*, p. 95.   [74] Ibid., p. 58.

[75] Here Nussbaum's argument echoes classical Marxist arguments about working class consciousness and the ways in which these are expected to naturally track changes in their prevailing social and economic conditions.

The perfectionist, and so controversial character, of Nussbaum's list of capabilities thus makes it of limited use with respect to helping us to resolve hard cases of cultural conflicts, particularly those that involve disputed customs that are in some sense 'traditional'. Capability theory also supports state action or government policy as the primary means of supporting women's capabilities, suggesting that a range of suspect choices could easily be deemed impermissible as a matter of law, despite the apparent consent of some group members. Thus, in the case of women who seem to reject one or more of the basic capabilities, or who agree to a practice or custom that permanently jeopardizes a list good, a more stringent test must be applied, according to Nussbaum: 'What we would need to show is that women who have experienced the full range of the central capabilities choose, with full information and without intimidation... to deny these capabilities, politically, to all women.'[76] By imposing a maxim of moral universalizability here, Nussbaum practically guarantees the censure of a wide range of traditional sex roles and practices, and invites the use of law and other state and transnational state apparatuses (i.e., to protect the capability in question). To bring women up to a threshold level of human capability requires not only extensive legal, social, and economic restructuring, then, but also tremendous *cultural* change. Nussbaum hints at the scale of change necessary when she comments that applying the capabilities approach will cause a number of cultural practices and arrangements to be deemed unjust, on the grounds that they undercut one or more core human capability (or make its attainment impossible). Yet she utterly fails to discuss the consequences of these changes or their implications for the justice claims of ethnic, religious, and cultural minorities. She also dismisses the prospect that some models of sex differentiation could incorporate different but equal capabilities for men and women on the grounds that such an arrangement no doubt incorporates some systematic form of inequality.[77]

Nussbaum's particular conception of the good life is thus a curious combination of Aristotelian idealism, political liberalism, and Kantian ethics, in which the pivotal values are those of autonomy and choice, embedded in a thick account of human flourishing. It is not an unattractive vision.

---

[76] Nussbaum, *Women and Human Development*, p. 153.

[77] Nussbaum raises the possibility that a 'separate spheres' model of the sexes might conceivably endorse 'the same general normative list of functions [for men and women] but [stipulate] that males and females should exercise these functions in different spheres of life.' Nussbaum's response to this is that 'it is likely that women's subordination will not be adequately addressed as long as women are confined to a sphere traditionally devalued.' Nussbaum, *Sex and Social Justice*, p. 51 and p. 52.

Nussbaum is surely right that people generally prefer more choice and control over the circumstances of their lives than not: the conversations with poor Indian women that she invokes to illustrate the role of capabilities in well-being—in which they almost uniformly praise the positive effects of greater choice in their lives—certainly resonate as true. However, the difficulty of Nussbaum's project is that it does not merely assert that autonomy and choice are important goods; rather, autonomy—and the capabilities and opportunities that support it—is an *ultimate good*. This claim, if it can be defended at all, will require extensive normative justification, particularly if it is to apply to diverse cultural groups.

As it turns out, then, certain choices are simply not choices at all in Nussbaum's capability scheme. Women cannot freely choose to participate in practices or arrangements that may diminish their own capabilities or well-being, understood largely in terms of their capacities for autonomy; and if they do, the state ought to step in to prevent them. According to Nussbaum's rationalist view, women will seek to secure their own basic physical and material well-being, and that of their children, first, *before* they venture out to seek a wider range of goods or to develop other capabilities. Women will (or ought to) choose to develop and maintain capabilities that enhance their ability to make choices and lead reasonably self-directed lives, according to the theory; they will (or ought to) choose to secure basic capabilities and the circumstances that support these (nutrition, shelter) before they pursue other capabilities and goods, such as those associated with traditional cultural roles. But what of choices that do not fall into line, such as a life of religious devotion, which may include deliberate sacrifice of several of the capabilities Nussbaum cites, or even suffering? Adaptive preferences theory might explain some of these choices or rankings, but surely not all. Nussbaum's own conception of flourishing thus does not acknowledge its dependence on a controversial *ordering* of choices; but we do not have to look very far to see that this ordering of preferences and choices is not to be counted on.

Like the possible consent view, where the capabilities approach faces its toughest challenges is in responding to the hard cases of toleration, namely cases in which practices are not overtly harmful but constrain the freedom of some individuals. Nussbaum is right to draw our attention not only to the formal structures that condition women's inequality but also to the social arrangements that make it difficult or unlikely for agents to imagine or take advantage of opportunities, and to develop their capabilities. However, women's responses to their own cultural practices and social restrictions are multifaceted and complex; they will not often follow the predictable trajectory of Nussbaum's list of core capabilities. Women may make choices that appear inexplicable from the point of view of the list, but these may be eminently rational within the cultural and religious context in which they find themselves. This is not to suggest that women's apparent choices must simply be endorsed and supported—far from it. Rather, it is to assert that any approach to social justice for women that bills itself as both firmly universal in scope *and* inclusive of cultural diversity will have to listen to women's own accounts of the cultural and religious practices that shape their lives, and what proposals they would make for their reform. Nussbaum gestures in this direction when she writes that the list of capabilities is deliberately 'specified in a somewhat abstract and general way, precisely in order to leave room for the activities of specifying and deliberating by citizens and their legislatures and courts'.[78] But there is enough that is determinate about the list that certain practices and arrangements would be deemed simply impermissible. As I argue in subsequent chapters, an effective approach to mediating conflicts of culture, particularly those dealing with contested sex roles and arrangements, will need not to dismiss certain of women's choices in advance as irrational, or deem them merely the result of adaptive preferences.[79] Even human rights law concerning women's rights must avoid this mistake: if the intended beneficiaries of a theory of rights (or capabilities) ultimately reject the normative content of the rights to be protected, or view it as incompatible with their central evaluative commitments and projects, this should surely make us pause.

RETHINKING HUMAN RIGHTS FOR WOMEN?

O'Neill's possible consent view and Nussbaum's capabilities approach, unlike the liberal a priori, juridical, and laissez-faire views of the last chapter, urge us to interrogate the social contexts in which cultural practices are developed and sustained. This will be an important dimension of any process that aims justly to mediate disputes about gendered customs and arrangements. Yet even these approaches take too little account of cultural members' own understandings of their lives, customs, and conflicts, relying instead on

---

[78] Nussbaum, 'On Hearing Women's Voices: A Reply to Susan Okin', *Philosophy and Public Affairs*, 32/2 (2004), 193–2005, pp. 197–8.

[79] Indeed, it is possible that the degree of paternalism vis-à-vis traditional cultural groups that is required by the capabilities approach violates some of the core capabilities whose protection Nussbaum cites as justification for state interference, namely the capabilities and freedom for practical reason and affiliation.

more formal and abstracted processes for determining the legitimacy of disputed practices. As such, both overlook the extent to which cultural arrangements are actively contested and subverted, often by persons with seemingly little power. These are also problems that arise generally in connection with human rights strategies for protecting women. Human rights protocols are necessarily formal and abstract, because they must be seen to be generally applicable or universalizable; they cannot (so their defenders generally say) permit local variations for instance, without risking undercutting these rights generally. They do not readily allow exceptions, even when the intended rights recipient might in fact reject the individual right in question (e.g. favoring group sovereignty over a particular individual right, as has sometimes happened in the case of indigenous peoples). Despite the categorical nature of human rights, however, we have seen that tensions and even outright contradictions exist between different protected rights—for example, between the right to religious freedom and certain women's human rights.

While these difficulties speak to the conceptual challenges faced by human rights approaches to protecting women, the practical consequences are no less important: attempts to apply rights which appear to conflict in some way with other human rights, and so which intended beneficiaries might have cause to reject, have not been especially effective. This is why one transnational women's rights organization, WLUML, aims to confront such tensions at their source, as Sunder explains:

While traditional human rights law is content not to challenge despotism in the private, religious and cultural sphere—indeed, it more often defends despotic religious practices—WLUML is confronting injustice within the contexts of religion and culture. WLUML's approach is in part strategic: The network recognizes that religious claims are particularly hard to challenge, and therefore expends effort to deconstruct religious claims as, in part, contingent and political. Perhaps more importantly, WLUML recognizes that many women will resist rights if they are only possible outside the context of religious and cultural community. Thus, it pursues strategies that would reconcile religion and rights, making it possible for women to have both.[80]

Given the normative and practical difficulties of empowering and protecting women through human rights—and in particular, fostering lasting reform of sexually discriminatory cultural practices and arrangements—we might wonder whether international human rights protocols are the best tool for effecting change. My discussion here suggests that sometime they are not. However, human rights can and do play an important role in certain struggles by women for political, legal, and economic justice. Is it possible to rethink

---

[80] Sunder, 'Piercing the Veil', p. 1441.

the human rights paradigm so as to make it more effective and relevant for evaluating and reforming practices in the social and private spheres? Or is the human rights framework too general and abstract, and not sufficiently sensitive to contexts of cultural and religious diversity, to be of much help to women? These are large questions, and in what remains of this chapter, I can only gesture at some of the better responses that have been offered by scholars thinking critically about human rights in theory and practice.

In opening up the question of the effectiveness of the human rights paradigm for protecting and empowering women, I should say that I am not discounting the real benefits that human rights law has had for women in many different contexts, nor am I suggesting that we simply dispense with them in future. These and other charges are sometimes made when the substance and effectiveness of women's human rights are in any way questioned or criticized: for example, Ann Meyer writes that 'one finds Western academics who endorse religious cultural rationalizations for gender apartheid and ignore or downplay the extent and seriousness of human rights violations affecting women.... Western apologists for gender apartheid impute imperialist and anti-religious attitudes to advocates of women's international human rights law.'[81] Similar, but less inflammatory, is Susan Okin's reference to 'the subject of Western academic feminism's hesitant or ambivalent approach to the issue of violations of women's rights in other cultural contexts'.[82] Needless to say, raising questions about the coherence and strategic usefulness of women's human rights discourse is not to be confused with supporting a return to gender apartheid.

Some key conceptual shifts in human rights law could, arguably, make human rights protocols more relevant and effective tools for protecting and empowering women. First, immanent critics agree that human rights law must somehow incorporate recognition of the particular obstacles to securing women's rights and needs in diverse religious and cultural settings. Most crucially, there needs to be some institutional recognition of the fact that gender roles and status are not determined in the abstract, but rather that they are shaped by a complex range of factors. Merely endorsing provisions that purport to protect women's rights *without* examining the broader context in which these rights are to be implemented almost certainly dooms these rights to ineffectiveness:

[D]e facto rights cannot be secured unless the interlocking relationships among gender, class, race, ethnicity, national identity, and the structures of state power are taken into

---

[81] Ann Elizabeth Mayer, 'A "Benign" Apartheid', p. 291.
[82] Susan Okin, 'Feminism, Women's Human Rights', p. 42.

account.... Women's ability to exercise their rights under international (and national) law is shaped not only by gender, but by such factors as: class; race; ethnicity; the role of the state in constructing gender ideologies and relations of power; and bilateral and multilateral economic and political relations.[83]

When women's status and potential remedies for their inequality are viewed in a vacuum, important contextual factors are neglected. In India, for instance, advocated efforts to introduce a uniform civil code for family and personal law, which many Hindu feminists have advocated for over the years, is justifiably viewed with suspicion by non-Hindu women as an attempt to legally subordinate minority religions. And in Canada, many Native women have turned away from mainstream feminist politics, including efforts to improve women's rights protections, on the grounds that these efforts fail to recognize that the racist Canadian state—not patriarchy—is the main source of their oppression.

One of the most important factors that needs to be addressed in rethinking women's human rights is that of religion. As mentioned earlier, religion and the right to religion are generally treated procedurally in international law, without inquiring much into the content of particular religions, or the effect of protections for religious or customary law on the lives of group members. Without a more direct engagement with religions as living—and changing—practices and ideologies, there is little recourse when conflicts between religious freedoms and other individual rights (such as women's equality rights) arise.[84] The view that religion is simply beyond the purview of national and international legal scrutiny is reinforced by the tendency to view religion as fundamentally private. However, as women's human rights scholars and activists have consistently argued, there are real dangers that follow from placing so-called private areas of life, chief among them religion and religious-based forms of sexual discrimination or mistreatment, beyond the scope of national and international human rights law. In particular, certain human rights provisions protecting women's rights are undermined by the failure to look seriously at how cultural and religious norms bear heavily on women's status, family arrangements, and their de facto power or powerlessness.[85] While there has been some limited success in getting international

[83] Donna Sullivan, 'Gender Equality and Religious Freedom: Toward a Framework for Conflict Resolution', *New York Journal of International Law and Politics*, 24 (1992), 795–856, p. 803.

[84] See for example Sunder, 'Piercing the Veil'.

[85] See Friedman, 'Women's Human Rights,' in which she comments that 'calling for government accountability in ['private'] areas of life requires a considerable reorientation of human rights law' (p. 20). See also Christina Cerna and Jennifer Wallace, 'Women and Culture', in *Women and International Human Rights Law*, Vol. 1, eds. Kelly Askin and Dorean Koenig

law to look at how women's rights may be violated in the private sphere—for example, to address the phenomenon of domestic violence—attempts to bring religiously sanctioned sex roles and arrangements into broader legal question have failed.

Opening religious and cultural practices generally up to the scrutiny of national and international law need not entail either coercion or exercises in rights-trumping. Rather, it is possible, at least in some forums, to treat this process as a kind of dialogue, with cultural and religious practitioners in conversation with legislators and those engaged in drafting and revising international human rights law. Participants in such a dialogue could, and should, look closely at the places where religious and cultural practices stand in tension with international law and human rights norms more generally, and examine the competing claims at stake. Some human rights scholars are beginning to develop innovative approaches consistent with this idea of a dialogue between religion and law. For example, legal scholar Donna Sullivan proposes a discursive legal framework drawing on 'international and regional human rights norms' for determining the legitimacy of religious restrictions on human rights.[86] And political theorist Avigail Eisenberg has developed an argument suggesting how cultural and religious claims might be better adjudicated in legal contexts, focusing on the scrutiny of individual and group 'identity-related' differences in the face of calls to restrict, or conversely, protect, aspects of culture and religion.[87]

Nor, in the dialogue I have in mind, need the emphasis always be on searching out points of difference or conflict between rights and norms on the one hand and practices on the other. Legal thinker Abdullahi Ahmed An-Na'im, for example, proposes that those politically engaged with human rights can and should help to discover points of overlap between religious cultures and human rights principles, supporting 'cross-cultural work to provide the necessary internal legitimacy for human rights standards'.[88] On his view, finding local or indigenous traditions that can help ground particular human rights deepens the legitimacy of those rights. Responding to the fact

---

(Ardsley, NY: Transnational Publishers, Inc.), who write (p. 629) that the 'private sphere, which deals with issues such as religion, culture, the status of women, the right to marry and divorce and remarry, and the like, is a domain in which the most serious challenges to the universality of human rights arise'. Also see Christine Chinkin, 'Cultural Relativism and International Law', in *Religious Fundamentalisms and the Human Rights of Women*, ed. Courtney Howland (New York: St. Martin's Press, 1999).

[86] Sullivan, 'Gender Equality and Religious Freedom,' p. 855.

[87] See Avigail Eisenberg, 'Identity and Liberal Politics: the Problem of Minorities Within Minorities', in *Minorities Within Minorities*, eds. Avigail Eisenberg and Jeff Spinner-Halev (Cambridge: Cambridge University Press, 2005), and her 'Diversity and Equality'.

[88] Abdullahi Ahmed An-Na'im, 'Problems of Universal Cultural Legitimacy', p. 356.

of cultural and religious challenges to human rights, philosopher Charles Taylor suggests that a truly 'unforced consensus' on human rights might emerge by welcoming different or asymmetrical justifications for particular human rights, rather like Rawls' overlapping consensus.[89] And noting the interpretive nature of religion, Charlesworth suggests that religious traditions might try interpreting religious texts against the background of human rights, thereby developing 'a "human rights hermeneutic"'.[90] It follows from these and other proposals for rethinking human rights that dialogue geared toward addressing tensions, as well as overlap, between religious traditions and human rights law need (and should) not be a zero-sum game—that is, one in which *either* religious rights or certain competing individual rights (e.g. sexual equality) emerge triumphant. This satisfies no one. Rather, as Sunder writes, individuals are increasingly articulating 'a vision of human flourishing that requires freedom within the context of religious and cultural community', and which 'includes not only a right to equal treatment in one's cultural or religious community, but also a right to engage in those communities on one's own terms'.[91] The complexity and difficulty of the task of opening up religious practices and beliefs to deliberation and critical questioning cannot be overstated; but without it, a range of human rights instruments, including those intended to protect women, may lack legitimacy and real purchase.

In rethinking the theory and practice of women's human rights, a final important conceptual shift we might consider is that of coming to view rights as fundamentally *political* in character, in the sense of not standing above local, national, and transnational politics. Against the view that 'rights, including human rights, stop political argument and end political contest',[92] human rights—like all rights—are variously contested, interpreted, revised, and affirmed. This is so for a variety of reasons, as we have seen. Just as cultural practices are often resisted by ethnocultural and religious group members on political and strategic grounds, so too are particular norms and rights frequently challenged for strategic political reasons. Religious reasons may of course be invoked (by states, groups, or individuals) as a challenge to particular human rights, especially women's human rights, but this is not

---

[89] Charles Taylor, 'Conditions of an Unforced Consensus on Human Rights', in *The East Asian Challenge for Human Rights*, eds. Joanne Bauer and Daniel Bell (Cambridge: Cambridge University Press, 1999).

[90] Charlesworth, 'The Challenges of Human Rights Law', p. 411.

[91] Sunder, 'Piercing the Veil', p. 1408.

[92] Sarat and Kearns, 'The Unsettled Status of Human Rights', p. 9.

to say that other, political and strategic, reasons do not supply the main motivation.[93] On the other hand, it does not follow that those who dispute a given right are necessarily disingenuous in their beliefs or positions.[94]

How might paying attention to the political dimensions of human rights help to strengthen women's human rights? In the first place, by adopting a political reading of human rights we can make better sense of important debates within international human rights discourse regarding the relative status of different kinds of rights (e.g. civil and political rights vs. social and economic rights), and the impact that culture and religion should, or should not, have on rights.[95] A political understanding of human rights helps us to grasp some of motivations behind, for example, Islamic states' reservations to CEDAW, or certain Asian countries' rejection of civil and political rights in the name of Asian values, and so makes it possible to engage in a critical debate about these reasons. Attention to 'the political uses of claims of religious culture',[96] as Charlesworth calls it, is perfectly consistent with, and even in some sense required by, a human rights approach. In the case of women's human rights, recognition of the political dimensions of human rights is particularly critical, for these are often among the most contested human rights in both theory and practice. Because women's status and roles are often seen as critical to the traditionalism of religious culture, and are so deeply interwoven with group practices and arrangements, any proposed changes to these are natural targets for dispute and backlash. The ensuing power struggles are often plain to insiders, but without a good grasp of the political dynamics at stake in human rights debates, it is difficult to know how women's human rights can best be defended, or where necessary, reformulated. As anthropologist Arati Rao writes:

Without questioning the political uses of culture, without asking whose culture this is and who its primary beneficiaries are, without placing the very notion of culture in historical context, and investigating the status of the interpreter, we cannot fully

[93] For example, Mayer suggests in connection with Muslim states' reservations to CEDAW that 'religious piety ... may merely be a convenient pretext for denying freedoms that the government wishes to curtail for reasons of self-interest.' See her 'Current Muslim Thinking', pp. 136–7.

[94] As An-Na'im writes, '[d]ominant groups or classes within a society normally maintain perceptions and interpretations of cultural values and norms that are supportive of their own interests, proclaiming them to be the only valid view of that culture. Dominated groups or classes may hold, or at least be open to, different perceptions and interpretations that are helpful to their struggle to achieve justice for themselves.' An-Na'im, 'Toward a Cross-Cultural Approach', p. 20.

[95] Charles Beitz, 'Human Rights as a Common Concern', *American Political Science Review*, 95/2 (2001), 269–82, p. 271.

[96] Charlesworth, 'The Challenges of Human Rights Law for Religious Traditions', p. 41.

understand the ease with which women become instrumentalized in larger battles of political, economic, military, and discursive competition in the international arena.[97]

A political approach to women's human rights also signals that rights are not all-powerful, infallible, or unalterable; they are, instead, the result of political understandings, negotiation, and human compromise. True, human rights resonate deeply in many societies, and seem to express minimum standards for treating fellow human beings that many, and perhaps even most, persons could agree upon. But they are also differently interpreted and applied, contested, and sometimes rejected. We can make the normative claim that all *should* accept existing human rights, but it is not entirely clear what this would accomplish in the face of actual objections to the contrary, and the continuation of practices and arrangements that undercut those rights.[98] Nor will it help the task of reformulating or replacing existing rights that do not adequately grasp, for example, the sources of women's disempowerment; for this, a critical discourse about rights and obligations, and the contexts in which these rights are to be applied, is indispensable. To the extent that they are 'universal', then, human rights convey what are often contingent political agreements that are the result of much debate and negotiation. Women's human rights activists, both those who lobbied for CEDAW and those who continue to lobby for further rights, understand this well. Nonetheless, this interpretation will trouble some readers, because it signals that human rights are not sacrosanct. But as defenders of a political approach to human rights have argued, this view does not necessarily imply that human rights have no moral authority, or that that there is no moral or metaethical justification for them (as some pragmatist perspectives suggest). Rather, as Charles Beitz argues:

[H]uman rights are standards to which it is reasonable to hold political institutions accountable in the processes of contemporary world politics. They operate as prima facie justifications of transnational (although not only transnational) political action aimed at bringing about change in the structure and operation of domestic (and international) institutions. Any account of the authority of human rights must take note of the political contexts in which they operate, but this hardly means that the account would exclude moral considerations; in fact, it would depend on them.[99]

---

[97] Arati Rao, 'The Politics of Gender and Culture in International Human Rights Discourse,' in *Women's Rights, Human Rights: International Feminist Perspectives*, eds. Julie Peters and Andrea Wolper (New York and London: Routledge University Press, 1995), p. 174.

[98] As Ali writes, 'international human rights as well as domestic legal systems appear to function on the premise that formal equality translates into substantive equality. Nothing could be further from the truth.' See her 'Women's Rights, CEDAW and Human Rights', p. 73.

[99] Beitz, 'Human Rights as Common Concern', p. 280.

The challenge of making women's human rights instruments more effective is inextricably linked, then, with the task of ensuring that those rights adequately respond to women's needs and the circumstances of their lives. This requires ongoing, critical debate about which domestic and transnational instruments and actions would best serve to protect and empower women in diverse cultural and religious settings. Women themselves, as human rights activists have long urged, must be a part of this discussion. This means that women's voices need to be heard when revising existing rights and protections or conceiving of new rights and obligations; when determining the 'take-up' of particular human rights, and the duty-bearers of rights; and when identifying the particular obstacles women face in having their rights met.

If human rights discourse and practice were to become more critical, open, and inclusive of women's perspectives in these ways, this would be a good start. However, given the formal character of human rights, there are built-in limitations (as discussed earlier) to the role such instruments can play in protecting women from culturally based harms. As Radhika Coomaraswamy, United Nations Special Rapporteur on Violence Against Women, reminds us:

When it comes to a woman's private life, we would be mistaken in our belief if we were not to accept the fact that in many societies human rights is actually a weak discourse in the context of family and community relations. While international human rights law is propelled forward to meet the demands of the international women's movement, the reality in many specific societies is that women's rights are under challenge from alternative cultural expressions.... Regardless of all the international standards and accompanying national legislation, unless there is resonance in national civil societies, there is little scope for real transformation.[100]

If just and lasting change of cultural and religious traditions cannot be secured by domestic and international law alone, we will need to look at other means and processes that might, in the end, be more far-reaching. In the next chapter, I sketch out an alternative approach to mediating conflicts of culture surrounding gender roles and arrangements, one that is politically inclusive and aims to generate real transformation at the grassroots level. It is an approach that complements human rights approaches and yet avoids many of the pitfalls of the liberal responses to gendered conflicts of culture surveyed thus far. For hard cases of cultural conflict in which traditional or religious practices rub up against liberal norms, the best approach, I argue, is one that foregrounds dialogue, debate, and negotiation among cultural minorities themselves, and between these groups and governmental and nongovernmental entities. On

---

[100] Coomaraswamy, 'Reinventing International Law', p. 182.

normative grounds, such an approach is intuitively preferable, for it takes seriously principles of equal respect and equal regard. For practical and prudential reasons as well, deliberation that foregrounds negotiation and compromise as means for mediating disputes about contested cultural practices is to be preferred, for it acknowledges the gradual nature of tangible cultural change and reform. Provided that democratic and representative formats for deliberation are insisted upon—both within minority cultural communities and in negotiations between such groups and the state—a deliberative democratic approach can also help to lend support to vulnerable group members and ensure that the voices of cultural dissenters are heard.

4

Democratic Deliberation: Empowering Cultural Communities

Juridical and a priori liberal approaches to cultural conflicts, I argued in Chapter 2, wrongly focus on the compatibility or incompatibility of particular social customs and arrangements with liberal principles. Nor do such approaches adequately stress the importance of cultural communities' own active involvement in evaluating and transforming their social practices. In Chapter 3, we saw that some of these same mistakes are reproduced by human rights discourses. While appeals to human rights can be a useful and important part of strategies for demanding gender justice, these are in many cases too indeterminate, alternately endorsing women's rights and cultural group rights.

For proponents of Aristotelian and deontological liberal (including human rights) approaches alike, the presence of principled and or constitutional tensions between a 'suspect' cultural practice and a core liberal norm will most often result in serious scrutiny and likely censure of that practice. Some liberals, as we saw, are dubious about more dialogical methods of resolving such conflicts, because it risks reinforcing the positions of powerful members and silencing vulnerable individuals, namely women. Other liberals (such as Kymlicka, Carens, and Levy) believe that deliberation by cultural communities and the liberal state is a critical part of the process of reform, and preferable to policies of mere prohibition. Nonetheless, even for these thinkers, dialogue is conceived largely as a form of mediation that brings minority communities together with the majority community, rather than a way for cultural groups to work through issues more independently. Also for these liberals, liberalism imposes necessary constraints on both the form and outcome of deliberative solutions to cultural disputes. Where cultural practices and arrangements are seen to violate liberal principles protecting individual rights (such freedom of religion or sexual equality), there is simply very little to discuss; as Kymlicka puts it, 'the logic of multiculturalism involves accommodating diversity within the constraints of constitutional principles of equal opportunity and individual rights.'[1]

---

[1] Kymlicka, *Politics in the Vernacular*, p. 174. Valadez's approach to intercultural dialogue is the exception here, as he does envision flexibility in the application of liberal democratic rights

These liberal accounts of intercultural dialogue between majority and minority communities differ from the more open-ended deliberation that some defenders of deliberative democracy urge, and which I develop in this chapter. The difficulty with the more constrained liberal approaches begins with the framing of the problem, namely, as (in part) a problem of either license or prohibition. Rather than starting from the question, 'which minority cultural practices should the liberal state permit, and which ought it to prohibit?', as many liberals do, I suggest that those committed to resolving a cultural conflict begin by asking a series of questions about the disputed custom and the social contexts in which it is practiced[2]: Why and how has a particular custom come to be questioned or contested? Who is insisting that a practice takes a particular (traditional or amended) form, and who benefits from this? Whose authority is challenged, and whose is reinforced, by a dispute over a particular custom, or by the introduction of a new form of that custom? These questions are best posed not only of the cultural minority community, but also of the majority culture. Thus, as Sarah Song urges, we also need to ask whether and how majority cultural norms and institutions make possible and even reinforce sexist practices within minority communities, not least because 'intercultural interactions may provoke hardening of hierarchies within minority groups, as in cases where group leaders shore up traditional decision-making structures within the community in the face of external challenges to those structures'.[3] Preliminary answers to these questions can help to contextualize the dispute at hand as well as help to direct attention to problems of power and subordination.

THE CRITERION OF DEMOCRATIC LEGITIMACY

Beyond these initial suggestions for how we might begin to reframe cultural conflicts, it is necessary to ask *what just procedures* for mediating cultural conflict in plural liberal societies might consist in. Along with other proponents of deliberative democracy, I suggest that just procedures for

---

by cultural groups. However, as noted in the last chapter, the actual outcomes of such dialogue are likely to be considerably more constrained than Valadez supposes, given the extensive list of nonnegotiable liberal rights and principles that he cites, as well as his autonomy-based justification of the value of culture.

[2] The answers will, of course, depend upon who is asking and answering. I address the question of just who ought to participate in and direct deliberations about contested customs later in this chapter.

[3] Sarah Song, 'Majority Norms, Multiculturalism, and Gender Equality', p. 476

resolving disputes about cultural practices are ones that affected citizens on the whole endorse as fair and politically legitimate, within the broad constraints of democratic legitimacy.[4] This claim is predicated on the assertion that individuals should be permitted to shape or contest their social and cultural arrangements through democratic means—and indeed, that this is fundamental to democratic legitimacy. Nor is this claim uniquely relevant to liberal minority communities. Although formal democratic mechanisms may not be present, even in the most insular of communities in liberal democracies we see evidence of dissent and efforts to modify customs, and attendant defenses of these efforts. The central political inclusion of cultural group members in deliberations about contested practices is, I argue, essential to the legitimacy of the proposed reforms. Moreover, such inclusion is also necessary to ensure that proposed reforms are viable and practicable. The procedural legitimacy of processes aimed at resolving cultural conflicts is furthermore linked to the viability of reforms, since excluded members may dispute the validity of political outcomes. A democratic process for mediating conflicts of culture must therefore ensure, as far as possible, that no 'stakeholders' are prevented from participating in deliberations or from attempting to (democratically) influence the outcome.[5]

While acknowledging that justice and democratic legitimacy are by no means synonymous, there is good reason to link the two concepts closely in considering the justice or injustice of procedures for evaluating and reforming cultural group practices. By contrast, the claim that just procedures are merely those that square with liberal principles does not necessarily satisfy the criterion of democratic legitimacy. Similarly, unlike instrumental accounts of just procedures, which insist that procedures are just provided they produce morally just *outcomes*, the view that just procedures are in effect democratically legitimate procedures—understood not in terms of simple majoritarian politics but rather in terms of deliberative and democratic processes—attributes an independent value to genuinely democratic processes.[6] Open and democratic procedures for deliberation and decision-making, in addition to permitting participants to shape the substance of

---

[4] I defend democratic legitimacy over other conceptions of political legitimacy at greater length in Chapter 8.

[5] I borrow the term 'stakeholders' from theorists of associative democracy but use it in a more general sense than they do, to mean anyone with a demonstrable and direct interest in the outcome of political deliberation. See Hirst, *Associative Democracy*, and Hirst and Khilnani, *Reinventing Democracy*.

[6] See Christopher Griffin, 'Debate: Democracy as a Non-Instrumentally Just Procedure', *The Journal of Political Philosophy*, 11/1 (2003), 111–21. However, whereas Griffin argues that '[a] political procedure is intrinsically just when the rules and practices constituting it treat persons appropriately' (p. 120), I maintain that democratic political inclusion in deliberation and decision-making is a requirement of just procedures.

proposals, also allow participants to question and modify (within limits) the procedures for mediating conflicts.

Applied to disputes about cultural practices and arrangements, democratic legitimacy requires that members of cultural communities whose customs are the subject of concern—or who claim special dispensation for these—play a central role in evaluating, and where necessary, proposing reforms of their own social practices and arrangements. The political inclusion of all those who are or could be affected by decisions is thus a further crucial component of the legitimacy of procedures for mediating cultural conflicts. Whether group members consider the outcomes of such procedures to be legitimate and therefore binding will be largely determined by whether they accept the process itself as valid and fair (and political exclusion surely tops the list of reasons to reject political processes as unfair). Yet admittedly, linking legitimacy to political inclusion in this way is controversial for a number of reasons. There are valid concerns (expressed, as we saw, by Nussbaum, Okin, and O'Neill) about the propensity for even the most well-intentioned deliberation to silence some members of religious and cultural communities and reinforce the power of others. More immediately, political inclusion is often what is ultimately at stake in cultural disputes; therefore, to stipulate wide political inclusion of group members in deliberations about a contested custom or arrangement is to foreground, and possibly compound, the conflict at hand. Membership disputes in indigenous communities are an obvious example of this, as are debates in traditional and orthodox religious communities about whether women members should be enfranchised in group power structures.

An important limitation of any democratic approach to resolving conflicts of culture concerns the problem of genuine as opposed to purely formal inclusion. Even where political exclusion of some group members, such as women, is not explicit, it may be difficult to ensure that those who have been historically disenfranchised actually participate in deliberation. In some traditional communities, women in particular may be reluctant to step forward, either out of fear of retribution, or because social custom simply discourages them. The deliberative norms or constraints I develop in the latter part of the chapter will speak to this problem, but the difficulty of establishing real political inclusion remains. There is also the concern that those who do participate in deliberation and decision-making about contested practices may simply endorse existing practices, as a consequence of lacking the necessary distance and critical reflexivity required to scrutinize their cultural arrangements. This is the problem of adaptive preferences. As we saw in the last chapter, Nussbaum's answer to this challenge is ultimately that we ought to defend and foster core human capabilities as universal principles to offset the adaptive effects of traditional cultures. These principles, which she claims have an 'independent moral argument' to support them, are therefore not to be rejected simply because some women, no doubt lacking adequate experience of a full range of capabilities and options, claim they do not value a given capability.[7] Applied to plural, liberal states, however, the issue of adaptive preferences has somewhat less purchase, since the majority culture offers a range of life options for women, and few groups are so isolated that their members cannot imagine other possible lives, or evaluate certain of their customs in reflective or critical light. Members of cultural minority communities within liberal states are arguably no less likely than are members of majority cultures to critically engage their own cultural frameworks. Arguably, the problem of adaptive preferences—which of course applies to both majority and minority communities—is best faced by supporting people's agency in a range of contexts, rather than by dismissing their stated preferences. I try to demonstrate this point in the chapters that follow.

Beyond the issue of the legitimacy of processes that evaluate contested customs, there are good practical reasons to defend the norm of political inclusion as essential to the just resolution of conflicts of culture. Strategically speaking, community members' input is necessary to help form a clear picture of the actual or *lived* form of contested social practices and the experiences they comprise. Without an accurate representation of how particular customs are practiced and affect different individuals, it is difficult to conceive of reforms that will help to protect and empower vulnerable individuals. Cultural members are well placed to articulate how different practices and arrangements in their cultures have evolved and which social relationships perpetuate oppression. Where no attempt has been made to involve cultural members in conceiving of relevant and plausible reforms, liberal reform policies may hold out the promise of formal sexual equality in contexts in which a group's social and cultural structures consistently undermine it. As gender injustice is likely to persist in areas of private life, it is all the more important to glean women's views about what actually goes on in this sphere.

Part of the preliminary answer to the question, 'What constitutes a just procedure for mediating disputes over contested cultural practices?' is thus that such a procedure would require and foster open and fair debate among participants in the dialogue about contested customs. In part, this means ensuring that procedures for discussion and decision-making are designed to give participants roughly equal positions in deliberation. A just procedure for negotiating disputes about cultural roles and arrangements would thus

[7] Nussbaum, 'On Hearing Women's Voices', p. 201. See also Ch. 2 of *Women and Human Development*, which is dedicated to exploring the issue of adaptive preferences.

need to try, so far as it is possible, to gauge the power differences among cultural group members and between these members and other, nongroup participants in deliberation. This in turn requires assessing who is excluded from politics-as-usual, the structural reasons for this, and how these factors might be mitigated—at least for the purposes of inclusion in democratic dialogue.[8] Later in this chapter, I introduce and defend three further norms—those of nondomination, political equality, and revisability—that I propose should guide the deliberative process so as to help ensure fair terms of deliberation. Crucially, my argument presupposes that deliberation about contested cultural practices takes place against the background of a liberal democratic state that protects fundamental individual rights and freedoms, and which prohibits physical harm or other cruel treatment through criminal law. However, as I discuss, my approach does not require that political deliberation ultimately yield proposals for reform that privilege liberal norms of individual autonomy and choice, or which endorse a *substantive* (and so normatively controversial) liberal standard of sexual equality.

THE DELIBERATIVE TURN

In recent years, dialogue and deliberation as means for resolving a range of political and cultural conflicts have been proposed by a number of political theorists and philosophers who draw variously upon different strands of liberalism, Kantian ethics, Habermasian communicative ethics, and emerging theories of deliberative democracy. Richard Bellamy, Seyla Benhabib, Simone Chambers, Bhikhu Parekh, Charles Taylor, James Tully, Jorge Valadez, Melissa Williams, and Iris Young, amongst others, have all advanced dialogue as a response to cultural disputes, ranging from casual proposals for reciprocal exchanges between citizens of different cultural communities to detailed descriptions of prospective intercultural dialogues. Some have suggested that a genuine commitment to cultural pluralism requires that some of the seemingly fundamental tenets of liberal society be left open to discussion: Carens, for example, advocates a dialogue between Aboriginal and nonAboriginal Canadians about the nature and meaning of justice for these different communities;[9] Tully argues that the constitutions of socially diverse democracies

---

[8] Michael Rabinder James gives an account of the structural aspects of *inter*cultural dialogue requiring attention in discussions of strategic and communicative action. See his 'Communicative Action, Strategic Action, and Inter-Group Dialogue', *European Journal of Political Theory*, 2/2 (2003), 157–82, esp. pp. 174–6.

[9] Carens, *Culture, Citizenship, and Community*, p. 197.

should reflect the different political and constitutional traditions of their national communities, and urges intercultural dialogue as a means of framing such pluralistic arrangements;[10] Benhabib proposes a 'complex multicultural dialogue' that places individuals at the center of 'processes of cultural communication, contestation, and resignifiation...within civil society'[11]; and Parekh conceives of a dialogue between minority and majority communities addressing contested practices—a process of 'intercultural evaluation' that begins from the core or 'operative public values' of a society.[12]

I share many of these thinkers' intuitions about the importance and value of concrete dialogue among affected citizens as the most democratically legitimate and just means of mediating tensions surrounding contested cultural practices, and will build upon them here. However, few of these writers have specifically proposed dialogue-based solutions as an alternative to liberal universalism; indeed, some proponents of deliberation simply invoke dialogue as a means for facilitating the discovery of genuinely universal values (or, relatedly, for determining the proper limits of liberal tolerance). For instance, Parekh writes that '[w]e stand a better chance of arriving at a genuinely universal morality consisting of *common* regulative principles and a rich *plurality* of ends and ideals if we derive it...from a critical dialogue between cultures'.[13] By contrast, the proposals I outline in this chapter begin from the conviction that deliberation and negotiation are indispensable tools with which to resolve cultural conflicts, but that, properly understood, these tools are incompatible with a normative commitment to liberal universalism of the sort employed by mainstream liberal approaches, and endorsed by some deliberative democracy proponents.

The deliberative approach to cultural conflicts that I advance thus differs in a few respects from the approaches of the thinkers mentioned above, and from deliberative democracy theory more generally. First, rather than locating the source of democratic legitimacy strictly in formal political deliberation, as most proponents of deliberative democracy theory do, I argue that the *scope* of democratic activity is much wider than this, and so should cause us to rethink the bases of democratic inclusion and legitimacy.[14] Nonformal democratic

---

[10] Tully, *Strange Multiplicity*, ch. 6 (esp. pp. 183–4).

[11] Benhabib, *The Claims of Culture*, p. 101.

[12] Parekh, *Rethinking Multiculturalism*, pp. 270, 272, 292–3, and *passim*.

[13] Bhikhu Parekh, 'Moral Philosophy and its Anti-Pluralist Bias', *Philosophy and Pluralism*, ed. David Archard (Cambridge: Cambridge University Press, 1996), p. 134.

[14] In a parallel argument, John Dryzek has argued that democratic activity in the public sphere reaches further than we suppose, shaping political norms and discourse more generally. Citing feminism and environmentalism as examples, he writes that, 'discursive engagement in the public sphere can influence state action in many informal ways. These ways include changing the terms of discourse in ways that eventually come to pervade the understandings of governmental

expression, such as forms of cultural resistance, retrieval, and reinvention in the private and social realms, also speak to the issue of a social custom's legitimacy or illegitimacy. Liberal political institutions can help to expand and support this informal democratic activity by supporting the safe public articulation of concerns and cultural expressions both within cultural communities and in the wider society. Proponents of deliberative democracy have long argued that liberal states need to deepen their democratic practices and find ways to better include all citizens in political deliberation, but rarely do they consider such practices beyond the ambit of the public sphere. They do, of course, argue for greater inclusion in political institutions, as well as for the transformation of these institutions in accordance with normative principles of equality and mutual recognition.[15] Beyond this insight of deliberative democrats, however, I argue that to expand democratic inclusion, we will need to rethink what democratic political activity comprises, and proliferate the spaces for such activity.

Second, where it is necessary to try to mediate cultural conflicts in more formal political forums, I argue that we should adopt a model of democratic deliberation that engages participants' strategic interests and needs, rather than insisting, as deliberative democracy theorists normally do, that citizens' moral or normative differences must provide the proper and indeed exclusive focus for democratic deliberation. On the deliberative democratic approach, these differences are mediated through processes of moral argumentation and justification. A more political approach, by contrast, permits and even encourages frank deliberation about citizens' needs-based and interest-based disagreements, which I argue often reflect the key motivating concerns behind cultural disputes. A more politically focused framework for mediating cultural conflicts better reflects the practical, strategic, and *intracultural* nature of many actual cultural disputes about social customs in liberal democratic states, as I argue.

The deliberative democratic approach to mediating conflicts of culture advanced here is grounded in a democratic conception of political legitimacy that stresses the importance of wide political inclusion. The participation of 'stakeholder' members of cultural groups in deliberations about contested practices makes it more likely that proposed reforms will be relevant and informed by people's lived experiences. Their political inclusion is also required to establish the legitimacy of deliberative processes and outcomes. This

actors'. See Dryzek, 'Deliberative Democracy in Divided Societies: Alternatives to Agonism and Analgesia', *Political Theory*, 33/2 (2005), 218–42, p. 234.

[15] See for example Seyla Benhabib, 'Deliberative Rationality and Models of Democratic Legitimacy', *Constellations*, 1 (1994), 26–52.

latter justification is bound up with the claim that citizens (generally) are not to be bound by principles to which they have not consented, or to which they could not give consent. Here I draw from Habermas's test for the normative validity of principles, whereby 'only those norms can claim to be valid that meet (or could meet) with the approval of all concerned in their capacity as participants on a practical discourse'.[16] As we saw earlier, neither juridical liberal nor traditional liberal human rights approaches accord adequate importance to such mechanisms of ensuring political inclusion and the normative legitimacy of political processes and their outcomes.

PROBLEMS WITH DELIBERATIVE DEMOCRACY AS USUAL

Tensions between cultural practices and liberal norms expose not only intercultural tensions, but also considerable intracultural disagreements over the interpretation, meaning, and legitimacy of particular customs: communities themselves disagree about the purpose and proper form of given practices and arrangements. In part this is due to the evolving and malleable character of customs, and the strategic character of many of these disputes. Some liberals and deliberative democracy theorists have recently acknowledged the fungible nature of cultural practices and arrangements. Both Benhabib and Parekh, for instance, insist on the essentially fluid and contested character of social customs, and emphasize the narrative form of cultures as a whole. As Parekh writes:

A culture has no essence. It includes different strands of thought, and reformers are right to highlight those that have been marginalized, suppressed or misconstrued by the dominant interpretation of their tradition. Furthermore, every tradition can be read in different ways, none of them definitive and final.[17]

Similarly, Benhabib emphasizes the complexity and contestability of social and cultural identities, and claims that a process of multicultural dialogue better responds to this reality than does a liberal, juridical model.[18] These accounts of culture, social identities, and customs as constantly in flux, capture much more accurately the practice of culture. They do not, however, emphasize the *political* dimension of conflicts as much as they should, and

---

[16] Jürgen Habermas, 'Discourse Ethics: Notes on a Program of Philosophical Justification', in *The Communicative Ethics Controversy*, eds. Fred Dallmayr and Seyla Benhabib (Cambridge, MA: MIT Press, 1990), p. 90.

[17] Parekh, *Rethinking Multiculturalism*, p. 175.

[18] Benhabib, *The Claims of Culture*, p. 71.

as a consequence, risk overlooking the extent to which disputes about the validity of cultural practices reflect either external pressures or else challenges to communities' internal decision-making structures, from within and outside the group.

This brief characterization of cultural conflicts also generates at least two clusters of objections to the adequacy and fit of deliberative democratic frameworks for mediating such disputes. Below, I discuss these two challenges briefly and the deliberative models of politics that are most vulnerable to them. Subsequently, I try to show why we should opt for an *amended* model of public deliberation to help mediate conflicts of culture, one that conceives of conflict resolution not in terms of a process of rational, moral argumentation, but instead emphasizes the political dimensions of disputes, stressing strategies of negotiation and compromise.

Critics of deliberative democracy theory, both immanent and otherwise, have issued a range of criticisms of idealized models of discourse and deliberation relevant to the issues at hand. These center on the following problems: Who is to participate in deliberation? Who is included, silenced, and who speaks for whom? What norms are presupposed by the deliberative scheme, and are these genuinely shared norms, or do they result in acts of exclusion? How is deliberation to be conducted—whom does it privilege, and whom does it disadvantage? What kind of outcome is sought? If the answer is thick consensus, whose views would this stifle? These objections are especially salient in socially diverse contexts, and are more important still in situations of cultural conflict. In many cases, it is deliberative democracy theorists themselves who have raised and responded to these criticisms. For example, in connection with challenges centering on the issues of political inclusion and exclusion, Iris Young rejects the assumption that particular representatives can speak for whole communities or social groups in democratic politics.[19] James Bohman notes that although idealized versions of deliberative democracy require 'the inclusion of everyone affected by a decision', failure to account for the effect of social inequalities on civic participation and political inclusion can render the norm of inclusion entirely ineffectual.[20] Potential participants may also be excluded from deliberation, or else silenced within a deliberative setting, through the introduction of onerous normative constraints on the form and content of deliberative communication. For instance, the insistence that participants must adhere to norms of reasonableness

---

[19] Young, *Inclusion and Democracy*, pp. 121–2.

[20] James Bohman, *Public Deliberation: Pluralism, Complexity, and Democracy* (Cambridge, MA: MIT Press, 2000), pp. 16 and 18.

and/or rationality by giving 'public' reasons—reasons that are morally universalizable and so accessible to public reason—may further render deliberative designs inhospitable or closed to some citizens. Cultural minorities whose traditions of communication and standards of justification are at odds with these norms, including some religious minorities, are especially likely to have their discursive or reasoning styles discredited or disqualified.[21] And especially where norms of rationality and reasonableness are stipulated as *criteria for inclusion* in public deliberation, they can have an exclusionary effect, as John Dryzek and others have observed.[22] But it may not be the case that 'deliberative democracy requires a full commitment to public reasoning' of the formal, idealized type.[23] Norms of reasonableness and universalizability can be rejected as *conditions for participation in public dialogue*; as Knight and Johnson argue, deliberation must have more 'expansive conditions of entry' if it is to help mediate conflicts arising in plural states.[24]

Deliberative models of politics that emphasize normative and reasoned public discourse have also been roundly criticized for stipulating that deliberation should result in moral consensus, on the grounds that this assumes a greater degree of overlap and agreement among citizens than is warranted in socially diverse societies. And indeed, many proponents of deliberative democracy do interpret the normative criterion of public reason as requiring that participants in deliberation appeal to a common good.[25] To forge moral consensus from citizens' divergent convictions, needs, and interests typically requires an appeal to a conception of the public good that may deny the scope of citizens' differences. Deservedly, these normative requirements of consensus and shared rational grounds appear to be losing support among at least some deliberative democracy proponents, who increasingly agree that moral consensus is not a sensible goal for public deliberation in socially plural

---

[21] Young discusses the example of storytelling as an important communicative strategy that is likely to fail rigorous normative, discursive requirements, in *Inclusion and Democracy*, p. 75.

[22] John Dryzek, *Deliberative Democracy and Beyond: Liberals, Critics, Contestations* (Oxford: Oxford University Press, 2000), p. 58. See also James Bohman, 'Deliberative Democracy and Effective Social Freedom: Capabilities, Resources, and Opportunities', in *Deliberative Democracy: Essays on Reason and Politics*, eds. James Bohman and William Rehg (Cambridge, MA and London: MIT Press, 1997/9).

[23] John Ferejohn, 'Instituting Deliberative Democracy', Nomos XLII: *Designing Democratic Institutions*, eds. Ian Shapiro and Stephen Macedo (New York: New York University Press, 2000), p. 76.

[24] Jack Knight and James Johnson, 'What Sort of Equality Does Deliberative Democracy Require?', in *Deliberative Democracy: Essays on Reason and Politics*, eds. James Bohman and William Rehg (Cambridge, MA: MIT Press, 1997/9), p. 287.

[25] Joshua Cohen, 'Deliberation and Democratic Legitimacy', in *Deliberative Democracy: Essays on Reason and Politics*, eds. James Bohman and William Rehg (Cambridge, MA: MIT Press, 1997/9), p. 77.

societies.[26] Even Habermas has recently acknowledged that conditions of deep moral pluralism in liberal democratic states make it difficult to discover 'generalizable interest' or to reach agreement on issues with normative content.[27] And although he remains committed to a conception of rational moral consensus, Habermas now accords more importance to bargaining and compromise as strategies in deliberation.[28]

Rather than moving toward more pragmatic and strategic models of conflict resolution, as I would urge, some deliberative democrats simply advocate replacing the goal of moral *consensus* with that of reasoned, normative agreement and/or moral *compromise*.[29] Dryzek, for instance, declares that '[i]n a pluralistic world, consensus is unattainable, unnecessary, and undesirable', but he rejects a model of political deliberation as essentially negotiation and bargaining, which he thinks reduces politics to 'strategic action'.[30] Bohman also eschews the goal of normative consensus but holds out moral compromise as the aim of dialogue; deliberation aimed at moral compromise, he claims, is a far cry from modus vivendi–style politics involving mere 'strategic bargaining' and 'trade-offs'.[31] Similarly, in his discussion of what he calls the process of 'intercultural evaluation', Parekh situates intercultural dialogue firmly against the backdrop of an appraisal of society's core public values, and encourages appeals to universal values as well as to the common good.[32] And Benhabib, while subscribing to a complex, constructivist or 'narrative' account of culture, insists that a broad framework of 'normative universalism' is perfectly compatible with her model of multicultural dialogue.[33] Democratic dialogue should seek to address cultural differences, which Benhabib claims 'run very deep and are very real', but she assures us they are best negotiated through a process of moral argumentation structured according to norms of rationality and publicity. While moral consensus may only rarely be achievable, it should not be jettisoned as a goal, for 'consensually attained moral norms' are, according to Benhabib, possible even in deeply plural societies.[34]

[26] Dryzek, *Deliberative Democracy and Beyond*, pp. 47–8; Ferejohn, 'Instituting Deliberative Democracy', pp. 79–80; and Richard Bellamy, *Liberalism and Pluralism: Towards a Politics of Compromise* (London and New York: Routledge, 1999), p. 110.

[27] J. Habermas, *Between Facts and Norms*, trans. William Rehg (Cambridge, MA: MIT Press, 1996), p. 165.

[28] Ibid. 166.

[29] Dryzek endorses 'reasoned agreement' as a goal of deliberation in *Deliberative Democracy and Beyond*, p. 47.

[30] Ibid. 170.

[31] Bohman, *Public Deliberation*, p. 91, and Bohman, 'Public Reason and Cultural Pluralism', *Political Theory*, 23/2 (1995), 253–79, esp. p. 266.

[32] Parekh, *Rethinking Multiculturalism*, pp. 292–4 and 341.

[33] Benhabib, *The Claims of Culture*, p. xi.

[34] Ibid., p. 7, pp. 134–43, and 144–5.

By contrast, according to the alternative model of democratic deliberation for mediating conflicts of culture that I defend here, even the expectation of minimal moral consensus, or moral compromise, may, in some circumstances, be unrealistic and undesirable. Both the goal of moral consensus amidst social and cultural diversity, and the problem of political exclusion, point (in my view) to the need for a reframing of deliberative democracy as more explicitly political, particularly insofar as it is used to mediate cultural conflicts. If public deliberation is instead conceived of as (exclusively) reasoned, moral argumentation about policies and norms that reflect citizens' moral beliefs, the strategic interests and motivations of participants will fade from view. In the case of disputes over the validity of cultural practices, we see that this conception of deliberation frames even manifestly strategic disagreements in a moral light by encouraging-or even requiring-that participants present their claims in terms of moral differences and beliefs. While in some cases this might help move participants to a fair resolution of the conflict, in other instances it serves to make disputes less tractable. More importantly, however, when strategic interests are translated into moral arguments or recede from the space of politics, power relations may be effectively camouflaged, with the result that some individuals are left more vulnerable or powerless.

It is not the case that the more politically focused model of deliberative democracy I defend necessarily rejects moral argumentation, or always privileges strategic and interest-based concerns. Rather, it seeks to expand the possible scope of deliberation, and to make it possible for strategic kinds of concerns to come to the surface in formal deliberative forums. Nor do I mean to suggest that the distinction between moral and strategic concerns is hard and fast, for they very often merge: for instance, in the context of cultural disputes, one may well have a (higher-order) interest in seeing one's culture maintain traditional ways. Moreover, over time, some kinds of shared interests and need-based claims can take on a settled normative status: for example, persons who share a strategic interest in maintaining male-only inheritance or succession probably also come to believe that this is the most natural and fitting social arrangement, and as so defend it accordingly.[35]

---

[35] There is some parallel here between my argument and certain variants of moral contractarian theory, and (moral) choice theory, such as that of David Gauthier (see Gauthier, *Morals by Agreement* [Oxford: Oxford University Press, 1986], and Paul Voice, *Morality and Agreement: A Defense of Moral Contractarianism* [New York: Peter Lang, 2002]). However, unlike many contractarians and choice theorists, I reject the reduction of moral values to mere preferences or interests. My claim is instead that there is a more fluid interplay between interests and moral commitments than deontologists in general, and proponents of discourse ethics and deliberative democracy in particular, acknowledge.

Equally, citizens' moral commitments may lead them to push particular strategic concerns. The relationship between strategic and interest-based concerns on the one hand and moral beliefs on the other is thus in many instances a fluid one. But on the political approach to deliberation I develop here, strategic interests are not to be disqualified or bracketed, but rather, can serve as a valid focus for dialogue, negotiation, and political compromise. Provided certain constraints are in place (which I discuss shortly), deliberative dialogue and decision-making that focus on participants' interests and needs can produce democratically legitimate outcomes that both protect and empower vulnerable cultural group members in tangible ways.

Some deliberative democracy proponents doubt that cultural identity claims per se are compatible with norms of public reason, particularly the principle of universalizability, and so argue that these should be set aside in deliberation.[36] Bracketing cultural identity claims, however, does not seem the best answer here. Many democratic theorists have suggested that cultural claims do have a place in formal political deliberation, but that they should be framed as moral arguments in a context of reasoned, normative argumentation. Undergirding this assertion is the belief that cultural differences are, *au fond*, moral differences; this view is pervasive throughout much political theorizing about cultural groups, yet is oddly underdefended. In his discussion of intercultural disputes involving Aboriginal peoples, for example, David Kahane insists that 'justly resolving intercultural disputes requires that one treat cultural differences as deep: no single definition of justice can be fully adequate to the understandings of disputants, and communication across cultural differences will, at best, be approximate'.[37]

Another way in which some cultural disputes come to be characterized as necessarily moral is through the assertion that cultural arguments should enjoy a normatively privileged status in deliberations about contested practices. Most notably, Avigail Eisenberg has proposed the development of legal and political processes and institutions to fairly assess what is at stake in intercultural disputes. In particular, she recommends a public procedure for adjudicating cultural minority claims that would give the greatest weight to what she calls citizens' 'identity-related differences'.[38] Importantly, for

---

[36] For a reply to these objections, see Jonathan Quonq, 'Are Identity Claims Bad for Deliberative Democracy?', *Contemporary Political Theory*, 1/3 (2002), 307–28.

[37] David Kahane, 'What is Culture?: Generalizing About Aboriginal and Newcomer Perspectives', in *Intercultural Dispute Resolution in Aboriginal Contexts*, eds. David Kahane and Catherine Bell (Vancouver and Toronto: University of British Columbia Press, 2004), p. 32.

[38] Eisenberg calls this the 'difference-based approach'; see her 'Diversity and Equality.' Eisenberg first developed this in 'The Politics of Individual and Group Difference in Canadian Jurisprudence', *Canadian Journal of Political Science*, 27/1 (1994), 3–21.

Eisenberg, the adjudication of these identity claims ought to be a public and transparent process; the courts are one place in which this adjudication is already taking place. Moreover, Eisenberg contends that justifying practices in dispute by appealing to identity-based reasons (which are then evaluated) can be constitutive of greater cultural recognition: 'publicly discussing minority identity claims could be one important form of "recognition" in that it allows minority groups a means to defend their practices and traditions in terms of what may matter most to them, namely that these practices are key to their understanding of themselves and their way of life'.[39] In those instances where historical injustices and discrimination have wounded communities deeply, it seems possible that public deliberation and reason-giving that highlights the values and identities of harmed groups can help to restore their sense of wholeness. However, as noted above, there is a danger that members of cultural groups may also defend practices by invoking traditions, beliefs, or identities that are in fact only secondary or tertiary in importance to the issue at hand. Eisenberg seems to downplay this concern when she writes that the 'enthusiasm to frame arguments in terms of identity or identity-related interests suggests that individuals and social groups often view the harm of laws that restrict their cultural or religious practices as, in the first instance, harms to their identity'.[40] Deliberation so conceived, I argue, can have a distorting effect on the actual issues and conflicts at stake, which may have more to do with the concrete needs and interests of group members, as well as questions of power and authority.[41] If this is so, then attempts both to resolve cultural disputes by foregrounding participants' identity claims in a process of adjudication, or, as on the deliberative democracy model, emphasizing the evaluation of participants' moral and normative claims and beliefs in a process of moral argumentation, may fail to get to the heart of conflicts. Not only do we risk reinforcing the ontological status of cultural identity claims—overlooking 'the politics of culture', as Jim Johnson notes[42]—but we risk silencing or ignoring cultural group members whose concerns are not centrally about their group identity, but instead about arrangements or practices that disadvantage, constrain, or harm them in some way.

My aim here is not to deny that cultural conflicts in plural liberal states may sometimes concern deep differences of value; rather, my contention is merely that disputes with this underlying cause are rarer than is often supposed. As I illustrate shortly, conflicts of culture often entail conflicting strategic interests,

---

[39] Avigail Eisenberg, 'Public Institutions and the Assessment of Cultural Identity', p. 9.

[40] Ibid., p. 9.

[41] This is not to deny individuals' needs and interests have a normative dimension, nor that questions of power and authority are bound up with moral claims. The point is one of emphasis.

[42] Johnson, 'Why Respect Culture?', p. 413.

very broadly construed[43]; the desire to maintain a traditional family structure and a gendered domestic division of labor—with all the power and conveniences that this brings—may, for example, underlie the insistence that girls receive different (religious) schooling than boys. But this is of course not always the case. Some seemingly resource-based conflicts, like debates over fishing rights between First Nations peoples and the federal and provincial governments, are also about a community's identity. Cultural conflicts may thus have both a moral and a strategic dimension. For example, disputes over membership among Native peoples in North America typically combine concerns about who counts as a member of the group (in light of family or blood ancestry, religion, etc.) with concerns about how a community's resources are to be divided—such as access to tribal lands, hunting rights, housing, or any dividends or wealth the band might have. Value-based and pragmatic motivations may also fuel efforts to recreate group identities: immigrant communities sometimes seek to retrieve a cohesive sense of ethnic or religious identity both because it is something they have reason to value, and because it may serve as a basis for organizing politically to protest concrete social and economic injustices, such as high unemployment among their members, racist discrimination in housing or education, and so forth. As Veit Bader reminds us, '[p]rojects of collective identity definitions, quite generally, take place in situations of competition and struggle for resources and benefits that are defined and experienced as scarce'.[44]

To suggest that we demote the moral dimensions of deliberation in this way is controversial. Much more so than rival liberal models of politics, deliberative democracy endorses explicitly normative and reasoned discussion between rational, uncoerced, and equal participants as a means of resolving disagreement and conflict. This conviction in the normative basis of politics, as Bohman argues, links together diverse models of deliberative democracy: 'they all reject the reduction of politics and decision making to instrumental and strategic rationality'.[45] Through deliberation, participants are expected not simply to communicate their beliefs, but more importantly, to reflect upon and transform these in dialogue with others.[46] Dialogue is supposed to clarify our own evaluative attachments, as well as our deepest shared commitments.[47] Valadez draws a sharp distinction between deliberation and traditional problem-solving methods:

[43] For a parallel but more detailed argument about the strategic motivations of actors in cultural disputes, see Johnson, 'Why Respect Culture?'.

[44] Veit Bader, 'Culture and Identity: Contesting Constructivism', *Ethnicities*, 1/2 (2001), 251–73, p. 261.

[45] Bohman, *Public Deliberation*, p. 5.

[46] Dryzek, *Deliberative Democracy and Beyond*, p. 30.

[47] See for example Simone Chambers, *Reasonable Democracy: Jürgen Habermas and the Politics of Discourse* (Ithaca, NY: Cornell University Press, 1996), p. 11.

What makes public deliberation distinct from other forms of negotiation such as bargaining and market behavior is that, while the latter take for granted that participants are primarily motivated by the maximizing of their self-interest, in the former participants have to make a genuine commitment to reach a position that takes into account the needs of the larger political community and that may involve compromise and the overriding of one's self-interest.[48]

However, as argued above, to assume the fundamentally moral character of cultural conflicts is to risk misconstruing what is actually at stake. A model of political deliberation that privileges moral discourse may give individuals and groups ample incentive to present their interest-based concerns in terms of cultural identity claims that may or may not speak to the crux of the issue. Arguments that appeal to cultural identity have increasing purchase in constitutional democracies committed to policies of cultural pluralism; groups are sometimes rewarded politically for framing their arguments in such terms. By contrast, the desire to maintain one's own status or the status of one's sub-group within the wider community, to shore up one's position of power vis-à-vis others, or to further one's own financial gain, do not make for good reasons in moral deliberation. Defenders of idealized models of deliberative democracy sometimes acknowledge these motives and argue that they should be deemed illegitimate on the grounds that they would fail the test of public reason (and so cannot count as valid justification for policies).[49] Benhabib, for example, acknowledges that strategic reasons are often uppermost in the minds of deliberative participants yet insists nonetheless that moral argumentation is necessary for normative validity.[50] But attempts to neutralize unjust motives and pernicious interests by excluding certain kinds of reasons a priori from public discourse—as illustrated, for example, by the deliberative approach advocated by Amy Gutmann and Dennis Thompson[51]—may simply push these underground without in any way lessening their grip on political life.

An idealized model of deliberation that either denies the force of participants' interests and relative power in determining dialogical outcomes, or else rules out certain kinds of reasons in advance in the hope that these will not impact deliberation, may succeed only in reinforcing the advantages enjoyed

---

[48] Valadez, *Deliberative Democracy*, p. 39.

[49] Joshua Cohen defends an ideal of deliberative democracy as centrally about political justification. See his 'Procedure and Substance in Deliberative Democracy', in *Deliberative Democracy: Essays on Reason and Politics*, eds. James Bohman and William Rehg (Cambridge, MA and London: MIT Press, 1997/9).

[50] Benhabib, *The Claims of Culture*, p. 143.

[51] See for example Amy Gutmann and Dennis Thompson, *Democracy and Disagreement* (Cambridge, MA: Harvard University Press, 1996).

by powerful participants in deliberation. Nor is it clear that deliberation consisting mainly in the exchange of moral claims about one's cultural identity and values is more likely to yield fair and practicable solutions to the sorts of conflicts in which cultural groups are often embroiled—namely, disputes about the application and legitimacy of religious personal and family laws, land and resource claims, group membership laws, and the like. Arguments that appeal strictly to group cultural identity may in fact serve as impediments to compromises in political deliberation,[52] for the same group identity can be invoked to support very disparate views about traditions, and so may not, by itself, illuminate or resolve anything.

If I am right that struggles over the meaning and validity of contested cultural traditions in liberal states are more centrally about the concrete interests of group members and the distribution of power and decision-making authority in these communities, then arguably any sound procedure for mediating cultural conflicts ought to recognize this. In practical terms, this suggests that reason-giving in deliberation ought not to be restricted to normative claims, nor privilege identity claims, but rather should permit—and even at times foreground—the strategic and pragmatic concerns and needs of cultural members. This reorientation of the deliberative democratic framework might also help to mitigate what Valadez has called the 'epistemological inequalities' that afflict idealized models of public deliberation.[53] Deliberative democrats set high standards for reasoned, moral argumentation and justification whose success will arguably depend in part on access to education, information technologies, political networking, and so forth. As Valadez notes, these 'differences in capacities to use available resources could lead to inequalities in the ability to defend one's needs and interests in public deliberation'.[54] On the more strategic approach to deliberation, by contrast, the goal is a more *transparent* and politically inclusive process in which cultural group members can present their everyday concerns about particular practices and arrangements. These concerns and interests, and the moral justifications that may *or may not* attach, are then subjected to critical scrutiny and evaluation in democratic processes of dialogue and negotiation. Political deliberation about contested practices would in the first instance aim to provide an accurate picture of the different *lived forms* of contested cultural practices, as well as some account of the concrete, practical interests of participants to the deliberation. These understandings are then used to

---

[52] Daniel Weinstock, 'Is "Identity" a Danger to Democracy?,' in *Identity, Self-Determination and Secession*, eds. Igor Primoratz and Aleksandr Pavkovic (Aldershot: Ashgate Publishing, 2006).

[53] Valadez, *Deliberative Democracy*, p. 77.   [54] Ibid. 78.

develop relevant policy reforms, initiate debate, and ultimately, to generate negotiated political compromises.[55]

AN AMENDED MODEL OF POLITICAL DELIBERATION

A key feature of the amended deliberative framework for resolving cultural conflicts that I develop here is the principle of democratic legitimacy. Democratic legitimacy in turn requires wide political inclusion; it is not usually secured by simply consulting with minority community leaders, but rather may require that a plurality of group members with divergent interests and circumstances be consulted.[56] Deliberative democratic procedures can provide spaces for these voices, as well as aid in amplifying criticisms of particular practices and arrangements within communities by supporting their safe public articulation. Sometimes, where government is not too discredited, the state can help in the establishment of deliberative forums; in Britain, for example, neighborhood panels set up by local government authorities in areas with a high density of racial, religious, and cultural minorities helped to democratize local decision-making structures, facilitating greater community input.[57] It may also be possible, as Ayelet Shachar proposes, to 'empower at-risk group members' by allocating formal legal jurisdiction over certain cultural practices and arrangements to some social groups, provided that democratic processes of decision-making are observed.[58] Alternative dispute resolution models offer still another resource for inter- and intracultural

[55] Aggregative procedures like voting may play a part in this process. As James Johnson argues, the incompleteness of deliberation as an approach to political disputes means that 'aggregation devices will be an unavoidable component of any democratic institutional arrangement'. See his 'Arguing for Deliberation: Some Skeptical Considerations', in *Deliberative Democracy*, ed. Jon Elster (Cambridge: Cambridge University Press, 1998), p. 162. James Bohman also comments that many deliberative democrats concede to the necessity of voting and representation, but that these are seen as normatively 'second best' since both mechanisms introduce the possibility of serious distortions of deliberation'. See his article, 'The Coming of Age of Deliberative Democracy', *The Journal of Political Philosophy*, 6/4 (1998), 400–25, p. 416.

[56] Spinner-Halev also cautions against consulting solely with male leaders in 'Feminism, Multiculturalism, Oppression, and the State', p. 108. Okin makes a similar point in 'Reply'.

[57] John Stewart, 'Democracy and Local Government', in *Reinventing Democracy*, eds. Paul Hirst and Sunil Khilnani (Oxford: Blackwell, 1996), p. 51.

[58] Shachar, *Multicultural Jurisdictions*, p. 132. My argument for a deliberative approach to resolving cultural conflicts is largely compatible with Shachar's proposal for a system of 'joint governance', under which cultural groups and the state would have responsibility for different aspects of community governance. Whereas I focus on the public deliberations that might produce reforms, however, Shachar focuses on legal and, to a lesser extent, political institutions and procedures in her proposed power-sharing scheme.

public deliberation aimed at resolving cultural conflict, and the best of these take seriously the differences in cultural communities' approaches to disagreements and dialogue.[59] Indeed, such models suggest ways that even parties in acute conflict, and with a history of mistrust, can partake in dialogue in a spirit of respect and mutual recognition.

The inclusion in deliberation of all stakeholders who want to participate is therefore not an afterthought to legislated reforms but rather a critical part of the process of democratic conflict resolution. In some case and at some stages of intracultural conflicts, deliberations may include *only* members of cultural communities whose practices have been thrown into question—particularly if the group is reasonably democratic in its internal structure. At other times, the principle of democratic legitimacy suggests that group members would likely constitute the majority of participants. Indeed, there is no reason why some cultural communities could not be essentially self-governing over large areas of their social affairs, as suggested by proponents of indigenous self-determination and advocates of associative democracy, amongst others.[60] For other groups, however, particularly deeply hierarchical or non-liberal cultural groups (including certain religious communities), strictly internal resolution of cultural conflicts will violate the principle of democratic legitimacy, because some members are systematically excluded from participation in political life. As I argued in Chapter 2, such exclusions should caution us against more laissez-faire approaches like those of Spinner-Halev and Kukathas.[61]

Where cultural conflicts are worked out in an intercultural dialogue, perhaps brokered by a state or semistate body (e.g. South African Law Commission holding consultations on the reform of customary marriage), unequal power relations between majority and minority community participants can jeopardize the legitimacy of the dialogue and subsequent outcomes. These power differences derive from any number of sources, most notably discrepancies in formal political power and social and economic clout. As Valadez notes, deliberative inequalities and differences in political efficacy can also result from differential access to resources (education, information technologies, media, etc.), which in turn shape citizens' political capabilities.[62] As a result, '[e]ven if all cultural groups are guaranteed formal rights

---

[59] See for example, *Intercultural Dispute Resolution in Aboriginal Contexts*, eds. Catherine Bell and David Kahane (Vancouver and Toronto: University of British Columbia Press, 2004).

[60] Hirst, *Associative Democracy*, pp. 13, 60, and *passim*.

[61] Spinner-Halev, 'Feminism, Multiculturalism Oppression, and Kukathas, 'Are There Any Cultural Rights?'

[62] Valadez, *Deliberative Democracy*, pp. 73 and 77–8.

of participation in public deliberation, inequalities in epistemic resources create significant asymmetries in their capacity for functioning effectively in forums of public deliberation'.[63] There are ways to remedy these political and epistemological inequalities, as Valadez suggests, but here there are no easy solutions. Challenging structural inequalities that disadvantage some participants in deliberation is not as simple as according equal speaking and voting rights; as Nancy Fraser reminds us, political inequality often has its roots in both cultural and economic forms of subordination.[64]

It is because political inequality is so deeply interwoven with other dimensions of social and economic inequality that strategies for empowering group members must do more than *formally* enfranchise less powerful members in important community decisions. For example, there is evidence that certain kinds of economic reform initiatives targeting women (such as micro-credit programs) may increase female bargaining power within the family, giving them greater say over cultural roles and traditions. This is an example of how women's political voices can be extended as well as how new spaces for democratic resistance might be opened up. As noted earlier, in some cases, state institutions can play an important role in expanding spaces for democracy, as for example by establishing consultative bodies that include and make possible regular consultations between ethnic and religious minorities and the state. More generally, some rights legislation, as Mark Warren has argued, can also extend opportunities for greater political voice, and 'court decisions that equalize and expand individual rights tend to expand democracy'.[65] Democratic activity does not necessarily need state support, however; indeed, resistance to the state can often be a catalyst for new forms of democratic resistance by cultural minorities. For instance, in the run up to the vote in the French National Assembly in February 2004 banning religious symbols in public schools—widely understood to be targeting the Muslim headscarf—Muslim women turned out in the thousands in Paris and other cities across France and Europe, wearing their headscarves in protest at the impending decision.[66]

Crucially, decision-making about contested cultural practices should also routinely bring to the table individuals and groups that are not necessarily members of the cultural group in question, but who nonetheless have a demonstrated stake in the outcome of proceedings regarding a contested

---

[63] Valadez, *Deliberative Democracy*, p. 45.

[64] Nancy Fraser, 'Rethinking Recognition: Overcoming Displacement and Reification in Cultural Politics', in *Recognition Struggles and Social Movements: Contested Identities, Agency, and Power*, ed. Barbara Hobson (Cambridge: Cambridge University Press, 2003), pp. 29–30.

[65] Warren, 'A Second Transformation of Democracy?', p. 242.

[66] 'Headscarf Ban Sparks New Protests', BBC News world (web) edition, January 17, 2004.

custom. For example, in the case of the reform of customary marriage in South Africa, consultations included representatives from legal reform groups and women's rights activists, scholars, and government policymakers, all of whom advanced arguments for reforms that they thought could aid disempowered women and foster communities' well-being. Some will balk at the suggestion that those outside the cultural groups in question should be involved in decisions about the reform of its customs; however, in part this inclusion is a nod to the permeable boundaries of different cultural communities in plural, liberal states, as well as to the common constitutional norms that bind them. The identities of participants to deliberations may also cross different communities: biracial or bicultural individuals and those who leave and re-enter a community may not be considered fully 'of' a group in the eyes of some, but they may nonetheless have an interest in the reform of customs. Additionally, NGOs—such as legal reform groups, women's rights activists, and human rights advocates—may have a stake in the reform of traditions that are harmful or disempowering for their constituents. The inclusion of social activists, and even government and political representatives (some of them, of course, also members of the cultural group in question), can also bring much-needed political pressure to the reform process and provide solidarity and support for cultural dissenters.

Participants in more formal deliberative processes initially use the framework of discussion and consultation to clarify and better understand contested social customs and practices, and to outline the different interests and needs at stake. The democratic tools of negotiation, bargaining, and compromise—crucial alternatives to deliberative democracy's traditional focus on reasoned, normative argumentation—come next. By enabling participants in deliberation to give frank and concrete reasons in support of particular customs and proposals for or against change, it becomes easier to expose unjust reasons and to foreground the abuses perpetuated by particular practices. Moreover, by framing the process of conflict resolution in terms of debate about the concrete purposes, gains, or benefits, and disadvantages of cultural traditions, it becomes difficult fully to mask the strategic concerns and interests at work. These interests, whether articulated by those who hold them or by critics, are then subject to critical evaluation in policy debates about the proposed reform of customs, and are reflected in the ensuing political compromise. Such a deliberative approach would still encourage debate and decision-making about norms and the social practices that they help to shape; indeed, good normative reasons may even remain more persuasive in public deliberation than interest-based reasons if the latter fail to speak to the needs of other citizens.

Proponents of deliberative democracy have generally suggested that negotiation, bargaining, and compromise should be used in public deliberation
only when conditions of social pluralism preclude common moral premises
and consensual outcomes. For Habermas, only when normative discussion is
unfeasible or collapses as a result of incommensurable moral differences do
bargaining and compromise become acceptable (temporary) procedures in
decision-making.[67] Bohman likewise mistrusts bargaining as a method and
goal of deliberation on the grounds that it requires participants to treat their
beliefs as mere interests, which he claims is both normatively unreasonable
and impractical.[68] And for Benhabib, ever confident in the rational and moral
nature of dialogue, strategic bargaining is mostly an unnecessary step down
from moral discourse, which is bound by 'norms of *universal respect* and
egalitarian reciprocity'.[69] By contrast, I argue that as a part of deliberations that
focus on the tangible aspects of cultural practices, strategies of negotiation,
bargaining, and compromise may sometimes be the best methods to adopt in
disputes about the validity or future status of a contested cultural practice,
from both a normative and pragmatic standpoint. These strategies comple-
ment deliberation that openly but critically engages participants' interests,
without necessarily privileging or catering to those interests. In the context of
deliberations which strive to give equal political voice to participants, and in
which participants can openly challenge the rationale (and purpose) behind
cultural assertions and make claims about the benefits and harms of social
practices, strategies of negotiation and compromise can signal the recognition
that stakeholders have valid concerns, differences, and interests which are
nonetheless irresolvable at the level of moral agreement.

An important objection to my emphasis on negotiation and compromise
in cultural disputes is that agreements struck on the basis of interests, rather
than moral consensus, will only last as long as participants' interests continue
to be served by them. There are three reasons why, in my view, this concern
does not ultimately tell against strategies of political negotiation and compromise as a means of negotiating cultural tensions. First, when cultural
conflicts (either intra- or intercultural) prove intractable, whether because
of fundamentally incommensurable moral beliefs or else clashing interests,
a democratic process of dispute mediation aimed at securing compromises
is often the only way to resolve the impasse. Especially if serious harm is
at issue, some action will need to be taken. It is normatively preferable—from
the standpoint of democratic legitimacy, but also from the point of view of
many of those involved in the conflict—that persons who are to be bound by

[67] Habermas, *Between Facts and Norms*, pp. 165–6.
[68] Bohman, *Public Deliberation*, p. 90.
[69] Benhabib, *The Claims of Culture*, p. 11.

particular reforms or arrangements have a direct say in shaping or transforming them. Where moral consensus in response to inter- or intracultural
conflicts is not possible (which, I have argued, is often the case), processes
of mediation, bargaining, and political compromise may be the only way to
include all stakeholders, and to reach a negotiated solution among diverse
participants. Second, the temporariness of many of the political compromises
reached about disputes over cultural practices may in fact be a benefit, insofar
as it permits cultural group members to revisit reforms as practices and beliefs
change and evolve. And finally, as suggested earlier, some interest-based
agreements and compromises can come to take on a settled normative status
over time: the decision to reform African customary law so as to permit
women to inherit property, even if forged out a balancing of interests, may
eventually (for many) come to enjoy normative acceptance, and indeed, to be
viewed as more just than previous arrangements.

CHALLENGES TO DEMOCRATIC APPROACHES TO CULTURAL CONFLICTS

My claim that a democratic and manifestly political approach to mediating
conflicts of culture is in many cases preferable to a process of moral argumentation and deliberation is not uncontroversial. Many worry that the power
relationships internal to cultural communities will make fair inclusion of
silenced or marginalized members unlikely, and strengthen the hand of self-
styled leaders who invoke the culture and identity of the group as justification for
their own dominance. Indeed, the space of culture lends itself well to precisely
these kinds of power plays. As Norwegian anthropologist Unni Wikan argues,

> Culture is often portrayed as if it possessed uncontested and uncontestable authority,
> whereas authority actually rests with those who hold power. Some people have the
> right—or seize the right—to define what is to count and for what, and the result, the
> authoritative 'truth', is often called culture. Culture and power go hand in hand, in
> every society, at all times.[70]

Acknowledging the truth of this remark, I propose that we deal with concerns
about the silencing and exclusion of some group members in the following
ways: by discussing strategies for ensuring equal opportunities for political
inclusion; by requiring nondomination in political deliberations; by making
it possible to revisit agreements if and when it becomes necessary; and finally,

---

[70] Wikan, *Generous Betrayal*, p. 87.

by suggesting ways to empower relatively vulnerable members of cultural groups by supporting and expanding other, informal, kinds of democratic (and 'legitimating') responses and activity.

Wikan's concerns nonetheless stand as a challenge both to more conventional versions of moral deliberation and to my amended proposal for more politically focused dialogue and decision-making. In terms of the former, immanent critics have shown that in public deliberation in multicultural liberal societies, some racial, ethnocultural, and linguistic minority communities can be at a tremendous disadvantage. Young argues that certain discursive norms and expectations of deliberative democracy are at odds with minority groups' presentation styles, with the result that their contributions go unheard. What count as good reasons in public debate—and indeed, even the 'rational' approach to discussion and problem solving—may also conflict with certain communities' (particularly indigenous peoples') modes of reasoning and ways of discussing problems.[71] By moving the emphasis in deliberation from reasoned consensus to concrete problem solving and compromise—including, if necessary, negotiated solutions through bargaining—it is possible that some of these discursive obstacles could be lessened, in my view. But here, as noted earlier, deliberative inequalities also surface, for there is unequal access to those social, educational, and political capital resources (such as good education, public funds for their community associations, and the media) that enable participants to wield more authority in decision-making processes. In the next section, I propose the introduction of deliberative principles that can help mitigate these inequalities. Together with the goal of expanding the points of entry into democratic life, as well as our sense of what constitutes 'legitimate' democratic activity, I argue that this approach can help to amplify the political voice of those traditionally marginalized from formal politics.

PRINCIPLES OF NONDOMINATION, POLITICAL INCLUSION, AND REVISABILITY

How might politically focused deliberation avoid or reduce the problem of internal domination—the silencing of some persons in dialogue about cultural disputes? Both intergroup and intragroup power plays are a real challenge to

---

[71] See for example Michelle LeBaron, 'Learning New Dances: Finding Effective Ways to Address Intercultural Disputes', and Kahane, 'What is Culture?' in *Intercultural Dispute Resolution in Aboriginal Contexts*, eds. David Kahane and Catherine Bell (Vancouver and Toronto: University of British Columbia Press, 2004).

fair deliberation. In answering this challenge, it is important to note that political negotiation and bargaining do not somehow suspend all norms of respect and reciprocity among participants. Quite the contrary: procedures can and should be implemented which prevent any one participant or faction from dominating deliberation or its outcomes. On the view I defend, negotiation and bargaining as strategies in political deliberation are in the first instance subject to the norm of democratic legitimacy. Additionally, the procedures of political deliberation ought, I argue, to be bound by three further normative principles, those of *nondomination, political inclusion,* and *revisability.*[72]

The principle of nondomination is intended to prevent participants (especially those with greater social or economic power) from coercing other participants in a dialogue situation. As Iris Young notes, nondomination is closely connected to political equality, and is indeed a precondition of the latter.[73] Coercion may undercut political equality by excluding some individuals from deliberation; preventing less powerful interlocutors from presenting concerns or proposals through threats of unfavorable repercussions; or controlling voting through similar means. Nondomination may seem a very minimal constraint but is nonetheless an important foundation for democratic political dialogue. In disputes over the validity of cultural customs and arrangements in liberal states, there is always the danger that traditional cultural leaders or elites will seek to silence dissenters through pressure tactics or more overt forms of oppression. Yet even where intracultural disputes are not at issue, nondomination in deliberation is still an important principle, for the reasons outlined above.[74]

The principle of political inclusion is more controversial both because it is ambiguous in content and may potentially shape decision-making more directly than the principle of nondomination. Following Bohman's discussion of political equality, I argue that in the context of deliberative democracy, the requirement of political inclusion denotes the presence of real opportunities for all citizens to participate in debate and decision-making. This means not only ensuring that such opportunities are available, but also making every effort to prevent 'extra-political or endogenous forms of influence, such

---

[72] The norms I posit here over lap with certain of those specified by other proponents of deliberative democracy. Iris Young, for example, posits that inclusion is a requirement of normative legitimacy. However, unlike some deliberative democrats, I do not claim that these norms are deliberatively conceived, nor do I suggest that they should be open to negotiation. Rather, I argue that they are justified as deliberative constraints because of their central role in supporting democratic legitimacy in settings where cultural and political authority is contested and subordination is widespread.

[73] Young, *Inclusion and Democracy,* p. 23.

[74] Bohman's variation of this principle, the 'non-tyranny constraint'—which draws on the work of James Fishkin—is, similarly, a way of preventing concentration and abuse of power in deliberation generally. Bohman, *Public Deliberation,* p. 35. Both Young and Bohman view non-domination as a pivotal requirement of democratic deliberation. See Young, *Inclusion and Democracy,* p. 23; and Bohman, *passim.*

as power, wealth, and preexisting social inequalities' from impacting deliberation and its outcomes.[75] Who can participate in deliberation, as Joshua Cohen has observed, ought not to be determined by their access to power and resources.[76] We can and should use the ideal of political equality to shape discussion and decision-making procedures, by guaranteeing wherever possible that participants have equal access to formal political deliberation and that their contributions *count*—for example, by balancing interests in negotiations and employing equal voting procedures. Similarly, as Young has argued, the principle of political inclusion can be used to challenge deliberation that is not truly democratic:

[D]emocratic norms mandate inclusion as a criterion of the political legitimacy of outcomes.... Even if they disagree with an outcome, political actors must accept the legitimacy of a decision if it was arrived at through an inclusive process of public discussion. The norm of inclusion is therefore also a powerful means for criticizing the legitimacy of nominally democratic processes and decisions.[77]

Political inclusion as a requirement of deliberation about cultural conflicts is a still more complex matter, especially if we take this principle, as I do, to require substantive opportunities for participation and influence in political deliberation and decisions.[78] One reason it is difficult is that, as Amartya Sen has observed, '[p]articipation in civil interactions and political activities is influenced by cultural conditions'.[79] More pointedly, who can participate in political life is, for many, culturally determined, perhaps most especially in the case of traditional cultural groups. Often the very role and status of certain subgroups—for example, whether women ought to have a political voice—is at issue. Moreover, who counts as a member of what cultural group is not always clear: sometimes membership is contested as a way of denying the justice claims of minorities within the group. Even if internal agreement about membership and roles is reached, the difficulty of ensuring that marginalized segments of communities are fully included is daunting. In addition to insisting on guidelines for fair and representative inclusion in formal political consultations, the political enfranchisement of marginalized and vulnerable members of communities can be fostered through the deliberate *expansion* of informal sites of social and political debate and contestation.

[75] Ibid., p. 36.

[76] Cohen, 'Deliberation and Democratic Legitimacy', p. 74.

[77] Young, *Inclusion and Democracy*, p. 52.

[78] Knight and Johnson ('What Sort of Political Equality...?') use the term 'equal opportunity of political influence' to capture these criteria. See also Warren, who defines the norm of equal inclusion as the requirement that 'every individual potentially affected by a decision should have an equal opportunity to affect the decision' ('A Second Transformation of Democracy', p. 224).

[79] Amartya Sen, 'How Does Culture Matter?', in *Culture and Public Action*, eds. Vijayendra Rao and Michael Walton (Stanford, CA: Stanford Social Sciences [Stanford University Press], 2004), p. 40.

As noted earlier, sometimes this involves state initiatives, such as economic reforms empowering women, or legislation and court decisions overturning sex discrimination in inheritance and divorce. Government funding for social and community services, local media sources with a broadly democratic outlook, and community groups that foster debate about the changing face of cultural practices, are a few more examples of ways in which the liberal democratic state can directly facilitate the expansion of spaces of democratic activity.[80]

The third principle that I propose ought to shape political deliberation about cultural conflicts is that of revisability. Specifically, decisions and compromises, once reached, may be revisited at a later point when warranted. Revisability may facilitate compromises, for participants and groups understand that if and when they need to redress problems or settlements it will be possible to do so.[81] But the main advantage of an assumption of revisability in the context of deliberation about cultural conflicts is that it acknowledges the gradual character of real change and the ways in which a range of processes *outside* legislation—processes of a social, cultural, and economic nature—contribute to the transformation of customs and cultural arrangements. A revisable deliberative process for evaluating disputed customs and initiating reforms can be responsive to the fluid character of many social practices. Internal criticism of practices and arrangements by group members often spark their reform, and by allowing policy decisions about customs to be revisited we remain open to this input. As a recent United Nations report on gender justice observes, 'the history of internal contestation reinforces what should be the starting point for thinking about issues of multiculturalism and rights: that cultures are not monolithic, are always in the process of interpretation and reinterpretation, and never immune to change'.[82]

The revisability condition implies a further constraint that helps determine *what counts as a just outcome* of political deliberation: just as outcomes are not legitimate if they depend on the systematic exclusion of sections of the community seeking to be heard, so they are not legitimate or tenable if they undercut the future ability of citizens to deliberate on these or other issues,

---

[80] I agree with proponents of associative democracy who argue that voluntary associations should be supported through taxation. Strategic funding of cultural community groups can increase the organizational and political capacities of such associations.

[81] Simone Chambers also emphasizes the importance of leaving deliberative agreements open to revisitation, in *Reasonable Democracy* (pp. 103–4) and 'Discourse and Democratic Practices', in *The Cambridge Companion to Habermas*, ed. Stephen White (Cambridge: Cambridge University Press, 1995), p. 248.

[82] Maxine Molyneux and Shahra Razavi 'Gender, Justice, Development and Rights', *Report of the United Nations Research Institute for Social Development Workshop* (2003).

if and when policies are revisited. This Kantian-style constraint[83] would be violated, then, by the adoption of a policy that legally prohibits all women in a particular society or community from voicing their views in public or from voting. The ban on female political participation would in any case also violate the constraints of democratic legitimacy, political equality and, probably, noncoercion. However, skeptics might ask, what of a situation where women appear to endorse or at least not to protest such a rule? My response to this is that it is difficult if not impossible to imagine a scenario in which such a policy could be *arrived at democratically*, under conditions of nondomination and nonintimidation. Wherever customs and cultural arrangements subordinate women and harm them in tangible ways, there are signs of resistance; these are not always easy to recognize, however, especially as they often occur in informal, even private, spaces. As Anne Phillips writes:

> It is highly unlikely that a discussion conducted on genuinely inclusive lines would fail to throw up evidence of internal opposition to practices that constrained women's freedom or subjected them to arbitrary male power;...particularly...in the light of...the interpenetration of different cultures and different ethical ideals...[T]he very process of inclusion encourages people to stretch their sense of what is desirable and possible, enabling them to articulate previously repressed interests and concerns.[84]

On the view defended here, then, participants to deliberation debate the meaning, relevance, and future status and form of contested social practices, and try to negotiate political compromises. Deliberation is bound by minimal norms, and ultimately aims to secure democratic political solutions, including, where possible, concessions for contending parties.[85] In many cases, deliberation about the development of cultural practices would be linked to processes of legislative reform, through public hearings and community consultations and the like, and therefore subject to further procedural and even constitutional norms. In these deliberative forums, members of cultural groups are invited to give their accounts of particular practices in their own communities, noting how they have evolved, what exceptions to rules are made, and what changes might be beneficial. There are also opportunities to protest the perceived injustice of community practices and arrangements, and to discuss ways these might be transformed. Among the various stakeholders participating in deliberation, those less powerful members of cultural communities are motivated to agree to reforms that they perceive as offering them

---

[83] Here I draw on O'Neill, especially *Bounds of Justice*.

[84] Anne Phillips, 'Multiculturalism, Universalism, and the Claims of Democracy', in *Gender Justice, Development, and Rights*, eds. Maxine Molyneux and Shahra Razavi (Oxford: Oxford University Press, 2002), p. 134.

[85] Bellamy also advocates a politics of negotiation and compromise for democratic societies in *Liberalism and Pluralism*.

opportunities and protection, particularly against the power of their own leaders, who may discount their interests or well-being. Community leaders are, arguably, motivated to agree to political concessions when social practices and arrangements that are important to them are in jeopardy (i.e., of potential legal restrictions or reforms), or when they need to protect their own power base. As Shachar argues, the goal of political compromise that would shape the deliberative process sketched here gives participants cause to consider 'next best' options when it comes to demands for the reform of cultural practices and arrangements.[86]

The deliberative democratic framework for resolving conflicts of culture advanced here is thus a purposive conversation in which citizens debate the meaning, relevance, and future status of contested social practices and try to reach negotiated political compromises. Such debates are not restricted to traditional political institutions but might include forums sponsored by local community and cultural associations, media, and more spontaneous public responses to incidents in the community. Ongoing structures for deliberation are best, since when understandings break down, it is not easy to develop the necessary institutional forums to respond to the anger and sense of marginalization expressed by minority groups. (The lack of permanent community consultation structures in France was revealed, for example, following the widespread riots of October–November 2005, which were triggered by the deaths of two immigrant youths.) Those involved in deliberations speak from their partial, situated perspectives, with their beliefs and interests intact— though these may of course change. Deliberation conceived in this way is not expected to yield any thick normative consensus on shared values, or to dissolve moral disagreements. Instead, participants try for contingent and revisable agreements that endorse a plan for the reform of customs that in turn reflects a compromise between the interests and justice considerations of different factions of the cultural group, state representatives, and other stakeholders.

SOME CHALLENGES TO THE DELIBERATIVE APPROACH TO CONFLICTS OF CULTURE

Proponents of 'differentiated citizenship', such as Kymlicka, Young, and Carens, have argued that liberal states need to extend *legitimating* political voice, not just toleration and 'culture-blind' citizenship, to minority groups.

---

[86] Shachar, *Multicultural Jurisdictions*, p. 143.

For instance, arguing against a uniform or culturally undifferentiated conception of citizenship—what he calls 'unitary citizenship'—Carens contends that 'a commitment to equal citizenship rights requires distinct legal rights for cultural minorities'.[87] Setting aside the question of just what sort of collective rights would foster equal citizenship in a plural liberal democracy, those political systems in which cultural minority citizens are consistently marginalized or disenfranchised clearly do not meet minimal criteria of justice. Real political voice, on this view, requires ongoing and systematic forms of political inclusion: consultation with minority communities; the existence of forums—both established and ad hoc—in which minority citizens and cultural associations can communicate their perspectives and needs in more than just token ways; designated voting blocks (e.g. race conscious redistricting); and in some cases, forms of self-government. In Canada, the Royal Commission on Aboriginal Affairs, which sponsored hundreds of consultations with members of Aboriginal communities over several years, is an example of this type of sustained dialogue (however imperfect). Britain's Commission for Racial Equality, although subject to criticism, has sponsored numerous meetings between government agencies and ethnic and cultural minority groups over areas of concern and dispute (including the Rushdie Affair), and so also illustrates this kind of political inclusion. Real political voice for cultural minorities can be established in these and other ways by insisting on consensus-building and compromise as centerpieces of political dialogue. This approach signals that participants' views are not simply to be bracketed or dismissed, and that dialogue is an ongoing process, not a one-time affair.

I have argued that inclusion can foster political trust and make possible practical political compromises. But is this enough? Should the more democratic and inclusive model of political deliberation advocated here not also aim for something resembling moral consensus? If we conceive of cultural conflicts as primarily political in character, and acknowledge the irreducible social and cultural diversity of most liberal democratic states, then a thicker or more substantive form of agreement as the goal of deliberation is ill-advised. Other democratic theorists have also come to this conclusion. Bellamy, for instance, has defended ideals of negotiation and political compromise, which he predicts will lead to practices of reciprocal accommodation; he rightly notes that where dialogue between cultural groups is concerned, '[t]he aim is an integrative as opposed to a distributive compromise, with the interests and values of others being matters to be met rather than constraints to be overcome through minimal, tactical concessions'.[88] Including representatives

---

[87] Carens, *Culture, Citizenship, and Community*, p. 166.
[88] Bellamy, *Liberalism and Pluralism*, p. 101.

of minority groups in deliberations about practices and arrangements of importance to them and to their communities is also a way of expressing formal respect and equal regard for these individuals (as citizens) and for their groups. This respect and inclusion will in turn go a long way toward increasing political trust between communities and also constructing negotiated political compromises over disputes about contested cultural practices.[89] Genuine political inclusion may of course more readily bring conflicts to the surface. However, if we think of the goal of political inclusion as that of fostering democratic legitimacy and 'fair and reciprocal compromise',[90] rather than reaching moral consensus, then exploring conflict should be understood as part and parcel of the process of mediating cultural disputes.

* * *

Liberal states are beginning to witness the expansion of sites of democratic activity beyond institutionalized, representative politics, thereby expanding the possibilities for political inclusion and participation. Political scientist Mark Warren describes this phenomenon in general terms as a trend marked by such changes as:

[T]he rise of social movements, dramatic increases in the numbers and activities of associations and interest groups, new forms of direct action, increasing use of referendums, devolution and deconcentration of decision-making and governance, stakeholder representation within bureaucracies, a growing use of the courts to press citizen interests, new experiments in collaborative governance and deliberative policy-making, more vigorous public debates about policies, increased public monitoring of government and corporate activities, new political uses of communication technologies, and small groups aggregated into networks that are now often global in scale.[91]

While it may seem that cultural minorities are not the most obvious participants in these expanded spaces of political life, there is evidence to the contrary. Among both immigrants and long-standing ethnic, cultural, and religious groups, there has been an expansion of both identity affinity groups (local, national, and transnational) and cultural community-based associations, many with explicit agendas for social and political change. Paragovernmental bodies whose concern is to represent and advocate on behalf of minority groups have also increased (e.g. the Ethnocultural Council of Canada, and in Europe, the European Union Migrants' Forum). While it is important to ask whether these kinds of political activities offer real access

---

[89] Melissa Williams's work on the topic of political trust in multicultural liberal states is especially pertinent here. See her *Voice, Trust, and Memory: Marginalized Groups and the Failings of Liberal Representation* (Princeton, NJ: Princeton University Press, 1998).

[90] Bellamy, *Liberalism and Pluralism*, p. 208.

[91] Warren, 'A Second Transformation of Democracy?', pp. 223–4.

to channels of power, their potential and actual function in supplying spaces for democratic deliberation and social critique should not be discounted.

Another objection contends that some more traditional cultural and religious minorities lack both the critical or reflective distance from their identities and cooperative spirit necessary to engage in productive and reasonable political dialogue. Intransigence and an unwillingness to consider other points of view are tremendously counterproductive in discussions aimed at increasing understanding and yielding compromises. But traditional minority communities are no less able to consider the perspectives of those outside their group than are unreflective citizens who believe that personal autonomy must take a recognizable liberal form. Indeed, as cultural or religious minorities in liberal states, they are surrounded by (and often fully conversant in) liberal and secular values and customs. Nor does productive dialogue necessarily require that one regard one's own beliefs as simply one perspective among many, no better or worse, as this objection seems to suggest. Rather than requiring a secular or highly detached outlook, successful political dialogue between different communities (as with any dialogue) minimally requires a willingness to listen to others, present one's own views, work toward solutions, and to negotiate and consider possible compromises. As Joseph Carens and Melissa Williams have recently argued in their discussion of some common concerns about Muslim minorities in liberal democracies:

We might ask whether the problem here lies not with the Muslims but with an understanding of democracy that would exclude or require fundamental changes from not only many Muslims but many other people as well, at least if applied consistently. This model of deliberative democracy requires that people abstract themselves from their identities. But there is an alternative model of democracy that simply requires that people listen and interact with each other. To treat other people with respect—which is a requirement of deliberative democracy—does not necessarily require that one suspend one's own commitments or distance oneself from one's own identity. Indeed, conversations are often most fruitful when people speak from their deepest selves.[92]

A further important challenge to deliberation points to the open-ended, and so possibly illiberal, nature of the political outcomes of this approach. My response to this concern is to reiterate the importance of taking seriously the principle of democratic legitimacy in the context of cultural diversity. The deliberative democratic approach to conflicts of culture insists on radically

---

[92] Joseph Carens and Melissa Williams, 'Muslim Minorities in Liberal Democracies: The Politics of Misrecognition', in *The Challenge of Diversity: Integration and Pluralism in Societies of Immigration*, eds. Rainer Bauböck, Agnes Heller, and Aristide Zolberg (Aldershot, UK: Avebury, 1996), p. 159.

democratic and inclusive processes of discussion and decision-making; as such, it cannot guarantee that deliberation about cultural conflicts will yield liberal outcomes. By contrast, the liberal views discussed earlier suggest that dilemmas of justice involving nonliberal cultural groups can be determined in the abstract, without the central participation of community members. Such approaches may ensure that liberal policies follow from deliberation—however ineffectual such policies may be in practice—but they cannot deliver democratically legitimate solutions. Similarly, the extensive normative constraints that some democratic theorists propose to impose on deliberation, and which reflect the ideal of deliberation as a process of moral argumentation, are in large part designed to make certain that results are just by measurable liberal standards. These constraints, I have argued, may be inconsistent with the inclusion of culturally diverse citizens, and can have the effect of diverting attention away from contested issues of power, authority, and legitimacy in cultural communities.

A final concern is that requiring broadly inclusive deliberations about contested cultural practices could negatively impact traditional communities that do not wish to change. This is related to the claim that imposing a democratic conception of legitimacy onto such communities fails to respect their cultural autonomy, which I address at greater length in the concluding chapter of this book. Similarly, some critics doubt whether ethnic, cultural, and religious groups, particularly traditional ones, actually *want* to negotiate compromises with mainstream society at all: what about religious fundamentalists? In a sense, this is an empirical challenge, although not one that has been especially well supported by empirical evidence. True, some groups desire to minimize contact with the liberal state (e.g. the Amish), and where there is no issue of internal oppression, there is no reason whatsoever to force them to cooperate with government commissions or deliberative bodies. Of course, where groups' interests are jeopardized—when a practice is to be regulated or restricted, or a group's language or aspects of the culture are dying out—there often exists a powerful incentive to negotiate.

To be sure, requiring democratic decision-making procedures for settling the status of disputed social practices and arrangements will trigger social changes within traditional communities; as Bohman observes, '[t]he cost of interaction in the public sphere may well be the loss of some cultural forms of authority. The self-interpretations of such cultures and their traditions will be thrown open beyond their authorized interpreters to a wider set of participants, even to non-members with whom they engage in dialogue'.[93] The requirement that cultural and religious groups concede to the democratic

---

[93] Bohman, *Public Deliberation*, p. 146.

participation of their own members in deliberation and decision-making about contested cultural practices may indeed be onerous in some cases. But as I have argued, disagreements about the validity of particular customs of traditional cultures frequently arise, within liberal societies, as a result of dissent *within* communities. Those who claim that the liberal state oppresses nonliberal groups by insisting that they take steps to democratize their internal decision-making procedures must also account for the fact of dissenting members seeking to be heard.[94]

There is, admittedly, a real tension between the principle of respect for cultural group autonomy and the norm of democratic legitimacy. Where cultural conflicts involve concrete and serious harm, it is hard to see why protecting cultural autonomy is necessarily more important than endorsing the right of all cultural group members to have a say in contesting, shaping, and if necessary reforming the practices and arrangements under dispute. In other words, there is good reason to endorse the principle of democratic legitimacy in designing means to mediate serious kinds of conflicts. Notwithstanding this tension between the principle of cultural autonomy and the principle of democratic legitimacy, then, a political process that aims to facilitate deliberation among members of cultural communities, representatives of groups in civil society, and state officials is arguably more democratic and equitable than the alternatives. Within the context of liberal constitutional democracies, demonstrating respect for cultural communities does not require that any or all practices, however much in tension with democratic norms, be accommodated. By putting members of cultural communities at the center of debates and decision-making processes about the future of their cultural practices, we express formal respect and equal regard for them as citizens and as members of groups.

CULTURE AND THE QUESTION OF AGENCY

In order to develop a deliberative procedure for mediating disputes about cultural practices that does not reinscribe power inequalities, we need to question the social and political contexts in which cultural practices are defended, criticized, reasserted, and revised. In some cultural communities, how is it that some members are able to dominate the process by which customs

---

[94] See for example Spinner-Halev's objections to state intervention in the internal decision-making processes of cultural and religious communities in 'Feminism, Multiculturalism, Oppression', p. 108.

are interpreted and appraised? If the group's traditional leaders are entrusted with this function, are competing voices in the community silenced, whose account of particular practices ought to be heard? Conceiving of a deliberative democratic framework for debate and decision-making is not enough, then; we also need to ask which disenfranchised individuals might need to articulate and press their concerns within the broader community, in both formal and informal contexts. Taking this problem one step further, we also must probe whether seemingly disempowered members of the group have outlets for criticizing, resisting, and amending specific practices and arrangements—however invisible these may seem to outsiders.

With respect to women's agency, social and cultural anthropologists have long noted that women's methods of resisting and modifying social customs in traditional societies may be indirect, manifesting in myriad subtle but important ways. Indeed, the strategies of powerless people generally often involve such indirect methods; for example, Scott, writing of resistance among the Malaysian peasantry, describes:

Everyday forms of peasant resistance.... Most of the forms this struggle takes stop well short of collective outright defiance. Here I have in mind the ordinary weapons of relatively powerless groups: foot dragging, dissimulation, false compliance, pilfering, feigned ignorance, slander, arson, sabotage, and so forth...[95]

Similarly, women in traditional cultures may make small but highly consequential decisions in order to underscore their protest, by waging acts of social transgression, or by temporarily abdicating their domestic and caretaking duties.[96] What possible supports or structures might empower women in their efforts to transform oppressive aspects of customs, and to help create more direct channels for such change? And how can women's critical evaluation and contestation of cultural practices have a real impact on their communities?

To ask these and other questions about the contexts in which social and cultural practices are negotiated, as well as about individuals' different capacities and opportunities to challenge and revise customs and arrangements, we will need to make certain conceptual shifts. First, as discussed in earlier chapters, we will need to eschew liberal a priori and liberal toleration paradigms

---

[95] Scott, *Weapons of the Weak*, p. 29.

[96] Anthropologist Erin Moore discusses women's indirect methods of resistance in her *Gender, Law, and Resistance in India* (Tucson, AZ: University of Arizona Press, 1998). Also see Usha Menon, 'Does Feminism Have Universal Relevance? The Challenges Posed by Oriya Hindu Family Practices', *Daedalus* (Fall 2000), 77–99.

altogether, for these do not foster dialogue about contested customs on equal terms, or on terms that enhance mutual respect and cooperation.

Second, we will need to reconceptualize cultural conflicts as struggles over social and political power, which in turn inform negotiations and disputes over roles, group identities, customs, conflicts over social arrangements, and so forth. Michel Foucault's analysis of power as a form of 'governing conduct' that is exercised in myriad ways by individual agents and institutions alike, and which comes to partly constitute the individual subjects over whom power is exercised, is useful here.[97] Foucault's more dynamic account of power reminds us that power is fundamentally a relationship—albeit often of very unequal proportions—and alerts us to the forms of resistance that are always possible, except in relations of total domination and slavery:

When one defines the exercise of power as a mode of action upon the actions of others... one includes an important element: freedom. Power is exercised only over free subjects, and only insofar as they are free. By this we mean individual or collective subjects who are faced with a field of possibilities in which several ways of behaving, several reactions and diverse comportments may be realized.... At the very heart of the power relationship, and constantly provoking it, are the recalcitrance of the will and the intransigence of freedom. Rather than speaking of an essential freedom, it would be better to speak of an 'agonism'—of a relationship which is at the same time reciprocal incitation and struggle...[98]

A more dynamic, agonistic account of power looks beyond purely juridical framework and asks about what lies behind rights. In contrast to the juridical liberal and human rights paradigms, a deliberative democratic framework does not assume or seek to establish that particular cultural traditions are fundamentally at odds with particular individual rights. Nor do rights bracket issues of power, for they are partly constituted through power relations and bear the imprint of institutional discourses and struggles. A deliberative democratic framework that is informed by an agonistic account of power can also readily account for the changing nature of customs in dispute, and insist that any reforms or proposals concerning such practices be open to renegotiation. Such a framework is responsive to a range of strategic and interest-based motivations of participants, which I have argued are central to cultural disputes. Finally, by using strategies of negotiation, bargaining, and compromise, deliberative democratic procedures for mediating and resolving disputes over the validity of social practices and arrangements can

[97] See especially Michel Foucault, 'Afterward: The Subject and Power', in *Michel Foucault: Beyond Structuralism and Hermeneutics*, eds. Hubert Dreyfus and Paul Rabinow (Chicago: University of Chicago Press, 2nd edn., 1983).

[98] Ibid., p. 221–2.

help ensure that different, contested understandings of these traditions are not only debated but are also represented in deliberative outcomes.

A deliberative democratic approach to cultural conflicts cannot guarantee liberal reforms, for liberal norms and principles do not, on the view defended here, trump nonliberal cultural values and claims. The open-ended character of democratic deliberation, and so of its outcomes, is a necessary consequence of according priority to the principle of democratic legitimacy in contexts of social and cultural diversity. But while a deliberative democratic approach does not purport to deliver liberal solutions, it does check the power imbalances and inequalities that can silence, or exclude, vulnerable individuals in political deliberation. A more democratic and egalitarian framework for evaluating and making decisions about contested cultural practices can, finally, also help direct attention to the challenge of *empowering* vulnerable members of cultural communities as opposed to simply *protecting* them in a paternalistic fashion.

5

Native Rights and Gender Justice: The Case of Canada

The uneasy relationship between claims for collective group rights, including demands for forms of self-government, and formal sex equality protections, has special pertinence to the political struggles of indigenous or Aboriginal peoples. In this chapter I explore this tension as it relates to an ongoing debate in Canadian politics over whether constitutional recognition of the right of First Nations peoples to self-determination is normatively and politically compatible with the 1982 Canadian Charter of Rights and Freedoms, which limits Aboriginal sovereignty.[1] Since the Charter formally protects individual equality rights in Canada, including the right of sex equality, whether these provisions should apply to First Nations peoples is a matter of no small importance. In the early 1990s, the question of whether the Charter should apply to future self-governing Native communities sparked a much-publicized rift between some Native women's groups and mainstream Aboriginal bodies, and ultimately served to erode support for the proposed political agreement that would have given both Québec and First Nations peoples greater autonomy (the Charlottetown Accord). In locking horns with the main Aboriginal associations over the issue of protections for women, Native women's groups brought into sharp relief some tensions between cultural, collective rights and individual sex equality rights.

Normative tensions do indeed exist between First Nations' peoples' demand that their inherent right to self-governance be recognized, and the liberal feminist and human rights-based claims that women's equality must be recognized through universal rights and domestic rights legislation. Nonetheless, I argue that the relationship between women's rights and Aboriginal sovereignty in Canada reveals a dispute that is less about the putative tension

[1] The terms 'Aboriginal', 'indigenous', and 'Native peoples' are used interchangeably here, and I also use the term 'First Nations (people)', collectively referring to the founding peoples with their own territory and languages (e.g. Algonquin, Mohawk, and so on). For a discussion of the evolution of these terms in the Canadian context, see Taiaiake Alfred, *Peace, Power, Righteousness: An Indigenous Manifesto* (Oxford: Oxford University Press, 1999), p. xxvi and p. 83.

between indigenous values and liberal individual rights than it is about political power and political voice. It is partly the history and ongoing context of colonialism, and the ways in which it has shaped power relationships in Native communities, which is responsible for creating the apparent impasse between indigenous sovereignty and individual rights protections.[2] Moreover, this context presents challenges for indigenous women who attempt to secure protection for their rights within broader struggles for indigenous sovereignty. When understood as primarily a political conflict, as I argue, the tension between sex equality protections and Aboriginal sovereignty becomes more tractable. Mediating this tension will, however, require a fundamental realignment in the power relations within First Nations communities (so as to give women greater voice) and between these communities and the Canadian state (so as to end its history of domination of Native peoples).

Far from revealing a fundamental and irresolvable normative conflict, then, the example of First Nations women illustrates the political nature of disputes between protections for culture and protection for women. Future negotiations concerning Aboriginal self-government, if they are to move beyond the apparent tensions between sovereignty and protection for the rights of 'internal minorities', will above all need to include marginalized members of Native communities in more meaningful ways, and also, in many instances, to leave them to work out their own solutions to internally contested practices and arrangements. However, First Nations women—whose views about sovereignty, gender protections, and justice were sidelined during the Charlottetown process of constitutional reform—will need to be fully enfranchised in these internal deliberations so that they can articulate their own vision of indigenous sovereignty and community well-being.

COLLECTIVE RIGHTS AND SEX EQUALITY: ABORIGINAL CANADIANS

The relationship between gender equality protections and Aboriginal sovereignty in Canada is a complex story that might be told in many different ways. I have chosen to focus on the period leading up to the referendum in 1992 on proposed changes to Canada's constitutional arrangements, known as the Charlottetown Accord agreement. The accord, which would have recognized

---

[2] See Marie Anna Jaimes Guerrero, 'Exemplars of Indigenism: Native North American Women for De/Colonization and Liberation', in *Women Transforming Politics*, eds. Cathy J. Cohen, Kathleen B. Jones, and Joan Tronto (New York: New York University Press, 1997), p. 206.

the inherent right of Aboriginal peoples to self-government and facilitated the shift to more extensive forms of self-government, was ultimately rejected. The reasons for its defeat are in part bound up with questions surrounding the protection of Aboriginal women's rights, which will be the focus of the discussion that follows. More generally, however, the accord's failure has its roots in a deep and well-founded mistrust on the part of Native peoples of the Canadian state and any agreements they might propose. The history of this relationship is a disgraceful one marked by policies of genocide, countless broken treaties, and Canada's ongoing failure to recognize the nationhood of Aboriginal peoples. Moreover, it was widely felt by First Nations peoples that they did not have a direct enough hand in the shaping of the accord itself, nor adequate input into the process surrounding the drafting. While the proposed agreement was in fact supported by leaders of many of the main First Nations organizations, thus, the lack of faith in the political process surrounding the drafting of the accord contributed to lower than expected support of the accord (among Native peoples) at referendum time.[3] It was during this critical period that the dispute within First Nations communities and leadership over whether Native self-government was compatible with liberal Canadian law— and ultimately with the sex equality clause of the Charter (15 [1])—also came to a head.

The Charlottetown process was the first serious initiative to establish Canada's constitutional recognition of the Aboriginal right to self-government. Canada's Aboriginal peoples comprise a diverse population of Native Indians, Métis, and Inuit across the country, with different languages, customs, values and forms of governance, and are further differentiated by region and by whether they live on or off Indian reserves. Despite their diversity, however, Aboriginal peoples in Canada have long been unified in their quest for formal, constitutional recognition of their intrinsic right to self-government. While self-government could take many forms, constitutional recognition of this right would in principle grant Aboriginal communities as much political and legal autonomy as they require to govern themselves according to their own values and traditions. Nor is this an unrealistic goal in the context of recent Canadian politics, particularly since Aboriginal peoples' inherent right of self-determination is already guaranteed by the state's 1982 Constitution Act (section 35 [1]). The Charlottetown Accord, because it stipulated Aboriginal peoples' inherent right to self-government, rather than just self-determination in general, would have paved the way for greater powers of self-government for Aboriginal peoples as well as for the province

[3] Thomas Isaac, 'The 1992 Charlottetown Accord and First Nations Peoples: Guiding the Future', *Native Studies Review*, 8/2 (1992), 109–14, p. 113.

of Québec. However, dissatisfaction with aspects of the agreement and with the political processes surrounding the accord led a majority of Canadians to vote against the proposed amendments, including a surprising majority rejection of the accord by Aboriginal peoples living on reserves.

Agreement amongst Native peoples in Canada regarding the objective of constitutional recognition of their inherent right to self-government has sometimes been accompanied by disagreement on the specific form that self-government should take and the best political means of securing it. Both the processes of constitutional negotiation and the proposals and accords pertaining to sovereignty tabled in 1992 elicited diverse responses from Native peoples and leaders, with some supporting and some rejecting the proposed amendments. One critical area of dispute was the precise relationship to Canadian law that Aboriginal peoples should seek to maintain within the framework of self-government. In negotiations with federal officials, it became clear that most Native leaders wanted their communities to have extensive powers of self-rule unfettered by Canadian law, including the Canadian Charter of Rights and Freedoms. The main Aboriginal associations—with the notable exception of the Native Women's Association of Canada (NWAC), as I discuss shortly—were in agreement on this point: the Assembly of First Nations (AFN), the largest Native organization, representing status Indians across Canada; the Native Council of Canada, representing nonstatus Indians; the Métis National Council; and the Inuit Tapirisat of Canada, all sought reassurance that future Aboriginal governments would not be answerable to Canadian law.

The rationale Native leaders gave for seeking independence—or indeed, immunity—from the Charter pointed to Aboriginal peoples' long-standing aspiration for genuine self-government and their belief that they must be able to govern themselves according to their own political ideals, institutions, and traditions. Related to this was the widely articulated objection that the genesis of the Charter itself was problematic in that it did not reflect a process of collaboration between First Nations peoples and the rest of Canada, but rather, was imposed from outside. As James Tully explains:

For the Aboriginal peoples ... the imposition of the *Charter* without their negotiation and consent, and without explicit recognition of the inherent right to govern themselves in accordance with their own laws and ways, or to opt into a suitably amended *Charter* if they chose, represented another act of imperialism in a long chain of abuses, giving the lie again to Canada's self image as a constitutional democracy. Like Quebecers, they were not opposed to *The Charter*, but to its imposition without consent and to its individualist and western bias which violated the principal of equality of peoples and their cultures.[4]

[4] See James Tully, 'The Crisis of Identification: The Case of Canada', *Political Studies*, 42 (1994), 77–96, p. 88.

At least on the face of it, then, Native leaders' misgivings about the Charter were due more to their view that it was not a document that emanated from Aboriginal political processes, or reflected serious consultation with their communities, than it was to any explicit desire to challenge specific individual rights.[5] However, as I argue shortly, the long-standing desire to be recognized as a self-governing people cannot be divorced entirely from the practical benefits that accompany unfettered powers of self-government.

Aboriginal leaders insisted that they sought the suspension of the Charter vis-à-vis Aboriginal governments primarily 'to keep options open for traditional forms of government such as those based on clans, confederacy, or hereditary chiefs'.[6] But at numerous junctures, the rights-based orientation of the Charter, with its assumption of the superiority of an elected representative democracy, was singled out as potentially at odds with Native political approaches. As Grand Chief of the AFN, Ovide Mercredi, wrote, 'Canada's idea of democracy is majority rule. Our idea of running governments is consensus by the people. Who is to say that Canada's principles are better than ours?'[7] One of the best summary accounts of these concerns appeared three years after the failure of the Charlottetown Accord:

Aboriginal leaders, and particularly the First Nations, leadership, have expressed reservations about the applications of the *Charter* to Aboriginal governments. The reasons are twofold. First, the *Charter* was developed without the involvement or consent of Aboriginal peoples and does not accord with Aboriginal culture, values and traditions. Second, the *Charter* calls for an adversarial approach to the resolution of rights conflicts before Canadian courts and there is a concern that this confrontational mode will undermine Aboriginal approaches to conflict resolution .... This is not to say that Aboriginal peoples have no concern for individual rights and individual security under Aboriginal governments. The concern rests more with the *Charter*'s elevation of guaranteed legal rights over unguaranteed social and economic rights, the

---

[5] Ovide Mercredi, former leader of the Assembly of First Nations, made the following clarification during the hearing conducted under the auspices of the *Royal Commission on Aboriginal Peoples*: 'The official position of the organization I represent is that whatever governments we establish have to respect individual rights, but in a manner that does not destroy the collective identity, the collective mind of the people themselves. And the resistance we have to the Charter of Rights and Freedoms had nothing to do with women's rights. It has to do with the concern that we have about the Charter imposing a political structure on our people that our people may not want.' *Public Hearings, Rounds I–IV, Royal Commission on Aboriginal Peoples* (June 26, 1992), p. 631.

[6] *Overview of the First Round*, Royal Commission on Aboriginal Peoples—Public Hearings (Ottawa, 1992), p. 41.

[7] Ovide Mercredi, in Mercredi and Mary Ellen Turpel, *In the Rapids: Navigating the Future of First Nations* (Toronto: Viking/Penguin 1993), p. 102.

emphasis on rights rather than responsibilities, the failure to emphasize collective rights, and the litigation model of enforcement.[8]

Returning to the immediate circumstances surrounding the rejection of the 1992 Charlottetown Accord, it is striking to note the very different perspective offered by some Native women and their organizations. In contrast to the position of male chiefs, some Aboriginal women, led in particular by NWAC, expressed misgivings about giving Aboriginal governments the discretion to suspend certain Charter provisions, especially those protecting women.[9] Many believed that Native leaders sought Charter immunity precisely so that they could reinstate sexually discriminatory criteria for band membership. It was precisely this power that had been abridged in 1985 by a piece of legislation that Aboriginal women generally welcomed, but many band council chiefs opposed and continue to oppose. This legislation—Bill C-31—overturned a discriminatory provision in Canada's Indian Act responsible for disenfranchising tens of thousands of Indian or First Nations women and their children, who routinely lost their Indian status if they married either 'nonstatus' Indian men or non-Indian men. The converse was not true of men, whose white or non-Indian wives and children automatically gained full Indian status and privileges upon marriage. Without formal Indian status, Native women and their children lost their treaty rights and numerous associated benefits, such as inheritance rights and permission to reside on reserve land. The practice of removing women's Indian status as a penalty for marrying non-Indian status men was not a long-standing Native tradition, but rather a function of Canada's 1869 Indian Act, which introduced a number of patriarchal conceptions and arrangements into Aboriginal communities—much like codified customary law in South Africa. Nonetheless, band council leaders used this legal device to prevent women and their non-Indian (or non-Indian status) husbands and children from sharing in the resources of Native communities, and were among the staunchest opponents of Bill C-31.

Native leaders' opposition to Charter limitations in the Charlottetown negotiations can also be explained in part by the fact that the Charter was instrumental in the development of Bill C-31. A Native woman disenfranchised by the discriminatory Indian Act provision, Sandra Lovelace, successfully brought her case to the United Nations justice committee with the help of the New Brunswick Human Rights Commission. The justice committee

---

[8] Peter Hogg and Mary Ellen Turpel, 'Implementing Aboriginal Self-Government: Constitutional and Jurisdictional Issues', *The Canadian Bar Review*, 74/2 (1995), 187–224, p. 213.

[9] Métis, Inuit, and northern Aboriginal women were less concerned with Charter protection, as they had not faced the discrimination that Indian women had experienced at the hands of band councils leaders. Katherine Beaty Chiste, 'Aboriginal Women and Self-Government: Challenging Leviathan', *American Indian Culture and Research Journal*, 18/3 (1994), 19–43, p. 21.

ruled in July 1981 that removing a person's Indian status was discriminatory under international law (specifically, it determined that this action conflicted with the International Covenant on Civil and Political Rights). Although not legally binding on Canada, the moral force of this decision was enough to soon prompt the introduction of Bill C-31, with the intention of eliminating the sexually discriminatory aspects of membership determination in the Indian Act and so also 'to bring the *Indian Act* into accord with the *Charter*'.[10] Between the implementation of the Act and 1990, in excess of 75,000 applications were received on behalf of a total of more than 133,000 Native persons seeking reinstatement of their Indian status, the vast majority of these women and their children.[11] Although certain effects of Bill C-31 were welcome to band chiefs—particularly the power it gives to Native bands to determine their membership rules—many resisted the reenfranchisement of so many women and children. Since 1985, some band councils have delayed or refused to offer such individuals land, housing, and other benefits. Nor is it simply a matter of lack of resources, for some of the wealthiest bands are also the biggest offenders in this respect: oil-rich band councils in the province of Alberta have managed to resist recognizing and resettling the vast majority of claimants who obtained legal reinstatement using the 1985 amendment.[12] In the period leading up to the Charlottetown referendum, some band councils readily admitted that they were looking for legal ways to override Bill C-31 and so disenfranchise recently reinstated persons of their Indian status, as well as forestalling future claims for reinstatement.[13]

It is not surprising, then, that in the period leading up to the Charlottetown referendum, many Native women voiced the concern that newly self-governing Native communities might seek to discriminate against women, particularly in matters of property rights and other benefits due to 'status' Indians in Canada. Indeed, NWAC estimated at the time that only about 2 percent of women displaced under pre-Bill C-31 discrimination have been permitted to return to their Indian bands.[14] In light of continued de facto discrimination, some said they could not trust their local band chiefs or national leaders to guarantee their sex equality rights at the local reserve level or to include

[10] Thomas Isaac and Mary Sue Maloughney, 'Dually Disadvantaged and Historically Forgotten?: Aboriginal Women and the Inherent Right of Aboriginal Self-Government', *Manitoba Law Journal*, 21/3 (1992), 453–75, p. 462.

[11] Ibid., p. 463.

[12] Joyce Green, 'Constitutionalising the Patriarchy: Aboriginal Women and Aboriginal Government', *Constitutional Forum*, 4/4 (1993), 110–20, pp. 113 and 115.

[13] Ibid., p. 115.

[14] Rudy Platiel, 'Native Women Fear Loss of Rights', *The Globe and Mail*, July 13, 1992.

such protections in proposed Aboriginal constitutions.[15] As the then- president of NWAC, the group leading the fight for sex equality protections, said:

Our Aboriginal leadership does not favour the application of the *Canadian Charter of Rights and Freedoms* to self government. The opinion is widely held that the Charter is in conflict with our notions of sovereignty, and further that the rights of Aboriginal citizens within their communities must be determined at the community level. As women, we can look at nations around the world which have placed collective and cultural rights ahead of women's sexual equality rights. Some nations have found sexual equality interferes with tradition, custom and history. There are many, many nations around the world which have refused to implement United Nations guarantees of sexual equality.... Canada...cannot exempt itself.[16]

Suggestions by mainstream Aboriginal leaders that the Charter was merely a remnant of Canada's colonial relationship with Native peoples and stood in conflict with the values and practices of traditional self-government were met with skeptical responses by Native women's lobbyists, who demanded a serious review of the Charter issue. Led by NWAC and supported by several provincial Native women's groups and the newly formed National Métis Women of Canada, many Aboriginal women pressed for assurances that their equality rights would be guaranteed in any imminent constitutional settlement pertaining to Aboriginal self-government. They also rejected the 'wait and see' approach urged by Native leaders: NWAC leaders, some of whom had themselves been reinstated to Indian status by Bill C-31, were reluctant to trust that women's equality rights would be safeguarded by Aboriginal governments in the absence of federal laws requiring them to do so.

Another reason why many Native women were skeptical of assurances that their equality rights would be respected in the context of self-government was that the dramatic increase in violence and sexual abuse in their communities had not been given the serious attention by Native leaders that women felt it urgently required. Reports of rates of domestic assault against Native women living on and off First Nations reserves that were several times the rate for non-Aboriginal women began to emerge in the early 1980s, and the lack of a sustained, institutional response by band councils angered and alienated many women from mainstream Native politics.[17] While not seeking

[15] Rudy Platiel, 'Aboriginal Women Divide on Constitutional Protection', *The Globe and Mail*, January 20, 1992. See also Green, 'Constitutionalising the Patriarchy', p. 113.

[16] Gail Stacey-Moore, 'Aboriginal Women, Self Government, the Canadian Charter of Rights and Freedoms, and the 1991 Canada Package on the Constitution.' Address to the Canadian Labour Congress, Ottawa, December 3, 1991, p. 7.

[17] A study by the Institute for Public Policy in Montréal confirmed that as many as 80% of Aboriginal women in Québec report being the victims of domestic violence (in *Overview of the Third Round: Exploring the Options*, Royal Commission on Aboriginal Peoples—Public

a constitutional solution to the problem of violence, many Native women viewed their leaders' poor track record on this issue as further reason to worry that access to the override section of the Charter for Aboriginal governments could mean a setback for women's equality rights. In consultations with members of the Royal Commission on Aboriginal Peoples—announced amidst the ashes of the defeated Charlottetown Accord—Native women spoke of male leaders urging them not to discuss publicly their communities' problems of domestic violence, alcoholism and sexual abuse with commissioners, in part because of fears that this would detract from critical negotiations on questions of self-government. Where commissioners agreed to meet *in camera* with Native women across the country, they were told of pressure tactics employed by band council leaders and chiefs to dissuade women from speaking out about violence and other problems in their communities.[18]

It remains unclear whether the Charlottetown Accord would have given future Aboriginal governments de facto immunity from the Canadian Charter in the absence of a formal agreement specifying such exemption.[19] Section 32 of the Charter states that the document is meant to apply to 'the Parliament and government of Canada' as well as all provincial governments; yet no specific mention is made of the applicability or inapplicability of the Charter to Aboriginal governments, as it predates the era of negotiations for Native sovereignty. Some legal scholars have suggested that '[d]espite the silence of section 32 on Aboriginal governments, it is probable that a court would hold that Aboriginal governments are bound by the *Charter*'.[20] Predicting this, Native leaders sought to include specific language in the Charlottetown Accord which promised that future Aboriginal governments would not be bound by the Charter provisions. Another proposal was that a separate Aboriginal charter of rights should ultimately replace the Canadian Charter with regard to Native peoples. Federal negotiators, unwilling to grant such full exemption from the Charter or to pursue the Aboriginal Charter idea very far, proposed a last-minute compromise solution whereby Aboriginal governments would be granted access to section 33 of the Constitution Act, known as the 'notwithstanding clause', if necessary. The province of Québec had already successfully negotiated access to this section on the grounds of its status as a 'distinct society'. The power to invoke the notwithstanding clause

---

Hearings, Ottawa, 1992), p. 10. The Canadian Panel on Violence Against Women later confirmed these rates of violence against Native women (cited in Green, p. 112).

[18] *Overview of the Third Round*, pp. 9–10.

[19] For a fuller discussion of whether the Charlottetown Accord as well as Aboriginal and treaty rights protected by the Charter might exempt Aboriginal governments from other aspects of the Charter, see Hogg and Turpel, 'Implementing Aboriginal Self-Government'.

[20] Hogg and Turpel, 'Implementing Aboriginal Self-Government', p. 214.

of the Charter could effectively enable Aboriginal governments to suspend those parts of the Charter that posed obstacles to collective Aboriginal self-rule. Native leaders agreed to this concession—despite protest from NWAC—and the change was duly included in the final draft of the *Consensus Report on the Constitution,* or the Charlottetown Accord.[21]

POLITICAL INCLUSION AND EXCLUSION

Concern about Charter exemption for future Aboriginal governments clearly had much to do with the feeling expressed by some Native women that their political voice was marginalized generally in Aboriginal politics and in Canada–First Nations relations, and consequently that women's rights would not be best protected by Aboriginal governments. Of the four main Aboriginal associations included in constitutional talks, none specifically represented Native women; NWAC, the largest and most important group representing Aboriginal women, was consistently excluded. Pointing to the male-dominated character of the main organizations, and to the relative marginalization of Native women's voices within these, NWAC and other groups argued that women's issues were not taken seriously; they cited as evidence men's control of the main national Native organizations, which had the effect of blocking serious discussion of sexual equality and sexual violence in particular. Under-scoring their opposition to Charter immunity, NWAC thus also expressed frustration with the unwillingness of other national Native organizations to listen to their concerns. Moreover, they blamed federal agencies for failing to fund their association and other national Aboriginal women's groups while funding mainstream, male-dominated groups. The discrepancy in funding for Native associations, NWAC argued, prevented their dissenting views from being heard, especially on the Charter issue.[22]

---

[21] Part IV (First Peoples), section 43, of the *Consensus Report on the Constitution* (Charlottetown Accord), August 28, 1992, states: 'The *Canadian Charter of Rights and Freedoms* should apply immediately to governments of Aboriginal peoples.... The legislative bodies of Aboriginal peoples should have access to Section 33 of the Constitution Act, 1982 (the notwithstanding clause) under conditions that are similar to those applying to Parliament and the provincial legislatures but which are appropriate to the circumstances of Aboriginal peoples and their legislative bodies.'

[22] NWAC received a small annual operating grant from the Assembly of First Nations, but the precariousness and inconsistency of this funding—and the suspicion that it was linked in some years to NWAC's political positions—prompted the group to argue that they needed their own direct government funding.

The dispute over whether the Charter should apply to future self-governing Aboriginal communities, according to some, reflected the already strained relationship between Native women's groups (specifically NWAC) and organizations with more political clout, especially the AFN. The different political priorities and strategies of these associations intensified the disagreement over the Charter's relevance to Native peoples. Some who watched the debate unfold suggested that NWAC's demands for guarantees for sex equality rights was mostly a manifestation of the growing schism between disenfranchised, disempowered members of Native communities—a disproportionate percentage of whom are women—and the male élite leadership of band councils and national associations. In connection with this concern about Native women's political marginalization, a pivotal part of NWAC's strategy was the group's launching of a legal challenge in the Federal Court of Canada in January 1992 claiming that they had been unjustly excluded from federal constitutional negotiations. NWAC sought an injunction against the referendum in the short term, and also demanded 'equal funding and an equal right of participation in the constitutional review process'.[23] These claims were denied. At the trial level, NWAC's case failed (in March 1992): the judge rejected the association's charges that government funding of the main Native associations and denial of equal financial support to Native women's groups compromised their freedom of speech or constituted sex discrimination.[24] However, NWAC appealed to the Federal Court of Appeals, which ruled in August 1992 that Native women's rights of political participation and speech were indeed negatively impacted by unfair government funding practices.[25] Despite this

---

[23] Jennifer Koshan, 'Aboriginal Women, Justice and the Charter: Bridging the Divide?', *University of British Columbia Law Review*, 32/1 (1998), 23–54, p. 43.

[24] 'Native Women Lose Bid For Spot At Talks: Exclusion From Constitutional Negotiations Doesn't Violate Rights, Judge Rules', *The Globe and Mail*, April 1, 1992.

[25] *Native Women's Association of Canada* v. *Canada* (1992), 4 C.N.L.R. (F.C.A.). The federal government appealed to the Supreme Court of Canada, which overturned the previous decision on October 27, 1994. In a summary of the 1992 case in the later suit, the political exclusion of Native women is made clear: 'During the constitutional reform discussions which eventually led to the Charlottetown Accord, a parallel process of consultation took place with the Aboriginal community of Canada. The federal government provided $10 million to fund participation of four national Aboriginal organizations: the Assembly of First Nations (AFN), the Native Council of Canada (NCC), the Métis National Council (MNC), and the Inuit Tapirisat of Canada (ITC). The Native Women's Association of Canada (NWAC) was not specifically included in the funding, but a portion of the funds advanced was earmarked for women's issues. As a result, AFN and NCC each paid $130,000 to NWAC and a further $300,000 was later received directly from the federal government. NWAC was concerned that their exclusion from direct funding for constitutional matters and from direct participation in the discussions threatened the equality of Aboriginal women.... They alleged that by funding male-dominated groups and failing to provide equal funding to NWAC, the federal government violated their freedom of expression and right to equality. The application was dismissed by the Federal Court,

moral victory, NWAC spokeswomen did not succeed in getting invited to the constitutional talks along with other Aboriginal leaders, because the issue of participation was deemed outside the court's power. On the eve of major political talks with Aboriginal leaders and provincial premiers on Canada's future prior to the October 1992 Charlottetown referendum, NWAC made a final, unsuccessful, bid for formal participant status at the constitutional negotiating table.

The implications of the continued exclusion of women's groups from constitutional negotiations were far-reaching: the draft Charlottetown Accord barely made mention of Native women's concerns, stating merely that 'the issue of gender equality should be on the agenda of the inaugural First Minister's Conference on Aboriginal Constitutional matters...'. Most critically, the final package agreed to in August 1992, at Charlottetown, granted future Aboriginal governments access to the controversial 'notwithstanding clause' (section 33), which in principle would allow them to suspend certain Charter provisions at their discretion.[26] Although some commentators (including some Native women associated with the mainstream Aboriginal organizations) believed that the final accord had adequate protection for Native women in the application of Aboriginal rights,[27] the issue of whether women's sex equality rights would be protected by the constitutional agreement remained. Undoubtedly, the lack of deliberate and systematic inclusion of Native women and their organizations in the process of drafting the accord, and in the constitutional talks generally leading up to Charlottetown, exacerbated the loss of political trust felt by women on this question. Ironically, Native women's demand to be included in constitutional talks was eventually heeded, several months after the defeat of the accord: in early 1993, NWAC was finally invited to participate at an intergovernmental conference on constitutional issues. But this came too late for the Charlottetown Accord, which was rejected in national referenda in October 1992.

Trial Division. The Federal Court of Appeal also refused to issue an order of prohibition. It made a declaration, however, that the federal government had restricted the freedom of expression of Aboriginal women in a manner that violated ss.2 (b) and 28 of the Charter.' [1994] 3 S.C.R. 627, F.C.A. decision 95 D.L.R. (4th) 106.

[26] *Consensus Report on the Constitution* (Charlottetown Accord), section 52, 'Gender Equality'.

[27] For example, Isaac writes that 'Aboriginal women had a number of clauses to protect and to ensure their equality in First Nations governments and in the application of Aboriginal rights (for example, see sections 35.5 (2), 35.7 and 2 (g) of the Canada clause).' See Isaac, 'The 1992 Charlottetown Accord', p. 113.

ABORIGINAL WOMEN: DELIBERATING ABOUT JUSTICE

This account of the tension between Aboriginal self-government and the protection of Native women's rights in the Canadian context has highlighted practical and political considerations as the driving force behind the dispute about Native women's rights in the Charlottetown process. For some band council chiefs and leaders of mainstream Native organizations, concerns about jurisdictional power, and in particular, the determination of band council membership rules and jurisdiction over access to band resources, were of paramount importance. Native women who spoke out against the immunity clause (and not all did) were vigilant about pointing out these motives, and equally clear that their own interest lay in protecting women's rights and in trying to secure a political voice for Native women. What was sorely lacking in this period was a democratic forum in which Aboriginal peoples and their leaders could engage in more substantive, and less pressurized, talks about how best to protect women's rights and secure their inclusion within the framework of Aboriginal governance. Forced to fight their own exclusion from constitutional negotiations, and the immediate dangers surrounding possible Charter immunity for Aboriginal governments, Native women and their organizations were also unable to come to a consensus position or to persuade the mainstream organizations (like the AFN) to change their stance.

For political and pragmatic reasons, NWAC and some other Native women's groups supported Charter compliance for future Aboriginal governments.[28] But it is not the case that Native women unreservedly embraced Charter protections and liberal sex equality rights.[29] Indeed, not all who spoke out against Charter immunity insisted on *permanent* Charter protection: some women left open the possibility that eventually adequate sex equality protections might be included in Aboriginal constitutions, and even proposed an Aboriginal Charter of Rights. Native women were thus by no means unanimous in their call for formal constitutional protection of their individual equality rights by means of the Charter, and disagreement continues today.[30] For example, chief Wendy Grant, vice chief of the AFN at the time of the original dispute, spoke out against NWAC's position and argued in favor of Aboriginal self-government free from the constraints of Canadian law. Like some other Aboriginal leaders, Grant characterized the conflict as

---

[28] Rudy Platiel, 'Native Women Fear Loss Of Rights'.
[29] Chiste, 'Aboriginal Women and Self-Government', pp. 38–9.
[30] Susan Delacourt, 'Natives divided over Charter: Women will not accept self-government without guarantees', *The Globe and Mail*, March 14, 1992.

fundamentally about different, even incommensurable legal and political systems, not about disparate commitments to women's equality: 'Your governments and laws are set up in such a way that it is a hierarchical government and—justifiably so—you've got to put protection in for the individual. But when you look at a traditional [Native] government, it's the other way: the collective is the driving force and the individuals rights are enhanced and protected by the collective which looks after those individual rights.'[31] Some leading Native women legal scholars, notably Mary Ellen Turpel, also disagreed strongly with NWAC's arguments.[32]

To the extent that there was normative (rather than merely strategic) disagreement among Native women over how women's well-being would be protected by future Aboriginal governments, it lay in the critique of the liberal feminist agenda that some First Nations women had begun to articulate, and the alternative, Aboriginal vision of justice they defended in its place. Individual equality, including the ideal of sexual equality, is viewed by some Native women as an inappropriate goal for First Nations peoples. As Native legal scholar Mary Ellen Turpel writes:

Equality is simply not the central organizing political principle in our communities. It is frequently seen by our Elders as a suspiciously selfish notion, as individualistic and alienating from others in the community. It is incongruous to apply this notion to our communities. We are committed to what would be termed a 'communitarian' notion of responsibilities to our peoples, as learned through traditional teachings and our life experiences.[33]

Even Aboriginal spokeswomen who opposed the Charlottetown Accord on the grounds that Charter immunity would leave them vulnerable were careful to emphasize that they were rejecting specifically *contemporary* forms of inequality and oppression within Native society, not the norms and beliefs of traditional Aboriginal society. Indeed, a frequent rhetorical strategy was to appeal to traditional Native values and forms of community governance, in which women play a central role. But the appeal to tradition was of limited use when it came to defending Charter protection and sex equality rights, for as First Nations women frequently note, gender equality (at least in its liberal iteration) is not an ideal held dear by indigenous communities.

Native women activists and leaders of the main Aboriginal associations disagreed and continue to disagree on both the status of equality as an ideal and the proper political priorities as concerns the goal of equality. Many,

---

[31] Quoted in Rudy Platiel, 'Gender Issue Sparks Native Disunity: Women's Group Charges Constitutional Proposals Will Undermine Female Equality', *The Globe and Mail*, July 20, 1992.

[32] See Mary Ellen Turpel, 'Patriarchy and Paternalism: The Legacy of the Canadian State for First Nations Women', *Canadian Journal of Women and the Law*, 6/1 (1993), 174–92.

[33] Ibid., p. 180.

particularly leaders of mainstream Aboriginal organizations, believe that *cultural* equality—specifically Native self-government—and not individual equality, should be the key objective. The political relationship to the rest of Canada which Aboriginal negotiators sought to establish was expected to instantiate such equality. By contrast, NWAC spokeswomen and some other Native women's groups supported a broadly (but not exclusively) liberal feminist conception of sexual equality in insisting on Charter protection. As we have seen, however, this position was largely driven by political exigencies. And even for the segment of the Native women's movement that defended formal gender equality, protection of women's rights must absolutely be made compatible with Aboriginal self-determination.

Some of the reasons given by Native women for supporting Aboriginal immunity from the Charter, and for rejecting formal sexual equality as a goal generally, have to do with what they perceived as problematic assumptions underlying the ideal of sexual equality. First, the very goal of sexual equality seems to imply, wrongly, that all women in Canada are somehow *similarly situated* and can rally around common prescriptions for the problems they face. Second and relatedly, many Native women express the belief that equality inescapably presupposes an ideal of *gender sameness* that clashes profoundly with Aboriginal notions of sexual complementarity and harmony.[34] Third, the emphasis on sexual equality seems to assume that *sexual oppression*, with its source in patriarchy, is the pivotal form of oppression and injustice women face, rather than racism and colonialism, and the social circumstances left in their wake (particularly the epidemic of violence currently facing Native communities).[35] Finally, some argue that the concepts of patriarchy and gender oppression underlying the paradigm of sexual equality presume that men are *opponents* rather than allies in the quest for justice, an idea Native women overwhelmingly reject.[36]

In addition to the problematic assumptions that seem to undergird the liberal ideal of sexual equality, the emphasis on individual *rights*, in the views of many Native thinkers and activists, is at odds with ideals central to Aboriginal society and governance. For example, as Turpel's earlier statement

---

[34] Ibid., p. 182. See also Arneil's discussion (2004) of statements made by women at the Roundtable of Aboriginal Women, convened by Status of Women Canada, at Ottawa, March 30–April 1, 2000.

[35] See Mary Ellen Turpel and Patricia A. Monture, 'Ode to Elijah: Reflections of Two First Nations Women on the Rekindling of Spirit at the Wake for the Meech Lake Accord', *Queen's Law Journal*, 15/2 (1990), 345–59, p. 358.

[36] Turpel, 'Patriarchy and Paternalism', p. 181 (Turpel acknowledges that some feminists are trying to move away from a notion of equality as sameness, p. 180, ff. 13).

makes clear, equality may suppose an individualistic rights framework that is at odds with indigenous social and political values. Egalitarianism is important to First Nations society and principles, according to Taiaiake Alfred, but is best seen as describing the relationship between leaders and their people, and as charactering social power relationships generally,[37] rather than the abstract relationship between all individuals or citizens generally. Instead of individual equality as a goal, then, many First Nations people, women included, point to the importance of well-being, harmony, and healing in their communities.

The critique of sexual equality advanced by some Aboriginal women is closely connected to concerns raised in connection with conventional interpretations of the notion of justice. Perhaps because the term is so often invoked in ways that assume a background context of liberal constitutional democracy—rightly or wrongly—the concept of justice is greeted ambivalently by some Native scholars. Patricia Monture, for example, notes that it is significant that there is no word for justice in many First Nations communities; it may be, she argues, that harmony, rather than justice, is the most important ideal in Native society.[38] Similarly, Alfred wants to retrieve a distinctively Aboriginal understanding of justice rather than merely applying a Western, liberal ideal of justice to Native communities:

The dominant Western conception of justice is rooted in a fundamentally individualistic, materialistic ideal of equity or sameness. By contrast, indigenous notions of justice arose within the context of belief in a universal relationship among all the elements that make up our universe.... The goal of indigenous justice is best characterized as the achievement of respectful coexistence—restoration of harmony to the network of relationships.... Indigenous ideas of justice differ from Western ideas in three basic ways: they are not a concerned primarily with questions of equity in treatment or distribution; there is not a universalizing or levelling imperative that may be used to justify the limitation of freedom; and the cultural framework that determines whether or not power is used appropriately includes not only the set of human relationships that form our society, but all other relationships as well.[39]

For many Native people, then, justice in Aboriginal terms foregrounds community well-being and harmony, as well as responsibilities and duties, not equality and individual rights.[40]

*　*　*

[37] Alfred, *Peace, Power, Righteousness*, p. 26.
[38] Patricia Monture-Okanee, 'Reclaiming Justice: Aboriginal Women and Justice Initiatives in the 1990's', in *Aboriginal Peoples and the Justice System* (Ottawa: Royal Commission on Aboriginal Peoples, 1993), p. 125.
[39] Alfred, *Peace, Power, Righteousness*, p. 42.
[40] See Turpel, 'Patriarchy and Paternalism'.

These important differences in the normative understanding of notions of justice and equality notwithstanding, it is interesting to observe how these concepts were nevertheless strategically deployed for particular political ends during the period of constitutional negotiations in 1992. Leaders of mainstream Native organizations did not mount an explicit challenge to the ideal of sexual equality in the run-up to Charlottetown. Rather, in response to some of their (antiaccord) dissenting rank-and-file members and NWAC lobbyists, spokesmen for the AFN argued that sexual equality was a matter for Native peoples themselves to work out in their own communities, altogether separate from issues of Aboriginal sovereignty. Moreover, Native leaders and band council chiefs lost no time in characterizing the rift between their associations and Native women's groups as one of clashing legal systems and political norms. Not only did they try to convey the message that traditional Native social, legal, and political institutions were best protected by a framework of collective Aboriginal rights, but some suggested that NWAC's sex equality concerns were proof of the extent to which European concepts and thinking had influenced Native society. Arguing in this vein, Mercredi, then AFN Chief, stated that many First Nations people 'challenge the Charter's interpretation of rights as weapons to be used against governments; we tend to see rights as collective responsibilities instead of individual rights—or at least see the strong link between the two'. Mercredi also argued that the legal system imposed by the Charter posed tensions with aspects of Aboriginal justice—'it doesn't include our communal vision'—and could pose obstacles to the authority of the traditional clan system and other institutions that Aboriginal communities might seek to reintroduce.[41]

Despite the possible perils of collective rights for Native women, NWAC and its provincial counterparts were somewhat less inclined than were Aboriginal leaders to portray the disagreement over the Charter as a conflict between collective rights and individual rights, for in principle they supported both. NWAC spokeswomen did however feel they needed to respond to attempts by national leaders to characterize collective rights as the only 'authentic' form of Aboriginal rights. To this end, they emphasized the importance of formal recognition of individual and human rights, which they warned should not be eclipsed by the quest for Aboriginal sovereignty.[42] Rejecting intimations by traditionalists that individual rights and collective rights were in some sense

---

[41] Mercredi, *In the Rapids*, pp. 96–103.

[42] Stacey-Moore, 'Aboriginal Women, Self-Government', p. 7. Arneil argues that even NWAC's position ought not to be understood as a straightforward endorsement of the liberal agenda: 'While the goal of women's empowerment may be consistent with the idea of liberal equality, it would be wrong to assume that they are the same or that individual rights is the conceptual framework that leads either aboriginal women (or the organizations that represent them) to seek greater power on

fundamentally incompatible, some Native women argued that explicit protection of their individual rights as women could and should go hand in hand with
the collective rights at the heart of Aboriginal self-government.

THREE NORMATIVE FRAMINGS

The rejection by some Aboriginal people of a liberal ideal of sexual equality
as the defining concept of justice for all women illustrates in a dramatic way
just why the choice between cultural group rights and sexual equality is so
problematic. And yet the positions of the main players in this fraught period
of Canadian constitutional history seemed to contribute precisely to a juxtaposition of cultural rights and individual (including sexual) equality rights. In
particular, three normative framings that emerged throughout this period—
and which arguably continue to characterize the debate—contributed to
a political impasse. The first of these calls for a return to traditional values
and social arrangements and insists that collective, cultural rights provide the
best framework for securing the balance and harmony within their communities. A second approach also endorses claims for collective, Aboriginal
rights, but accepts international human rights as morally binding on all
governments, including those of Native peoples. A third view defends the
legitimacy of collective Aboriginal rights but attaches the proviso that self-
governing groups must protect basic individual rights and freedoms with
domestic political instruments (like the Charter). These positions may seem
normatively incompatible in certain respects, but as I argue, when understood in
light of the political context and claims that inform them, it becomes possible to
see these views as negotiable and amenable to democratic compromise.

The View from Tradition

One initial response to NWAC's insistence on Charter protection for women's
rights was the appeal by some Native leaders to traditional Aboriginal models
of family and society. In particular, some Aboriginal spokespeople invoked
what is sometimes called the 'traditional Indian motherhood ideal' to suggest
ways of reconciling demands for sex equality (whether internal or external to

reserve, with respect to their male counterparts. In many instances, the explicit goal behind advocacy
for women's empowerment on reserve is not "equality" of "women" at all but the well-being of
communities...'. See Arneil, 'Sexual Equality and Cultural Protections', unpublished manuscript
(2003), p. 9.

the community) with Native cultural norms and social arrangements.[43] Typically, proponents of this view offer reassurances that women are respected and valued in their capacities as wives and mothers, and as full members of the community; different roles, on this view, need not mean unequal ones. Moreover, customary Aboriginal family roles for men and women are thought to contribute to social harmony and the preservation of communities' traditional identities. By contrast, liberal democratic social and legal norms are seen either as alien to, or directly undermining of, Aboriginal peoples' aspirations for cultural self-determination. This thought was voiced by some Native spokespeople during the 1992 debates, including one high-ranking woman leader, Chief Wendy Grant, who commented that 'divisions between First Nations people based upon the non-native fascination with extreme individualism simply support the assimilation of our people into the non-native culture'.[44] As this remark suggests, the view from tradition rejects liberal notions of individual rights in favor of a reassertion of Native cultural values and forms of social organization.[45] While this approach clearly reflects Native peoples' desire to direct the social, cultural and political life of their communities, it may also represent a backlash against dissenting members who demand social and political reform.

The Collective Rights/Human Rights Approach

A second position that emerged in the course of the debate on Aboriginal sovereignty and the Charter is what we might call the 'collective rights/human rights model'. Proponents of this view support the principle of self-government based on collective cultural rights, however, they concede that such governments are in turn morally bound to respect the basic human rights of their members, as specified by international covenants. Since the idea that 'women's rights are human rights' is gradually becoming a key aspect of human rights discourse, protection for women's basic rights could be expected to follow from the collective rights/human rights model. This is especially so if 'Aboriginal rights ... [as] in addition to fundamental human rights, not a replacement for human rights', and international law is seen as setting the standard for domestic equality protections, as Joyce Green proposes:[46]

[43] See L. E. Krosenbrink-Gelissen, *Sexual Equality as an Aboriginal Right: The Native Women's Association of Canada and the Constitutional Process on Aboriginal Matters, 1982–1987* (Saarbrücken, Germany: Verlag breitenback, 1991), p. 120.

[44] Rudy Platiel, 'Aboriginal Women Divide On Constitutional Protection'.

[45] See also Winona LaDuke, *All Our Relations: Native Struggles for Land and Life* (Cambridge, MA and Minneapolis, MN: South End Press, 1999).

[46] Joyce Green, 'Canaries in the Mines of Citizenship: Indian Women in Canada', *Canadian Journal of Political Science*, 34/4 (2001), 715–38, p. 731.

The fundamental rights of the excluded women must be guaranteed by the indigenous governments that exist as a matter of right in relation to the colonial state. Both Canada and indigenous governments must respect international law on the fundamental human rights of women . . . [47]

The breezy optimism of this position is, however, somewhat undercut by the notorious difficulty of enforcing international human rights law. Arguably, extensive and legally binding sex equality rights are best secured by a state's own formal constitution, which are in any case necessary correlates for securing human rights.

Some who supported the collective rights/human rights position during the early 1990s constitutional negotiations insisted that self-governing cultural minorities, namely Aboriginal peoples, should not be answerable to liberal democratic laws and norms. During the 1992 constitutional negotiations, many heads of the main Native associations and band council chiefs espoused views about the legal and political requirements of indigenous sovereignty that could best be characterized as fitting the collective rights/ human rights model: they advocated self-government for Aboriginal peoples, and nodded in the direction of international human rights standards. Indeed, their position was later adopted by Canada's Royal Commission on Aboriginal Peoples, whose final report contains perhaps the best articulation of this perspective; the commissioners endorse an approach which accepts that Aboriginal governments are subject to international human rights standards in their dealings with people under their jurisdiction. However, it argues that an Aboriginal government cannot be held accountable in Canadian courts for alleged violations of the Canadian Charter of Rights and Freedoms unless the Aboriginal nation in question has previously consented to the application of the Charter in a binding constitutional instrument.[48]

Although Aboriginal leaders eventually accepted the federal government's proposed compromise solution during the 1992 negotiations—that is, access to the notwithstanding clause of the Charter as part of the Native sovereignty package—they would have preferred complete amnesty from Canada's constitution. Native spokespeople however were careful to pad their claims for self-government with reassurances that they acknowledged the value of individual and human rights protections.[49]

---

[47] Ibid., pp. 734–5.

[48] *Final Report of the Royal Commission on Aboriginal Peoples*, 2, p. 228.

[49] Ovide Mercredi issued such reassurances repeatedly. See, for instance, Delacourt, 'Natives Divided Over Charter'.

The Equality View

A third approach to the dilemma of reconciling sex equality rights with collective, cultural rights is encapsulated by the stance advanced with considerable force by NWAC. This view endorses the goal of self-determination for Native peoples but emphasizes the importance of sexual equality protections and other individual rights provisions. Some versions of this perspective view women's equality rights and cultural self-determination as of equal importance. Similarly, this view might require that we consider not only Aboriginal group autonomy but also that we ask about its consequences for the autonomy of individual women members.[50] In the case of the Charlottetown process, NWAC spokeswomen and some other Native women activists emphatically rejected suggestions that women should even temporarily set aside their equality concerns for the purpose of forming a united front for Aboriginal sovereignty. Nor did advocates of the equality view accept traditionalists' claim that individual rights and collective rights are necessarily incompatible. Fears that the application of the Charter to Aboriginal governments would merely prolong the colonial relationship between Native peoples and the rest of Canada and obstruct traditional Native forms of self-governance may well have been justified; however, some Native spokeswomen argued that these were risks that Native peoples should be willing to take in order to secure the protection of the rights of all of their members, women included.

The equality view appears not to incorporate some Aboriginal peoples' misgivings and criticisms of the liberal ideals of sexual equality and sexual justice, as discussed above. However, this is not because Native women proponents of equality protections wholeheartedly supported liberal Canadian law, but rather because there was a pressing political need, in the minds of some, to stand firmly in favor of Charter protection (and individual rights protections) at this critical historical juncture. As one spokeswoman for the Quebec Native Women's Association commented:

It must be clearly understood that we have never questioned the collective rights of our Nations, but we strongly believe that as citizens of these Nations, we are also entitled to protection. We maintain that the individual rights of Native citizens can be recognized while affirming collective rights. This is why we would like to be in a position to rely on a Charter guaranteeing the rights and freedoms of all Native Citizens. The only model we have at the present time is the Canadian Charter of Rights and Freedoms.[51]

[50] See Caroline Dick, 'The Politics of Intragroup Difference: First Nations' Women and the *Sawridge* Dispute', *Canadian Journal of Political Science*, 39/1 (2006), 97–116, p. 109.

[51] Québec Native Women's Association, *Presentation to Hearing on the First Nations Constitutional Circle* (Montreal: QNWA, February 5, 1992). Cited in Isaac and Maloughney, pp. 471–2.

The fact that many Native women activists felt compelled to argue for Charter protection was thus largely a reflection of political circumstances in which they had neither significant political voice, nor access to democratic forums in which to deliberate about these issues and to try to effect political change.

The normative impulses of these positions appear to pull in opposing directions, and, as noted earlier, to create a policy impasse. To push past this roadblock, it is essential to recognize the practical and political circumstances that continue to inform the cases for Aboriginal sovereignty with, and without, the accompaniment of liberal equal rights protections. When understood as a fundamentally political dilemma, susceptible to deliberative negotiation and (compromise) resolution, this impasse looks much more tractable. Future deliberations about the best ways in which to protect and empower Aboriginal women and men within their communities may need to start *further back* than any of these three normative framings permit, and make possible a deeper questioning and interrogation of vested privileges, vulnerabilities, and power relationships in which both Aboriginal communities and the Canadian state are implicated. Unlike the South African Law Commission hearings on customary marriage, as we will see in Chapter 7, the Charlottetown consultations did not welcome discussions about the normative status of sexual equality, or disputed conceptions of justice. Future deliberations can and should do so.

Equally important, in order for negotiations to carry normative authority and actually contribute to a political compromise, future political deliberations will need to be much more politically inclusive than the constitutional negotiations in 1992. The Charlottetown process, much like the Meech Lake constitutional process before it, was far from open and transparent. One of the biggest complaints made of the process was that the final text of the accord was not made available in advance of the referendum; assurances were given to this effect, but the delay continued, and many suspected that this was deliberate. The lack of a final text that activists and ordinary Canadians could study and debate well in advance of the referendum was then one of the fatal flaws of the Charlottetown proposal, and a missed opportunity for citizens' direct participation in democratic debate. It also dovetailed with Native women's exclusion from the process and strengthened their misgivings about the dangers of Charter immunity. In September 1992, just a month before the referendum, Canadians were still without a final text to consider. This prompted a remarkable action on the part of NWAC: having recently (in August) received a favorable judgment from the Federal Court of Appeals—which had ruled that First Nations women were unjustly and detrimentally excluded from constitutional talks—the association asked for an injunction against the whole accord drafting process.[52]

One lesson to be learned from this case is that in the absence of real political inclusion, proposed compromises, not surprisingly, are likely to fail. Although sexual equality provisions were ultimately proposed to the Charlottetown Accord to try to assuage the concerns of Native women, their sense of exclusion was by this time too acute for this compromise to work; it was a matter of too little, too late (and too ad hoc).[53] Similarly, when the prospect of an Aboriginal Charter was raised, the response of some Native women was one of apprehension and mistrust. In large part, this was because their organizations—particularly NWAC and its provincial counterparts—did not have any direct political access to current constitutional negotiations, and so they could not trust that they would be included in talks on an Aboriginal Charter. In future negotiations, there is no reason why NWAC should not have a place at the bargaining table, alongside the other national Aboriginal associations.

Finally, aside from explicit inclusion in federal political negotiations over the future of Aboriginal sovereignty, Native women's formal and informal political activities will need to be supported in ways that they have not. Women's ongoing protest at the refusal of certain band councils to reinstate and accommodate women disenfranchised in the pre-Bill C-31 era can be assisted through funding for their legal battles. Native women's associations are also badly in need of consistent government funding, which has been reduced or withdrawn in recent years. And the inclusion of women's contributions and perspectives is particularly essential in ongoing efforts to develop an Aboriginal system of criminal justice in Canada. In particular, more could be done not only to incorporate their views but rather to make women's experiences of violence central to the very shaping of an Aboriginal criminal justice system.[54] A deliberative democratic approach to conflicts of culture along the lines developed in this book would foster just this sort of inclusion, and could allow Aboriginal participants, particularly women, to envisage and articulate new ways of protecting and empowering their own communities.

---

[52] Susan Delacourt, 'Text Being Altered, Native Women Say', *The Globe and Mail*, September 19, 1992. The bid for an injunction was unsuccessful.

[53] The proposed section of the Charlottetown Accord, s.35 (7), stated: 'Notwithstanding any other provisions of this Act, the rights of the Aboriginal peoples of Canada referred to in the Part are guaranteed equally to male and female persons.' However, questions still remained concerning the notwithstanding clause and whether future Aboriginal governments would necessarily be subject to all of the Charter's provisions in perpetuity.

[54] See for example Patricia Monture-Okanee and Mary Ellen Turpel, 'Aboriginal Peoples and Canadian Criminal Law: Rethinking Justice', *University of British Columbia Law Review*, special issue (1992); and Koshan, 'Aboriginal Women, Justice and the Charter'.

CONCLUSION

This account of Aboriginal women's efforts to secure sexual justice during constitutional negotiations on Native sovereignty brings into focus the deeply political character of tensions between sex equality and cultural rights, on at least two levels. First, the relationship between Aboriginal peoples and their organizations, and the Canadian state, is fraught with mistrust and domination. Against a background of colonialism, cultural oppression, and the racist laws and policies on the Canadian state, the opposition of the main Aboriginal organizations to a mitigated form of sovereignty was not surprising. Indeed, this sentiment is still echoed by Native scholars today:

> Clearly, any notion of nationhood or self-government rooted in state institutions and framed within the context of state sovereignty can never satisfy the imperatives of Native American political traditions. Harmonious cooperation and coexistence founded on respect for autonomy and the principle of self-determination are precluded by the state's insistence on dominion and its exclusionary notion of sovereignty.[55]

As Taiaiake Alfred's statement suggests, a relationship of domination between Aboriginal peoples and the settler society cannot provide the basis for co-operation and compromise solutions. A fundamental shift in the power relations between Native communities, and Native leaders, and their counterparts in the Canadian state must prefigure equitable democratic deliberations over issues of sovereignty and self-government.

Second, the dispute over how Aboriginal women's rights should be protected brought to the surface a difficult history within Native communities, one marked in many cases by women's political exclusion from band council governance and their disenfranchisement as a result of sexually discriminatory Indian membership rules. As the backlash against the legislation designed to rectify women's disenfranchisement, Bill C-31, was ongoing, it is no surprise that many Native women and their organizations would not agree to defer the issue of protection for women's rights to future (postaccord) negotiations. This highlights the importance of real political inclusion for marginalized and disenfranchised members of cultural communities in efforts to evaluate and reform customs—regardless of whether traditional practices or externally imposed laws (such as the Indian Act) are the cause of discrimination.

---

[55] Alfred, *Peace, Power, Righteousness*, p. 72.

As this case illustrates, groups that experience systematic forms of social, political, and economic subordination within a state system are by no means immune from practicing their own internal forms of discrimination and abuse. In Aboriginal communities torn apart by the loss of traditional social systems and ways of life, it is women who tend to face greater discrimination and powerlessness, and to suffer higher rates of poverty, unemployment, and physical and sexual abuse. The diminution of Native women's status and power has much to do with the racist and sexist laws (such as those encoded in the Indian Act) precipitated by European conquest and colonization. Patriarchal concepts and institutions introduced by British and French colonial authorities in Canada are widely credited with having compounded Native women's loss of authority in their communities, especially after the implementation of the Indian Act. However, Native women are also quick to point out that men in their own communities have made little attempt to prevent the erosion of women's traditional power base, and that these same men are now reluctant to relinquish control of Aboriginal political bodies or even to share their power with women.

In the case of First Nations women seeking to overturn the provision in the Indian Act responsible for the discriminatory dual system of determining Indian status that had disenfranchised so many of them and their children, many came to suspect that their biggest obstacle was the opposition of band councils and the heads of Aboriginal associations—*not* the federal government. While some Native leaders conceded the unfairness of the Indian Act provision, they did not want to see it settled by means of a judicial decision. Resisting the imposition of Bill C-31, some band councils and Aboriginal organizations urged that any changes or reforms should be the result of political consultation, and accompanied by guarantees from federal and provincial governments for increased financial assistance and land (in part to accommodate large numbers of reinstated members). It was no secret that council chiefs feared sharing economic resources and the loss of their power to determine band membership more than they feared women's complaints of discrimination and second-class citizenship. Clearly, against the backdrop of unaltered power relations in Aboriginal communities, and without guaranteed political inclusion for women, a negotiated political settlement would simply shore up the status quo.

For all of these reasons, the political enfranchisement of Native women will be critical to any future deliberations on Aboriginal sovereignty. Only they can speak to the specific problems they face as Native women, and the kinds of changes that will help them face these and empower them. The operative assumption in much rhetoric for political self-determination is that what is good for the collective is also good for individual members; indeed,

Aboriginal communities in Canada are often close-knit, and place great emphasis on the interconnectedness of family, generations, clans, and 'nations', and the importance of social harmony and 'healing'. Integral to traditional Native conceptions of community is the idea that family and clan members have different, but equally important, roles. Historically, women in Canadian Aboriginal societies have held revered roles primarily as mothers, caregivers, educators, and transmitters of culture; crucially, their needs and interests are not viewed as separate or indeed separable from those of her family and clan. But while arrangements based on extensive integration of individual and social interests may work well in communities with vigorous systems of social support and solidarity, the breakdown in such traditional structures in recent years has introduced a host of social problems. All too frequently, traditional roles and relationships that once helped to secure esteem and social power for Aboriginal women have become sources of disadvantage and powerlessness for them, particularly in light of the epidemic of violence facing Native communities.

There are good reasons, then, to foreground women's inclusion in democratic processes of deliberation and decision-making over the future of Aboriginal sovereignty in Canada. Nonetheless, there are also real risks associated with such a strategy. Deliberative modes of political negotiation and problem solving invariably leave open the possibility of power plays, interminable debate and political stand-offs, and also the possibility that participants to political dialogue may be silenced and intimidated. Given the open-ended nature of deliberation as advanced in this book, there are also real questions about whether political outcomes will necessarily favor liberal solutions. One way to help protect more vulnerable participants in political deliberation would be simply to require those cultural minorities (e.g. Aboriginal peoples) who seek forms of community autonomy and self-rule to include formal respect for the individual rights of their members as part of negotiated constitutional settlements, but to leave it up to them how precisely to do so. For example, it may also be possible to combine protections for individual rights (including sexual equality rights) with the legal framework of collective self-determination in a more synthetic way, by incorporating the different legal traditions in developing alternative legal paradigms. Recent efforts by Aboriginal scholars to forge a vision that accommodates individual and collective rights by emphasizing the idea of multitiered 'responsibilities to kin, clan and nation' as well as the importance of individual uniqueness are suggestive in this regard.[56] Whether such an arrangement would merely perpetuate the arrogance of colonial

---

[56] See for instance Russel Barsh, 'Indigenous Peoples and the Idea of Individual Human Rights', *Native Studies Review*, 10/2 (1995), 35–55, pp. 44–5.

domination, as Alfred's analysis suggests, is of course an open question. But a key advantage of a deliberative democratic approach to conflicts of the sort discussed here is that it leaves open the possibility of as-yet-undiscovered means of integrating protections for women and protections for culture. Native women's recent attempts to connect collective rights and individual rights by appealing to a reconceived conception of justice is suggestive in this regard. The idea of rethinking the non-Native received understanding of justice so as to make it correspond more directly to the realities of Aboriginal communities—their forms of social and political organization and their spiritual traditions—could also be an important part of this task.

It may be that at the end of any given deliberative democratic process, participants will opt for conventional liberal sorts of guarantees for women. Despite the potential that exists for retrieving egalitarian models of social and political relationships within Aboriginal culture, grounded in an indigenous conception of justice, many Native women remain keen to preserve formal constitutional guarantees for their individual rights. Scarcely five years after the defeat of the Charlottetown Accord, the final Report of Canada's Royal Commission on Aboriginal Peoples was published, and to the satisfaction of many Aboriginal women scholars and activists, the report contains definitive language urging the formal protection of Native women's equality rights. While not legally binding, the document will serve as a roadmap for future negotiations on Aboriginal sovereignty questions; as such, it makes it less likely that sex equality issues could simply be dropped from subsequent political talks on self-government, or indeed from Aboriginal government constitutions. The inclusion of specific language protecting Native women's equality rights in the commissioners' report must be seen as at least in part a result of their highly publicized struggle for guarantees for their sex equality rights in the early 1990s. However, while the report reiterates the federal government's position that the Charter should continue to apply to Native peoples, it confirms the view that future Aboriginal governments should have access to the controversial notwithstanding clause of the Charter. But in a partial concession to women's groups, the commissioners emphasized that in no case should Native communities use this discretionary power to suspend women's rights:

In our view, the Canadian Charter of Rights and Freedoms applies to Aboriginal governments and regulates relations with individuals within their jurisdiction. However, under section 25, the charter must be interpreted flexibly to account for the distinctive philosophies, traditions and cultural practices of Aboriginal peoples. Moreover, under section 33, Aboriginal nations can pass notwithstanding clauses for a period. At the same time, sections 28 and 35 (4) of the *Constitution Act*, 1982, ensure that Aboriginal women and men are in all cases guaranteed equal access to the inherent rights of self-government and are entitled to equal treatment by their governments.[57]

Native women's challenge to Aboriginal leaders on sex equality issues serves as a dramatic illustration of the ways in which the political priorities and strategies of women's equality advocates may differ from those of proponents of collective, cultural rights. The Canadian example is of special interest because it reveals the difficult decisions and trade-offs which those who advocate *both* gender justice and cultural protections and rights must make, and the far-reaching political consequences of their choices. The defeat of the Charlottetown Accord in October 1992 was by all accounts a steep price to pay to protest the deferral of political and legal protection for Native women's rights. Yet the support these women garnered from other citizens and advocacy groups suggests that many Canadians, women in particular, were concerned about the possible implications of Aboriginal rights for gender justice, particularly when constitutional talks relegated Native women to the sidelines. As such, this example serves as a poignant reminder that less powerful members of national minority groups—such as women—have good reason to press for political inclusion in negotiations to determine future arrangements of cultural rights and self-government.

[57] *Final Report of the Royal Commission on Aboriginal People*, 2, p. 168.

6

Personal Autonomy and Cultural Tradition: The Arranged Marriage Debate in Britain

This chapter reflects on concerns about the tensions between personal autonomy and cultural traditions, taking as its focus the example of arranged marriage and the debate it has spawned in Britain. My aim is to highlight the difficulties that attend a specifically *liberal* framing of the effect of certain traditional cultural practices on women's lives. As we saw in Chapter 2, this framing foregrounds the ideal of personal autonomy and related concepts of agency and choice. I begin by asking whether autonomy is useful as an ideal and regulative norm for determining the validity and permissibility of controversial cultural traditions, and if so, what kind of conception of autonomy is adequate for this task. I then discuss the U.K. government inquiry into the phenomenon of forced marriages among some British South Asians, paying particular attention to the framing of this issue in terms of autonomy, choice, and consent. The autonomy paradigm, I argue, has had the effect of steering public debate and policy about marriage in problematic directions. Fruitful discussion about both the reality of contested social practices—such as arranged marriage—and their purported validity thus necessitates a critical rethinking of personal autonomy and the closely related concepts of choice and consent.

The common liberal view that states should refrain from interfering with cultural minority practices so long as these do not violate the personal autonomy of group members faces important challenges. By their very nature, social customs may demand submission to the authority and expectations of others; whether individuals' acquiescence to cultural traditions can be understood as reflecting an instance of choice or decision within a person's broader life plan is therefore doubtful at best. Nor is this problem solved simply by claiming that a cultural practice is consistent with a group's exercise of autonomy—that is, the claim that the majority of a group democratically endorses a custom and so meets a broader test of democratic legitimacy. This is because democratic assent or refusal requires, for most liberals, evidence of a minimal level of personal autonomy. Where such autonomy is culturally impermissible or is expressed in ways that are not easy to recognize, how are the choices of group members to be authenticated? And are many or most so-called 'traditional' cultural practices that parents and older generations seek to maintain within liberal societies in some sense problematic, from a liberal standpoint?

LIBERALISM AND AUTONOMY

Perhaps more than any other value, liberal political theory emphasizes the importance of personal autonomy. Liberal thinkers of course differ widely in their understanding of what personal autonomy entails, and what form and degree of it is desirable[1]; but no liberal, as we saw in Chapter 2, disavows the value and importance of this ideal. Whether conceived in terms of the centrality of individual choice and legitimating consent—as Locke and later, political liberals, stress—or in terms of concrete capacities and opportunities for autonomy, as John Stuart Mill and some perfectionist liberals, such as Joseph Raz and Martha Nussbaum, emphasize[2]—liberals concur that a life without autonomy is not really much of a life at all. Not surprisingly, then, liberal thinkers share an intuitive distrust of social institutions and cultural practices or arrangements that apparently undercut personal autonomy either by restricting individuals' ambit of choice or, more insidiously, socializing them so as to make the formation (much less realization) of independent choices nearly impossible. Mill's well-known critique, in *On Liberty*, of the stultifying effects of social and religious mores and customs on free thought and individuality set the tone for later liberals' warnings of the dangers that restrictive cultural conventions might pose for individual autonomy.[3]

More recently, liberal proponents of multiculturalism have defended special group rights for cultural minorities by appealing to the importance of a secure culture for community members' autonomy. These same writers appeal to autonomy in order to indicate which practices and arrangements the liberal state (generally) ought not to support or protect; Will Kymlicka,

---

[1] See Gerald Dworkin's *The Theory and Practice of Autonomy* (Cambridge: Cambridge University Press, 1988), in which he identifies a range of different understandings of both personal autonomy and moral autonomy, many of which conflict.

[2] John Stuart Mill, *On Liberty* (Indianapolis, IN and Cambridge: Hackett Publishing Co., 1978); Joseph Raz, *The Morality of Freedom* (Oxford: Clarendon Press, 1986), and *Ethics in the Public Domain: Essays in the Morality of Law and Politics* (Oxford: Clarendon Press, 1994); Nussbaum, *Women and Human Development*.

[3] Mill, *On Liberty*, esp. Ch. 3.

for example, invokes autonomy in expressing misgivings about demands for greater accommodation by British Muslims, including state-supported religious schooling:

[T]here is a conflict here that must be faced, and which has implications for many aspects of society. Either we accept the ideal of autonomy as a fundamental human interest which the state should protect, or we don't. If we do, we will be led in the direction of a society which requires a broad liberal education for children and which accords priority to civil liberties. If we don't we will be led in the direction of a millet-like society which restricts the education and civil liberties of individuals in order to discourage the confusion and discontentment which comes from questioning religious practices.[4]

Note that the autonomy appealed to here is taken as straightforward and transparent, rather than multifaceted and contested. Similarly, Nussbaum, despite her endorsement of political liberalism, appeals to a thicker, liberal Aristotelian, conception of autonomy—one emphasizing capabilities for choices—in arguing that a range of practices harmful to women's agency ought to be prohibited. As we saw in Chapter 3, she has also criticized traditional forms of marriage that she argues remove core capabilities or capacities for fully human functioning, and suggests that these ought not to be supported.[5]

The importance of personal autonomy in liberal thought and practice helps explain why some contemporary liberals, such as Barry and Kukathas, are unsympathetic to demands for greater accommodation of cultural minorities: they fear that some groups will seek to restrict the freedom of their own members in illiberal ways, using cultural and religious traditions. These concerns have led to the suggestion that practices which severely constrain the choices of individuals through heavy-handed role socialization and restriction ought to be strongly discouraged or even prohibited.[6] But beyond this minimalist concern to protect individuals from outright violation of their civil liberties, many liberal thinkers, as noted in Chapter 2, also try to ascertain the validity of cultural practices by asking whether they restrict the capacity of individuals to develop and pursue a life of their own choosing. This appeal to a thicker or more substantive ideal of autonomy as *independence* in order to assess controversial practices is highly problematic in plural liberal democracies, I argue. An uncritical insistence on the absolute value of lives characterized by greater autonomy and self-direction can lead to a distorted and partial understanding of cultural customs that are the subject of political contestation, and so also ill-conceived policies for social reform and regulation.

---

[4] Will Kymlicka, 'Reply to Modood', *Analyse & Kritik*, 15 (1993), 92–6, p. 95.

[5] Nussbaum, *Women and Human Development*, pp. 94 and 230.

[6] See for example Barry *Culture and Equality*; Okin, 'Is Multiculturalism Bad for Women?'; and Nussbaum, *Sex and Social Justice*.

For liberals who eschew Kant's understanding of autonomy as a strictly *moral* capacity—according to which autonomous agents act in accordance with self-willed, universal moral laws—autonomy has come to refer to an ideal of a self-directed life. Individuals who can conceive of, and successfully identify, life goals and ambitions, usually in the form of a life plan, have gone some distance in demonstrating the capacity for autonomy, according to this view. Typically, a coherent life plan is thought to comprise goals that in turn reflect complex, higher-order (and rational) preferences. Some carry this requirement even further, as does Harry Frankfurt, and argue that autonomy requires second-order *volitions*, which enable agents to choose between conflicting desires (including higher-order desires).[7] On this view, the autonomous person is one who has freedom of the will—an agent who 'is free to will what he wants to will, or to have the will he wants'.[8] Accordingly, people who simply adhere to social pressures and family expectations irrespective of their own desires, preferences, and ideals are necessarily lacking in autonomy in important ways. Truly autonomous persons are individuals who stand apart from their peers in some sense: certainly Mill thought that individuality, nonconformity, and even eccentricity were the best markers of autonomy. Following in this vein, S.I. Benn suggests in his influential sketch of an autonomous person, 'Among the products of his creativeness therefore, is his own personality, something uniquely his own, what he has made from raw materials or notions, beliefs, principles and ideals supplied by his plural tradition. Unlike the heteronomous person, he is not merely an instantiation of a cultural mould or form.'[9] (The irony of this account is not lost on Benn, who recognized that the very idea of 'living by one's "law"' presupposes a particular tradition, a notion that is distinctively rationalist and liberal in character.)

Throughout the 1980s and 1990s, communitarian thinkers like Charles Taylor and Michael Sandel roundly criticized this particular liberal conception of the autonomous person as much too individualistic and 'atomistic'. Likewise, feminist writers such as Annette Baier and Carol Gilligan rejected the liberal individual as a misconceived construct, a psychologically truncated agent with no significant attachments and relationships. In light of these criticisms, some liberal thinkers have distanced themselves from the idealized, substantive vision of autonomy. While not eschewing the importance of

---

[7] Harry Frankfurt, 'Freedom of the Will and the Concept of a Person', in *The Inner Citadel: Essays on Individual Autonomy*, ed. John Christman (Oxford and New York: Oxford University Press, 1989), pp. 67–9.

[8] Ibid., p. 70.

[9] S. I. Benn, 'Individuality, Autonomy, and Community', in *Community as a Social Ideal*, ed. Eugene Kamenka (London: Edward Arnold, 1982), p. 50.

autonomy in some form, they ask how, as Jennifer Nedelsky writes, we might 'combine the claim of the constitutiveness of social relations with the value of self-determination'.[10] For these liberals, the ideal of autonomy is perfectly compatible with the recognition that human beings are also socially embedded, and that our social context places certain constraints on agents' independence. Joel Feinberg describes this liberal rethinking of autonomy thusly: 'The ideal of the autonomous person is that of an authentic individual whose self-determination is as complete as is consistent with the requirement that he is, of course, a member of a community.'[11]

This more moderate conception of autonomy which rejects maximum freedom as a perfectionist ideal, and instead emphasizes the social context in which individual agency is exercised, does not necessarily lead to a more sympathetic view of minority cultural practices and customs, however. Indeed, greater recognition of the socially constitutive nature of individuals has led some liberal philosophers to appreciate better the full force of early socialization, and accordingly, to propose limitations on it. Much discussion of the internalized obstacles to personal autonomy has followed from concerns about socialization. Robert Young, for example, reminds us that people who are free of external constraints may still fail to live autonomously if they are merely following strict social mores.[12] Schooling that encourages conventional feminine roles and behavior, on this view, 'interferes' with girls' autonomy and even their 'right of self-determination'.[13] Sometimes the effects of socialization on autonomy are not immediately apparent in that they do not involve direct indoctrination of children into traditional roles. The effects, however, may be no less far-reaching: Catriona Mackenzie, for example, writes of the ways in which 'a restricted or oppressive cultural imaginary may limit an agent's capacities for imaginative projection, and in so doing impair her capacities for self-definition, self-transformation, and autonomy.'[14]

One response to concerns about the negative impact of socialization on personal autonomy has been to argue that autonomy is not incompatible with

---

[10] Jennifer Nedelsky, 'Reconceiving Autonomy: Sources, Thoughts and Possibilities', in *Law and the Community: The End of Individualism?*, eds. Leslie Green and Allan Hutchinson (Toronto: Carswell, 1989), p. 221.

[11] Joel Feinberg, 'Autonomy', in *The Inner Citadel: Essays on Individual Autonomy*, ed. J. Christman (Oxford: Oxford University Press, 1989), p. 45.

[12] Robert Young, *Personal Autonomy: Beyond Negative and Positive Liberty* (New York: St. Martin's Press, 1986), p. 49.

[13] Sharon Bishop Hill, 'Self-Determination and Autonomy', in *Today's Moral Problems*, ed. Richard Wasserstrom (New York: Macmillan, 1979), pp. 129–30.

[14] Catriona Mackenzie, 'Imagining Oneself Otherwise', in *Relational Autonomy: Feminist Perspectives on Autonomy, Agency, and the Social Self*, eds. Catriona Mackenzie and Natalie Stoljar (Oxford: Oxford University Press, 2000), p. 143.

strong forms of socialization, but that agents need to acquire considerable reflexivity and self-definition in the face of such socialization in order to achieve minimal autonomy. Indeed, some philosophers have suggested that socialization could be specifically directed toward instilling such habits of reflection and self-criticism. Robert Young, for instance, endorses an ideal of 'persons developing their autonomy by way of gaining insight into how they came by their motivations (chiefly first-order desires and values) and then going on to make a conscious commitment to them or to a deliberate rejection of them'.[15] On his view, autonomy is a form of individual self-determination or sovereignty that is intrinsically valuable. Ironically, he believes that such autonomy may occasionally require strong forms of paternalism in order to guard against direct and imminent harm—including cases where a person ostensibly consents to being seriously harmed.[16] To be autonomous, according to this conception, is thus to be self-directed in one's life choices. This in turn requires freedom (as far as possible) from both external and internal obstacles and the development of capacities for critical reflection and decision-making: 'an autonomous life is one that is directed in accordance with an individual's own conception of what he (or she) wants to do in and with that life. Such an account requires us to think of autonomy as involving more than just the absence of constraints.'[17]

This understanding of autonomy, which we might call the self-determination view, is rejected as overly demanding by critics who doubt that we can ever have as much critical distance from our attitudes and desires as this model seems to require.[18] The assumption that we must overcome the effects of socialization in order to function as autonomous persons is, critics say, both a false requirement and hopelessly unrealistic.[19] In its place, some propose a more moderate conception of critical reflexivity as simply self-definition. Emphasizing both capacities and opportunities for self-definition, the philosopher Diana Meyers argues that 'the core of the concept of personal autonomy is the concept of an individual living in harmony with his or her "authentic self",' which in turn requires self-discovery, self-definition, and what she calls 'responsibility to self'.[20] The crafting of one's life plan in accordance with one's reflective desires thus lies at the core of this conception of autonomy: '[p]rogrammatically autonomous people have autonomous life

---

[15] Robert Young, 'Autonomy and Socialization', *Mind*, 89 (1980), 565–76, p. 576.

[16] Robert Young, *Personal Autonomy: Beyond Negative and Positive Liberty*, pp. 74, 78, and 87.

[17] Ibid., p. 49.

[18] See for example Diana Meyers' critique of Robert Young's account of autonomy in Meyers, *Self, Society, and Personal Choice* (New York: Columbia University Press, 1989), pp. 29–30.

[19] Ibid., pp. 40–1.   [20] Ibid., pp. 43, 49–50, 91, and 132.

plans. A life plan is a comprehensive projection of intent, a conception of what a person wants to do in life.'[21]

Meyers' account of autonomy, which we can call the 'self-definition' view, thus sees autonomy as a procedural capacity or competency (or set of competencies) that in turn enables individuals to lead authentic lives, one in keeping with their considered beliefs and preferences. This view of auton-omy might be compatible with at least some traditional cultural practices, provided these are real choices that reflect an individual's sense of self. But upon closer inspection, it appears to preclude strong forms of socialization, such as those found in many traditional cultural and religious communities. While this conception rightly rejects the possibility of complete transcendence over socialization, the notion of self-definition at its core is closely bound up with an ideal of a self-directed life that is thoroughly liberal. Meyers readily agrees that 'personal integration and life-plan innovation' are central to this view of autonomy, although she does not concede the normative content of this ideal of flourishing.[22] On her account, traditional sex-role socialization is anathema to personal autonomy: '[u]nconscious assimilation of cultural prac-tices' also makes it difficult for people to develop their own life plans and identify their own motives and desires.[23] It follows from this that restrictive social and cultural roles are just as problematic for this more moderate view of autonomy (i.e., of the autonomous person embedded within a community) as they are for the substantive 'free will' conception of autonomy.

In my view, neither the idealized, strong conception of autonomy as independence nor the more moderate views of autonomy as either, self-determination or self-definition and choice in the absence of external and internal obstacles, seem adequate to the task of illuminating what is at stake in social and cultural practices that are both traditional and critically contested. An idealized conception of autonomy as independence would probably lead us to reject practices such as arranged marriage, unless there was clear evidence of this custom accorded with the betrothed's reflective, higher-order preferences. But even the seemingly moderate account of autonomy as self-definition may preclude the possibility that affirming and 'choosing' traditional roles could count as autonomous agency. More gener-ally, the lack of different options and lifestyles in traditional communities would surely preclude the description of certain choices as autonomous,

---

[21] Ibid., p. 49.   [22] Ibid., pp. 61 and 41.

[23] Ibid., p. 207 and 181. See also Meyers, 'The Rush to Motherhood—Pronatalist Discourse and Women's Autonomy', *Signs*, 26/3 (2001), 735–73, in which she argues that traditional feminine socialization hinders women's capacities for autonomous decision-making with respect to whether to have children.

causing us to disregard decisions taken by individuals in socially confining settings.

The oversimple characterization of such traditional practices as arranged marriage as incompatible with liberal autonomy is thus not the exclusive purview of deeply normative accounts of autonomy, such as the substantive account of autonomy as independence; it is equally the consequence of more moderate, procedural accounts of autonomy. This point is perhaps best illustrated by Nussbaum's capability theory, which, as we saw in Chapter 3, points to restrictive social circumstances and the idea of adaptive preferences to explain why some of women's choices should be criticized and set aside.[24] Like Nussbaum's approach, the liberal conceptions of autonomy examined above consider both capacities for independent choice and the availability of diverse life options as a prerequisite for authentic decision-making and agency. While a thin version of the former condition may be compatible with traditional cultural arrangements, the latter is substantive in ways unacknowledged by liberals. Nor is it clear why the lack of available options and choice per se should be a definitive indicator of the presence or absence of autonomy for women.[25] While expanding women's social choices and options is no doubt beneficial, we need to see that in their everyday lives, women already do negotiate decisions even within constrictive social contexts.

Both the idealized conception of autonomy as free will and the more moderate conceptions of autonomy as requiring self-determination or capacities for self-definition and authenticity in the context of a socialized existence obscure the context of important decisions that people may make. Autonomous lives, on these liberal accounts, are ones in which the choices of individuals are clearly demarcated from their background context of social and cultural norms. This framing is particularly problematic when it comes to grappling with aspects of so-called traditional cultures, in which customs may represent more complex social dynamics between community and family pressures and individual reflection. Customs that have come under the scrutiny of the liberal state may equally represent religious self-assertion, or express rejection of perceived Western values and the exclusionary (or racist) policies of the host society. For example, the Muslim 'headscarf affair' involved this kind of resistance on the part of many Muslim girls and women in France,

---

[24] Nussbaum, *Women and Human Development*, p. 115, and Ch. 2 generally for her discussion of the problem of adaptive preferences.

[25] Uma Narayan, 'Minds of their Own: Choices, Autonomy, Cultural Practices, and Other Women', in *A Mind of One's Own: Feminist Essays on Reason and Objectivity*, eds. Louise Antony and Charlotte Witt (Boulder, CO: Westview Press, 2002 [2001]), p. 429.

Germany, and other European states.[26] The many factors that may contribute to the endorsement of a custom by a member of an ethnic or religious minority, and the different aspects of that 'choice'—which may or may not entail much in the way of visible reflexivity—are not well captured by the liberal autonomy conceptions discussed above. And in overlooking the complexity of individuals' own relationships to tradition, it would appear that the liberal autonomy framework would dispose the liberal state toward regulating or even censuring too wide a range of social customs that arguably should be accommodated.

ARRANGED MARRIAGE IN LIBERAL DEMOCRACIES

The custom of arranged marriage helps to highlight these questions regarding cultural tradition and autonomy, and also illustrates the limitations of the conceptions of autonomy discussed in the last section. A range of liberal and liberal feminist kinds of objections have been raised in connection with the custom, generally highlighting concerns about pressures that are put on girls and women to conform to traditional sex roles and arrangements, and the constriction of their freedom to choose when and whom to marry. Some worry that the framework of arranged marriage has intrinsically coercive features that are obfuscated by overly reverent and romanticized views of tradition. Okin, for instance, writes that

Some generally recognized human rights abuses have specifically gender-related forms that were not typically recognized as human rights abuses. Frequently, these abuses are perpetrated by more powerful family members against less powerful ones. For example, slavery is generally recognized as a fundamental violation of human rights. But parents giving their daughter in marriage in exchange for money or even selling her to a pimp has not typically been seen as an instance of slavery. If a husband pays a bride price for his wife or marries her without her adult consent; if he confines her to their home, forbids her to work for pay, or appropriates her wages; if he beats her for disobedience or mishap; these manifestations of slavery would not be recognized as violations of human rights in many parts of the world. In some parts, indeed, most of these acts would be regarded as quite within the limits of normal, culturally appropriate behavior in parents or husbands.[27]

---

[26] See for example arguments by Katherine Ewing, 'Legislating Religious Freedom: Muslim Challenges to the Relationship between "Church" and "State" in Germany and France', *Daedalus*, 129/4 (2000), 31–54, and Galeotti, 'Citizenship and Equality'.

[27] Okin, 'Feminism, Women's Human Rights, and Cultural Differences', p. 35.

Although I return to these concerns soon, I propose to discuss arranged marriage in political context rather than *tout court*. To do so, I focus below on the responses to this custom in contemporary Britain, where a public debate about arranged marriage was recently initiated by a Home Office inquiry into forced marriage. I pay particular attention to the assumptions about autonomy that informed the public framing of the issue of arranged marriage, and the policy questions and initiatives that emerged from the debate.

In Britain, with a large Hindu and Sikh population and an estimated 1 million Muslims (the majority of whom are South Asians), an estimated 10,000 arranged marriages take place each year. Arranged marriage is also, of course, the norm in many other countries, including some, such as India, which are constitutional democracies. In Europe, arranged marriage remains common in Muslim and Hindu communities; as there are over 23 million Muslims in Europe today, at least 6.8 million of whom reside in the European Union, the number of families and individuals involved is not insignificant.[28] While the vast majority of arranged marriages are understood to be broadly consensual, by some British estimates as many as 10 percent of these unions may be forced. Only a fraction of these come under the scrutiny of state agencies: annually in Britain, police and officials are asked to intervene in between 30 and 100 cases of girls who have been abducted (and sometimes drugged beforehand) by family members and forcibly sent back to India, Pakistan, or Bangladesh (where girls are permitted to marry from the age of 14 or 15) to be married.[29]

As in all other liberal democracies, arranged marriage is currently permitted in Britain. However, it is illegal to force a person into marriage; moreover, as Kukathas explains:

Under section 12 of the Matrimonial Causes Act 1973 a marriage can be annulled if it took place under 'duress', and the case of Hirani v. Hirani in 1982 established that the threat of social ostracism could place the individual under duress to a sufficient degree to determine that the marriage was not entered into voluntarily.[30]

Increasing reports of forced marriages, and the belief that a context of manipulation and coercion often surrounds the practice, have prompted outcries against the practice in Britain. A *London Standard* journalist demanded that the government should introduce legislation to ban customary marriages, following the death of a young Pakistani British woman: 'In every arranged marriage there is an element of compulsion that

---

[28] Ceri Peach and Günther Glebe, 'Muslim Minorities in Western Europe', in *Ethnic and Racial Studies*, 18/1 (1995), 26–45.

[29] 'Arranged Marriages Under the Spotlight', *Press Association Newsfile*, June 29, 2000.

[30] Kukathas, *The Liberal Archipelago*, p. 144.

should be wholly unacceptable in a civilized society, and young Rukhsana was its martyr ...'.[31] The case concerned a 19-year-old British Pakistani woman, Rukhsana Naz, who in 1998 was murdered by her mother and brother, who were subsequently tried and sentenced to life imprisonment in Nottingham Crown Court. Rukhsana had become pregnant by her boyfriend despite a forced marriage to an older Pakistani man at the age of 15, and for this she was killed. This case was the most extreme (and most high profile) example of a number of incidents that focused public attention on the custom of arranged marriage.[32] The British Home Office subsequently established a special Forced Marriages Working Group in 1999 to investigate the prevalence of specifically forced (as opposed to merely arranged) marriages and possible legal responses to this phenomenon.[33] The Group was composed of prominent Britons of South Asian descent, most notably the cochairs of the task force, Lord Ahmed of Rotherham and Baroness Udin of Bethnal Green.[34] Released on June 29, 2000, the final Report, *A Choice By Right*, estimates that about 1,000 forced marriages occur annually in Britain (or approximately 10% of the annual total).[35] The final report contains a number of recommendations for how government, police, and communities might better respond to the problem of arranged marriages, including increased social services and protection to help victims of forced marriage, and better training for service workers who may deal with cases of arranged marriage. It stresses the importance of community involvement in responses to forced marriages—particularly the need to include community-based organizations, especially women's groups—and urges better cooperation among the different agencies involved in dealing with the problem, such as child protection and domestic violence agencies. Finally, it recommends greater support and funding for safe housing and access to legal services for victims, and attention to the immigration laws that sometimes compound the vulnerability of women.[36]

[31] Brian Sewell, cited in Rachel Donnelly, 'Arranged Marriages Not Cultural Heritage but "Man-Made Law" ', *The Irish Times*, June 3, 1999, p. 13.

[32] Ibid.

[33] *The Daily Mail*, June 30, 2000, p. 27. Similarly, a report by the Council of British Pakistanis (Scotland chapter) estimates that 'around 10% of spouses aged between 16 and 25 are forced into marriages setup between immigrants from Pakistan and Pakistanis from Scotland without their consent', *The Herald* (Glasgow), July 7, 1999.

[34] The representative from the Southhall Black Sisters association resigned from the committee looking into arranged marriages in the British South Asian community on the grounds that some of the proposals it advanced would further disempower women in abusive families, but her concerns were registered in the process.

[35] *A Choice By Right: Report of the Working Group on Forced Marriages* (London: Home Office, U.K. Government, 2000) and *Forced Marriage Progress Report* (London: Home Office, U.K Government, 2001).

[36] *A Choice By Right*, pp. 22–5.

Following the release of an initial report on the phenomenon of forced marriages, the British Home Office task force decided to consult widely with South Asian community groups in order to gain a better sense of practices surrounding arranged marriage and the incidence and particular manifestation of forced marriages. This was part of a broader attempt to try to mediate between demands for cultural protections by South Asians who endorse the practice of customary marriages and concerns raised by state authorities and community groups in Britain. These consultations exposed community-wide criticisms of the use of force and intimidation in arranging customary marriages, and prompted calls for greater support services to protect vulnerable girls and women. At the same time, however, the consultations revealed wide support for the custom of arranged marriages and a sense of outrage that this custom should be confused or conflated with its forced variant. Traditionalists among the South Asian population in Britain have resented what they perceive as government and police interference with a central cultural practice in their communities. Significantly, even those segments of the South Asian community concerned about instances of coercion in marriage— women's and community groups as well as the Muslim Parliament of Great Britain—were, with few exceptions, intent on defending the custom of arranged marriage.

This response is consistent with a more general defense of arranged marriage as reflecting Asian cultural attitudes toward the critical importance and value of family; marriage is clearly a central part of this more traditional vision of family relationships, and the custom of arranged matches reinforces this institution. Although more Asian immigrant youth express an interest in the love-match ideal of relationships, in the limited studies that are available, it appears that many remain committed to the broader values that underpin the custom of arranged marriage.[37] And as some of its defenders maintain, the current form of arranged marriage in many places is closer to Western-style dating introduction services than it is to its historical predecessors.[38]

While the Working Group focused its attention on forced marriages— which it defined as 'a marriage conducted without the *full consent* of both parties and where *duress is a factor*'[39]—it is nonetheless important to note the

[37] See for example Nazli Kibria, 'The Construction of "Asian American": Reflections on Intermarriage and Ethnic Identity Among Second-Generation Chinese and Korean Americans', *Ethnic and Racial Studies,* 20/3 (1997), 523–44.

[38] South Asian newspapers at home and abroad commonly feature classified ads for arranged marriages, for example, prompting frequent analogies with Western-style ad dating. See for example Srikant Ramaswami, 'Marriages in Little India: Arranged Marriages, Union of Families', *Little India,* 5/7 (1995), 1–10.

[39] *Forced Marriage Progress Report—Update on the Joint Action Plan and Package of Care,* November 6, 2001.

broad characterization of arranged marriage that surfaced in the final report. The sharp contrast between arranged and forced marriages drawn by the task force focused on the absence—in forced marriage—of the consent of one or both parties to a marriage, and/or the presence of duress:

A clear distinction must be maintained between forced and arranged marriages. That distinction lies in the right to choose. The tradition of arranged marriage should be respected and valued.[40]

and

Arranged marriages are a successful and traditional method of parents taking a leading role in the future of their children. We do not wish to interfere with this role. However, a clear distinction exists between what constitutes an arranged marriage and what constitutes a forced marriage. In an arranged marriage, the consent of both parties is sought and given. In a forced marriage consent is not given.[41]

The emphatic distinction made between arranged and forced marriage was in part an attempt to reassure South Asian Britons that the former custom was not under attack, and so to secure the cooperation of community leaders.[42] Yet in insisting that arranged marriage and forced marriage shared nothing in common, a more nuanced analysis of the multifaceted forms of coercion that *may* operate in the custom of arranged marriage was simply not possible. And as Phillips and Dustin note, the government's framing of the issue of arranged marriage (through the Working Group) was in fact out of step with the ways that British courts have increasingly considered the social and psychological (rather than purely physical) circumstances of duress: 'The deference towards arranged marriage . . . is not in itself problematic. But when public authorities make the arranged/forced distinction so central to their initiatives, they have proved less sensitive than the courts to the complexities surrounding consent.'[43] Curiously, however, while leaving arranged marriage practically untouched, the Report acknowledges *forced* marriage may take many different forms: 'there is a spectrum of behaviours behind the term forced marriage, ranging from emotional pressure, exerted by close family members and the extended family, to the more extreme cases, which can involve threatening

---

[40] *A Choice by Right*, Summary of the report of the working group on forced marriage 2001, p. 3.

[41] *Forced Marriage—The Overseas Dimension*, Report of the Foreign and Commonwealth Office (U.K. Government, 2000).

[42] Anne Phillips and Moira Dustin, *U.K. Initiatives on Forced Marriage: Regulation, Dialogue and Exit*, Policy research paper, Nuffield Foundation (2003), pp. 10–11.

[43] Ibid., p. 16.

behaviour, abduction, imprisonment, physical violence, rape and in some cases murder'.[44]

A similar contrast was drawn by South Asian community groups involved in the consultation process. For example, the London-based Muslim Women's Helpline, a service organization dedicated to helping Muslim women in crisis, sharply distinguished between the custom of 'introduction' that characterizes arranged marriage and the coercion that marks forced marriage; they also emphasize that all adults have the right of choice under Islam, and should not be forced into any unions.[45] On one hand, it seems likely that women's service groups were keen to reinforce the notion that individual consent is what legitimates arranged marriage, and by doing so underscore the point that girls and women should not be forced to marry against their will. But more traditional lobby groups, such as the Muslim Parliament of Britain, also had good cause to emphasize the differences between arranged and forced marriage so as to reassure the task force and the British public that customary or arranged marriage falls well within the bounds of practices consistent with liberal democratic norms. The Rushdie Affair of 1989 had made plain the dearth of deliberative forums in British civil society in which Muslim groups could convey their dissent or argue for changes to existing laws, and relations with the state remained strained. This experience had left many British South Asians feeling mistrustful of government and the public at large, in the wake of the backlash against their communities.[46]

The oversharp contrast between arranged and forced marriage in Britain led to the recasting of arranged marriage as essentially a fully consensual form of marriage that differs only from mainstream 'love match' marriages in the role played by the family or community members in introducing prospective partners. One consequence of this characterization of arranged marriage was, as Phillips and Dustin note, 'to divert attention from more routinised and hidden forms of parental control that do not involve the dramas of imprisonment or abduction'.[47] And yet it seems undeniable that short of what would constitute forced marriage, less severe forms of pressure on young adults, particularly girls and young women, may also be present. While the Home Office report indeed discusses pressures that do not amount to coercion, it relies excessively on the act of consent as the single feature that distinguishes an arranged marriage from a union that is forced. This emphasis on consent

---

[44] *A Choice By Right*, p. 11.

[45] Interview with Najma Ibrahim, Muslim Women's Helpline, London, June 12, 2001.

[46] Adrian Favell, 'Multicultural Race Relations in Britain', in *Challenge to the Nation State: Immigration in Western Europe and the United States*, ed. Christian Joppke (Oxford: Oxford University Press, 1998), pp. 326–8.

[47] Phillips and Dustin, *U.K. Initiatives on Forced Marriage*, p. 16.

without a view to the circumstances (such as pressures and fear of reprisals on the part of families), helped ensure that a range of important but difficult questions about the practice went entirely ignored by the task force's work: Does the consent of both marriage parties suffice to assuage concerns about the autonomy of those being pressured to marry? Is it possible, as Narayan argues, for women to accept and in some sense 'choose' traditional arrangements in circumstances of tremendous pressure? And is it desirable or indeed possible to try to 'authenticate' the choices of girls and women in traditional cultural communities within liberal democratic states?

Construing arranged marriage in this way, however, it is possible that the task force may have hampered efforts to help girls and women in circumstances not as acute as those meriting the description of forced marriage. Indeed, looking only at clear cases of coerced marriage meant that the Working Group decided to focus on forced marriages involving overseas partners, rather than looking at the practices around traditional marriage more generally. This focus reflects the belief that forced marriages of Britons more often involve partners brought in from overseas (most often Pakistan, Bangladesh, and India) or a British national being sent overseas to marry, often using duplicitous and coercive means (stories of drugging teenage girls to ensure their compliance on flights to the Indian subcontinent were not uncommon). But as Phillips and Dustin have argued, the 'concentration on marriages involving overseas spouses feeds the view that all marriages arranged with overseas partners are suspect, and that all is well in the arrangement of marriages within the U.K'.[48]

While not warranting the regulation or policing of domestic arranged marriages, the findings of the Working Group and the testimonies of service groups working with women (and sometimes young men) in South Asian communities suggest that a broader and more candid discussion about this practice was needed. Decisions about whom children should marry are often hierarchical and may be filled with enormous pressure and manipulation; young men and women who are initially very reluctant to accept an arranged marriage may capitulate in defeat rather than lose the love and support of their families.[49] Invoking the simplistic dichotomy of arranged versus forced marriage, with the apparent act of consent distinguishing the former from the latter, these contextual features are left undiscussed. If a young woman agrees to a marriage partner chosen by her parents because she

---

[48] Ibid., p. 11.
[49] For one account of the difficulty of knowing when to intervene in such cases of extreme family pressure, as told from the perspective of a social worker, see Madeleine Fullerton, 'A Sikh Girl's Bridal Path', *New Society*, 64 (June 16, 1983), 428–9.

fears they will otherwise denounce or even disown her, does this count as consent? Or might such capitulation simply reflect—as Narayan's analysis suggests—the pragmatic compromises that women make in recognition of their desire to achieve certain ends or mixed bundles of goods, such as the support and acceptance of one's family? As these suggestions show, the British debate also had the effect of conflating the sheer variety of practices and values encompassed by the custom: some forms of arranged marriage are characterized merely by indirect family introductions, but many are not.

To explore the individual and social contexts in which cultural practices like arranged marriage take place, we will need to move beyond a simplistic understanding of consent as the single legitimating factor in marriage. In particular, there are good reasons not to exaggerate the extent to which arranged marriage manifests the free choices of fully autonomous agents, for at least two main reasons. First, by doing so we fail to ask about the circumstances surrounding arranged marriage, and particularly the conditions that may need to be present in order for agents to make real choices; as Anne Phillips argues, 'choice depends on substantive conditions. These include, at a minimum, having the political and civil freedoms that enable one to voice an objection, and the educational and employment opportunities that make exit a genuine choice.'[50] Second, to portray arranged marriage as a freely chosen arrangement agents make under the guidance of their parents may lead us to overlook more subtle forms of agency. In particular, it may cause us to ignore or even deny the possibility of agency for those living in constrictive or traditional environments. As Narayan writes:

The idea that women's values, attitudes, and choices can be impoverished and distorted by patriarchy should not be used so heavy-handedly as to *completely efface* the value and significance of these choices *from the point of view of the women who make them.* Despite undeniable distortions, these are in fact the values, attitudes, and choices that define for these women the lives they currently have and value, and the selves they currently are and in many ways want to remain.[51]

To understand why such grudging but ultimately willing acceptance of an arranged marriage might *not* constitute a violation of personal autonomy, we must first understand the value and practical benefits of this custom for different community members. Here the liberal autonomy framing of the issue in Britain is revealed as inadequate, for arranged marriage is not so much an arrangement that otherwise autonomous individuals opt into—or

---

[50] Anne Phillips, 'Multiculturalism, Universalism, and the Claims of Democracy', p. 136.
[51] Narayan, 'Minds of Their Own', pp. 422–3.

choose from among many options—so much as it is a framework for achieving other things of value, namely marriage, children, tradition, and family and social acceptance. Those best placed to address the issues raised by the social context of arranged marriage include, of course, community members themselves. But the Home Office inquiry, while encouraging discussion about the circumstances surrounding forced marriage, did not encourage this broader conversation. Indeed, arguably the Working Group did not want to engage cultural and religious differences at a very deep level, preferring instead to treat forced marriage as a criminal aberration that no group endorses. While this may have allayed concerns that arranged marriage might become the target of suspicion or regulation, it did little to engender the kind of confidence that more open community consultations on the issue would require.

In this way, arranged marriage was effectively normalized by the task force's discourse: by construing arranged marriage as a fully consensual arrangement undertaken by autonomous persons, the Working Group demanded that arranged marriage be understood as equivalent to Western models of marriage. In her examination of a legal case about arranged marriage brought to the European Court of Human Rights in 1985 (*Abdulaziz, Cabales and Balkandali* v. *United Kingdom*), Angie Means shows how the law functions to normalize customs like marriage by stipulating particular evidentiary norms and requirements when marriage is contested. In the case Means explores, the plaintiffs, all women, claimed that British immigration law was discriminatory in its interpretation of marriage and family, which they said made it difficult for them to bring their husbands (some of whom were married under traditional arrangements) to Britain. The women lost their case, with the effect that 'judges have been inclined to exclude spouses in cases of arranged marriage . . . [and] persons are generally excluded because they cannot offer convincing evidence that an arranged marriage is a real marriage'.[52]

Mere recognition of the validity of arranged unions, as in the case of the Working Group's report, does not necessarily challenge this normalization of marriage. If the litmus test for a custom's legitimacy is the extent to which the practice can be rendered compatible with prevailing public values (like consent), it will almost inevitably be presented and defended publicly in a normalized, liberal form.[53] Norms and values which are important to cultural

---

[52] Angelia Means, 'Intercultural Law: Justifying Rights to Others', unpublished manuscript (2002).

[53] Parekh defends arranged marriage as compatible with what he calls core, operative public values, but concludes that polygamy, female circumcision of children, and sati are not consistent with liberal democratic values and commitments. See *Rethinking Multiculturalism*, pp. 272 and 274–92.

group members, and the contested understandings of the social practices that these are bound up with, simply drop out of the public debate. And yet cultural differences in conceptions of self versus community and in attitudes toward important life choices are relevant to discussions of arranged marriage in ways not captured by the liberal framework. Defenders of arranged marriage frequently invoke a different psychological ideal in their communities, one that is more 'relational' and 'less individualistic' than dominant Western ideals of individual autonomy and individuation. Sawitri Saharso cites studies that indicate that notions of 'self' and the autonomy of self are peripheral to South Asians as compared with the central importance of family units and extended families.[54] A deeply intersubjective ethic of subjectivity is, on this view, inextricably linked with close-knit family structures and extended family clan systems, which stress interdependence and responsibility over independence.[55] A number of social, cultural, and psychological factors may therefore contribute to the desirability and acceptance of customary marriages in South Asian immigrant communities.[56]

The ideal of interdependence is not necessarily an unqualified good, of course. It may, for instance, make it difficult for British South Asian girls and women in particular to *refuse* certain arrangements or to explore nontraditional choices: as Saharso writes, they 'may find themselves hampered in their *psychological ability* to act autonomously'.[57] This concern has led some writers to argue that even on the thicker, more constitutive account of community, it is important to emphasize and support the basic autonomy of individuals, for 'to consider which particular attachments we should reshape, which to reject, which to choose, and which to promote, we need autonomy'.[58] However, if we employ a broader and thinner conception of autonomy, rather than a substantive conception of autonomy emphasizing self-direction and choice, we are more apt to capture important aspects of women's responses to cultural practices and arrangements. For instance, as Saharso notes, low 'interpersonal

---

[54] Saharso, 'Female Autonomy and Cultural Imperative', pp. 233 and 236–7.

[55] For an analysis of the importance of the ethic of responsibility in traditional and fundamentalist Muslim communities and its relationship to traditional family roles and arrangements, see Janet Afary, 'The War Against Feminism in the Name of the Almighty: Making Sense of Gender and Muslim Fundamentalism', *New Left Review*, 224 (1997), 89–110.

[56] A recent study of sixty young Asian Americans in Los Angeles and Boston showed that there is a strong preference on the part of young, second generation Chinese Americans and Korean Americans for marrying within their ethnic group or, failing that, other Asian Americans groups. Kibria, 'The Construction of "Asian American" ', 523–44.

[57] Saharso, 'Female Autonomy and Cultural Imperative', p. 228.

[58] Linda Barclay, 'Autonomy and the Social Self', in *Relational Autonomy: Feminist Perspectives on Autonomy, Agency, and the Social Self*, ed. Catriona Mackenzie and Natalie Stoljar (Oxford: Oxford University Press, 2000), p. 68.

autonomy' (or independence) may coexist with high 'intrapsychic autonomy,' or internal emotional strength and self-esteem.[59] Moreover, women make choices even from within highly restrictive, traditional environments, as Narayan argues. These less apparent aspects of women's agency are significant sources for helping to evaluate the validity of arranged marriage in liberal democracies such as Britain. Indeed, as I argue in the next section, these dimensions of self-hood and agency are particularly important to efforts by girls and women to revise and reinvent aspects of their own cultural traditions in ways that empower them.

FROM AUTONOMY TO AGENCY

As this brief exploration of arranged marriage suggests, there are good reasons to shift from asking whether contested cultural practices undermine or support personal autonomy, to asking about the range of actual and possible individual and social responses to specific customs and arrangements. A more adequate account of agency would acknowledge ever subtler expressions of reflexivity and action, such as subverting a cultural tradition from the inside. At the core of this broader understanding of agency that I propose to sketch here lies a procedural account of autonomy which emphasizes *degrees* of reflection about one's values and attachments, but does not insist that central aspects of one's identity must be submitted to significant critical scrutiny. This thinner, less idealized view of autonomy does not prescribe formal self-reflection about life choices but rather understands agency more broadly as any activity or expression that signals a response to a prevailing social norm, custom, role, or arrangement. Specifically, it attempts to draw attention to the myriad ways in which women in traditional cultures challenge, revise, and reaffirm aspects of cultural practices and arrangements, and argues that in so doing, they are exercising a form of procedural autonomy. Later I argue that these activities of resistance and affirmation speak to the validity and democratic legitimacy of contested cultural practices, such as arranged marriage.

Why should an account of procedural autonomy, however thinly conceptualized, be used to evaluate controversial social customs in liberal states?

[59] Saharso, 'Female Autonomy and Cultural Imperative', p. 235, and also Saharso, 'Is Freedom of the Will but a Western Illusion? Individual Autonomy, Gender and Multicultural Judgement', in *Sexual Justice/Cultural Justice*, eds. Barbara Arneil, Monique Deveaux, Rita Dhamoon, and Avigail Eisenberg (Routledge, forthcoming 2006).

First, without minimal procedural autonomy, cultural group members can be forced to participate in social arrangements through coercive means, without recourse to basic rights protections. In this respect, a conception of agency built upon a minimalist account of procedural autonomy shares with liberals an insistence on the importance of group 'exit rights'. Second, procedural autonomy is important to assessments about the validity of controversial social practices because it shapes individual agency in both private and public life. In their everyday lives, women must be able to resist and reshape roles and expectations that are oppressive to them without fear of repercussions such as physical threats and harm. Formal respect for the procedural auton-omy of women in traditional communities would mandate certain protec-tions against such harm, and support services funded by the liberal state whose aim would be to empower vulnerable women. If they are to resist, revise, and reform aspects of their cultural traditions, women's procedural autonomy therefore must be respected and protected; even rhetorical political support for this principle is a start. And finally, formal support of their procedural autonomy can help enable women to participate in the various forums of political deliberation in which their community's contested prac-tices and arrangements are discussed.

The philosopher Marilyn Friedman has also recently defended a proced-ural, content-neutral view of autonomy that she claims is compatible with the choices and lifestyles of women in more traditional communities.[60] On her view, 'autonomy competency is the effective capacity, or set of capacities, to act under some significant range of circumstances in ways that reflect and issue from deeper concerns that one has considered and reaffirmed'.[61] As with Meyers' moderate liberal conception of autonomy discussed earlier, what is necessary on Friedman's view is a minimal degree of self-reflexivity. This reflexivity does not so much signal a necessary distance from one's traditions, on her view, so much as it requires that one be capable of considering and affirming attachments and projects that one finds valuable: 'Autonomous choices and behavior must also be self-reflective ... they must reflect, or mirror, the wants, desires, cares, concerns, values, and commitments that someone reaffirms when attending to them.'[62] Importantly, however, unlike Meyers, Friedman intends for her conception of autonomy to include decisions and practices undertaken in fairly restrictive environments—ones in which independence is not especially valued or supported:

---

[60] Marilyn Friedman, *Autonomy, Gender, and Politics* (Oxford: Oxford University Press, 2003), p. 21.
[61] Ibid., p. 13.   [62] Ibid., p. 6.

Even if women affirm and choose according to norms of femininity in accord with which they were socialized, and even if these norms divert women from valuing and pursuing autonomy, women could still be content-neutrally autonomous so long as their choices in general accorded with and issued from their deeper wants and commitments. Even if a woman's deeper concerns include subservient roles and relationships and she lacks a commitment to her own autonomy as a value ... women could still be content-neutrally autonomous in pursuing the deep, traditional concerns other than the autonomy they happen to have.[63]

One intended effect of Friedman's view is that autonomy should become more 'widely applicable' in the sense that 'more people can qualify as autonomous'.[64] Despite the seeming flexibility and expansiveness of Friedman's procedural conception of autonomy, however, she introduces conditions that might circumscribe, rather than expand, the scope of legitimate traditional cultural practices. In particular, Friedman insists that consent should be the litmus test for the defense of cultural minority practices in both minority and majority cultures.[65] She rightly points out that both liberal societies and minority cultures within these societies tend equally to appeal to consent to establish the legitimacy of a practice, and suggests that this could be a point of convergence. But for Friedman, mere consent is not enough, for it is only meaningful against the background of extensive autonomy-enhancing conditions. In addition to transparent consent, Friedman stipulates two further conditions required for women's procedural autonomy:

First, women's choices would have to be made under conditions that promoted the general reliability of their choices. This would require that women be able to choose among a significant and morally acceptable array of alternatives and that they be able to make their choices relatively free of coercion, manipulation, and deception.

and

Second, women must have been able to develop, earlier in life, the capacities needed to reflect on their situations and make decisions about them.[66]

While the conditions Friedman proposes for evaluating the authenticity of women's choices do not seem especially strenuous, they take her further in the direction of a substantive, comprehensive conception of autonomy than she perhaps recognizes. This will effectively limit the range of practices that liberal states can permit, for as Friedman argues, 'if positive evidence reveals cultural conditions that impede the development of autonomy competencies in women or that prevent its exercise, then the consent of women living under those conditions does not justify the rights-violation

---

[63] Ibid., p. 24.   [64] Ibid., p. 23.   [65] Ibid., p. 187.   [66] Ibid., p. 188.

practices'.[67] The first of the two above conditions stipulated by Friedman appears to deny that women could value or affirm traditional roles and arrangements where the only real option is group exit; while this may be true for some women, it is surely not so for all women in minority cultural communities, particularly new immigrants. The second condition, while a laudable goal, is potentially demanding enough that it would require that liberal states eliminate certain forms of education, such as religious schooling that reinforces traditional sexual roles. Just how Friedman intends for this second condition to be applied in practice is not clear, but I argue that it could well lead liberal states to unjustly prohibit a wide range of educational and cultural practices.

Uma Narayan has also suggested that a number of cultural practices that do not warrant state intervention (in the form of prohibition) would probably fail Friedman's autonomy test, primarily because her conception of autonomy prohibits evidence of coercion and manipulation.[68] Although Narayan's claim that individual agency is compatible with even significant forms of coercion seems doubtful, her broader point that autonomy may be exercised within the context of very strong social constraints and pressures is insightful and instructive. Using the phrase 'bargaining with patriarchy' to describe the various ways in which women negotiate customs from within seemingly oppressive constraints, Narayan contends that 'there is active agency involved in women's compliance with patriarchal structures, even when the stakes involved in noncompliance and the pressures that enjoin compliance are very high'.[69] The example of arranged marriage belies the liberal feminist claim that women cannot exercise autonomy in 'oppressive cultural contexts', according to Narayan. Educated, upper-class Indian women often make pragmatic choices in favor of arranged marriage despite their own misgivings about aspects of the custom; they do so, Narayan argues, amidst tremendous family pressures, but do so in accordance with what they themselves value, fully aware of the trade-offs and implications of their choices.[70]

Although Friedman's thin account of procedural autonomy is helpful in certain respects, then, it neglects the forms of agency that are possible even within socially and culturally restrictive settings. It assumes—in a way that Nussbaum and O'Neill's perspectives do—that the availability of many different options (in a recognizably liberal sense) is necessary to authenticate the decisions of agents. One of the difficulties with this view, as Avigail Eisenberg

[67] Ibid., p. 192.
[68] Narayan, 'Minds of Their Own', p. 428.
[69] Ibid., pp. 421 and 422.
[70] Ibid., p. 424.

has argued, is that it tends to quickly frame a conflict between liberal rights and liberty and cultural communities' ostensibly incommensurable values and practices, and so to produce 'irreconcilable choices'.[71] Indeed, it would seem that this framing could have the effect of precipitating a reactionary defense of traditions in many communities—or a 'defensively self-protective' response, as Yasmin Alibhai-Brown has argued.[72] In part this is because this approach places the onus on minority cultural communities to show that their customs or arrangements do not violate these norms. Instead of using autonomy, and specifically, consent in this way, I suggest that we direct our attention to both the actual and possible expressions of agency in connection with cultural practices that have been drawn into question either by the liberal state or by some group members themselves. What is the range of actual and possible responses to the practice of, for example, arranged marriage, among South Asian Britons? What are some of the views that women in particular have voiced in response to the custom—concerns that they might have raised? And what social changes and supports might make it possible for girls and women who may not want an arranged marriage to express this desire without incurring serious 'psychosocial costs of exit'?[73]

To speak of agents' abilities to reflect upon and respond to social practices, and also their deliberative capacities to evaluate, endorse or accept, and reject customs, clearly entails some account of autonomy. My aim is to shift autonomy to a more ancillary role in debates about contested cultural practices, and to speak instead of 'agency,' which I understand as including a person's subjectivity more generally—including, for example, internal psychological processes, and responses that we would not necessarily characterize as illustrating easily recognizable forms of action and independence. To do so, I propose to endorse a modified version of Friedman's procedural account of autonomy, one amended by Narayan's critical insights. If we follow Friedman's feminist rethinking of this concept and dispense with the idea of personal autonomy as either a substantive, perfectionist ideal, or even as a capacity or competency that is demonstrated through self-directed actions and the formation of independent ideals, an alternative understanding of agency comes into view. This formulation acknowledges that individuals may affirm particular cultural practices (or aspects of practices) that are

---

[71] Eisenberg's comments are directed at Nussbaum's emphasis on women's autonomy and rights in *Sex and Social Justice*; see Avigail Eisenberg, 'Context, Cultural Difference, Sex and Social Justice', *Canadian Journal of Political Science*, 35/3 (2002), 613–28, p. 622.

[72] Yasmin Alibhai-Brown, 'After Multiculturalism', *The Political Quarterly*, special issue, 'Citizens: Towards a Citizenship Culture' (2001), 47–56, p. 47.

[73] See Oonagh Reitman, 'On Exit', in *Minorities Within Minorities*, eds. Avigail Eisenberg and Jeff Spinner-Halev (Cambridge: Cambridge University Press, 2005).

important to their own sense of themselves as members of families and communities and yet which entail a lack of obvious 'choice'. What is needed, on this account, for choices to count in some basic sense as *reflective* is the capacity to connect self-reflection with action: as Friedman writes, '[t]o realize autonomy, self-reflections must also be partly effective in determining someone's behavior'.[74] But for Friedman, autonomy also presupposes a coherent sense of self than is, I argue, strictly necessary: she emphasizes 'capacities not only for choices and actions that reflect superficial or momentary concerns but actions that bear a deeper connection to a perspective that constitutes her distinctive identity as an enduring self'.[75] Friedman hastens to add that self-reflective activity need not always be conscious, or even 'highly deliberate', and I agree,[76] but on my view, to count as an expression of agency, actions need only be reflexive to the extent that they reflect or help to secure something that a person has cause to value.

This more minimalist account of autonomy as requiring neither independence from one's social context nor, necessarily, a strong sense of self-definition within that environment is, I argue, flexible and expansive enough to include a much wider range of cultural practices and responses to those practices. It is moreover broad enough to encompass a range of evaluative activities and forms of expression that, as I shortly argue, speak more directly to the legitimacy or illegitimacy of cultural practices. If, following Narayan, we also reject certain of Friedman's strong side-constraints on anything that could count as coercion and manipulation, an even wider range of women's actions and decisions can be seen (and supported) as expressions of agency. Indeed, I would go along with Narayan here, who argues that '[c]hoices to engage in a "cultural practice," where the woman's values and identity are in part "invested and served by the practice," even if she does not care for certain aspects of the practice and lacks the power to negotiate modifications, would certainly meet [the] test for procedural autonomy.'[77]

The account of agency sketched here recognizes that people's relationships to their social and cultural arrangements and practices are complex and not best characterized as matters of either autonomous choice or oppressive constraints. In acknowledging that agency is possible even within highly restrictive social and cultural environments, this view may have distinct advantages in discussions about nonliberal or traditional cultural practices.

---

[74] Friedman, *Autonomy, Gender, Politics*, p. 5.   [75] Ibid., p. 7.

[76] Ibid., p. 8. Linda Barclay also raises and rejects the suggestion that 'a procedural notion of autonomy [necessarily] valorizes critical reflection and choice over and above the integrity and longevity of relationships ...'; see her 'Autonomy and the Social Self', p. 60.

[77] Narayan, 'Minds of Their Own', pp. 429–30.

Because it shifts our attention away from a substantive understanding of autonomy as the formation of coherent life plans, it directs us instead to look at individuals' own complex and myriad responses to social customs. A view of agency that includes not only choices, but also acceptance of roles and practices that are broadly reflective of what one values, can easily comprise resistance to (and reinvention of) traditional sex roles in traditional cultural communities. From girls' seemingly innocuous but nonetheless subversive modifications of conventional clothing styles in devout religious communities, to significant alterations of customs surrounding marriage, dowry payment, and sexual relations and child-rearing practices in culturally traditional communities—these and other forms of practices become recognized as possible sources of agency. We are prompted to ask not only about the ways in which individuals may resist cultural practices, therefore, but also about the many ways in which vulnerable group members may revise and reinvent certain traditions to empower themselves. Nor is this account of agency purely descriptive; for in attending to individuals' complex responses, it can also suggest creative strategies for reinventing customs. There is also, a normative dimension to such a view of autonomy, in that these responses can come to present a picture of the normative validity—or lack thereof—of particular practices and arrangements.

To this more optimistic picture of women's responses to cultural practices in traditional cultures, I add an important proviso. In addition to broadening our understanding of what counts as autonomy in more traditional cultural communities—and what this in turn reveals about the validity or nonvalidity of social practices—we must also seriously consider the tangible infrastructure that procedural autonomy requires. The idea of a moral minimum, introduced in Chapter 1, is critical here: group members ought not to be forced to comply with cultural practices that they reject; children ought not to be physically harmed in a permanent way; and existing laws prohibiting such force and demonstrable harm ought to be enforced. Criminal laws punishing those who attempt to coerce group members into cultural compliance, for example, forced marriages, are essential as supports for even minimal autonomy.[78] Protections for girls and women who make difficult choices to reject or to leave abusive marriages and family situations are also essential.[79]

---

[78] See also Okin, ' "Mistresses of their Own Destiny" '.

[79] There is a wealth of literature by South Asian women's organizations proposing particular supports for girls and women in abusive situations; see, for example, 'Growing Up Young, Asian and Female in Britain: A Report on Self-Harm and Suicide', Newham Asian Women's Project and Newham Innercity Multifund, 1998. There is also abundant sociological literature that also offers up policy proposals, such as, e.g., Margaret Abraham, *Speaking the Unspeakable: Marital Violence Against South Asian Immigrants in the United States* (Rutgers, NJ: Rutgers University Press, 2000).

Moreover, as noted earlier, liberal democratic states must ensure real exit options for cultural group members, as well as ensure that those who choose alternatives to traditional lifestyles and arrangements are not physically threatened or harmed, or subjected to psychological abuse (even though the social costs ultimately incurred by these individuals may be great). Liberal democratic states can and must help to supply tangible supports and infrastructure that protect such dissenting individuals (e.g. by providing safe-houses for abused women and runaway teenagers from immigrant communities or funding for local self-help initiatives).[80] These are background conditions for any future transformation of social practices, however, and do not supplant the work that needs to be done—through community consultations, deliberations, and inter- and intra-culturaldialogue—if customs and arrangements are to be responsive to members' changing lives and needs.

CONCLUSION: AUTONOMY AND DEMOCRATIC PRACTICE

I have argued that the substantive ideal of autonomy as independence and the more moderate views of autonomy as consisting of either self-determination or (less strenuously) self-definition would lead us to reject a number of cultural practices and arrangements prematurely. Traditional sex-role socialization is anathema to autonomy, on these accounts. Even Meyers' programmic conception of autonomy insists that the 'unconscious assimilation of cultural practices' makes it difficult for people to develop their own life plans or identify their own motives and desires.[81] Restrictive social and cultural roles are therefore just as problematic for the self-definition conception of autonomy as for the substantive free will conception of autonomy as a perfectionist ideal. In their place, I defended a minimalist, procedural understanding of agency that is both substantively thinner than these other accounts and broader in its scope, in terms of what 'counts' as agency. My hope is that this more complex and expansive conception of autonomy, and of the many places and forms in which agency is exercised, may help to direct our attention to the ways in which cultural group members—and women in particular—exercise self-definition and agency in their individual and social responses to social customs.

---

[80] For example, Britain is considering legislation that would add to existing sex crimes the crime of aiding abduction to assist a forced marriage; it would be punishable by a long jail term. Increased police monitoring and support for girls and women who refuse marriage matches has also been promised following the recent task force commissioned by the Home Office.

[81] Meyers, *Self, Society, and Personal Choice*, pp. 207 and 181.

When applied to the issue of arranged marriage, a procedural account of autonomy as requiring minimal self-definition and opportunities for refusal easily supports the claim that *forced* marriages violate individuals' autonomy in unacceptable ways. Such force clearly violates the minimal criteria of procedural autonomy, which includes the capacity to refuse unwanted arrangements without fear of harm and repercussions. As Kymlicka writes, a liberal state cannot 'allow the group to restrict the basic civil liberties of its members in the name of the "sacredness" of a particular cultural tradition or practice'.[82] But as we have seen, beyond the clear cases of forced marriage, the ideal of liberal autonomy is of little use in illuminating the goods at stake in arranged marriage. An idealized conception of autonomy as independence makes it difficult to conceive of (nonforced) arranged marriage as anything but an illiberal practice, for it is a custom that shifts responsibility for (and control over) one of the most central decisions of one's life to others. The thinner account of autonomy that I defend does not idealize autonomy or require independence per se, and as such is, I believe, a better starting point for exploring other, less visible, aspects of women's agency and empowerment in culturally traditional settings.

This more minimal account of procedural autonomy can also help us to explore three important dimensions of women's agency within arranged marriage that have been largely overlooked. The first of these concerns women's power within the family, extended family, and social networks to negotiate certain terms of marriage as well as to convey their expectations and needs. Sometimes this is much in evidence, as in the case of the authority and decision-making capacity of older or 'senior' women in a family. Usha Menon describes this power: 'senior women, secure in their positions within the family, engage with impunity in verbal and nonverbal displays of discontent: complaining loudly, withholding advice, and not cooperating are ways whereby confident and dominant women express their dissatisfaction and displeasure with what is happening within the family.'[83] There are of course dangers that accompany such power: it can be manipulative and fail to respect others' choices, and it is characteristically concentrated in the hands of some rather than shared. But it is not mutually exclusive with the exercise of counterveiling forms of power by others: even younger women, lacking authority in traditional families, may be able to express their opposition to any number of aspects of their lives through acts of resistance and subversion.[84]

---

[82] Kymlicka, 'Do We Need a Liberal Theory of Minority Rights?', p. 83.
[83] Menon, 'Does Feminism Have Universal Relevance?', p. 92.
[84] Moore, *Gender, Law, And Resistance In India.*

A second aspect of agency not recognized by the liberal autonomy framework is the way in which girls and women imagine, articulate, and begin to live out changed or altered forms of cultural practices. This can take the form of dramatic reinvention of, and resistance to particular social customs, such as the rejection of arranged marriage for oneself and the choice of a love match instead, or insistence on completing one's university studies and beginning a career prior to marriage, against family pressures. The role of cultural imagination in changing the lived experience of traditions such as arranged marriage is a critical factor here. Writing on this issue, Catriona Mackenzie has noted that although much attention has been focused on the social structures that impede women's autonomy, little attention has been given to the initial stage of change, in which 'innovative cultural imagery... (can play)... a liberating role'.[85] Such cultural imagery may only precipitate subtle kinds of adjustments, but might also lead to resisting or breaking stereotypes through unconventional choices. Such resistance is depicted, for example, by the decision of Jess Bhamra, a young Indian Briton played by Parminder Nagra, to pursue a professional football career in Gurinder Chadha's 2002 film, *Bend it Like Beckham*. It is also evident in one of the main cultural shifts in which British South Asian girls and women have participated, namely the practice of placing one's own ads in Indian immigrant newspapers seeking marriage partners.[86] This shift arguably changes the nature of arranged marriage for many, for it puts women far more at the center of the process than was previously the case.[87]

A final dimension of women's agency that is not captured by the liberal conceptions of autonomy discussed earlier in this chapter is the political response to forced marriage, both formal and informal, by South Asian women. Following the tragic death of Rukhsana Naz, the Muslim Parliament of Great Britain sponsored a national campaign—Muslims Against Forced Marriages—to alert South Asian communities of the important distinction between forced and arranged marriages, and to stress the need for mutual consent of the marriage partners. Women were an important part of this campaign. Similarly, some of the individuals included in the Home Office's

---

[85] Mackenzie, 'Imagining Oneself Otherwise', p. 143.

[86] Ramdas Menon, 'Arranged Marriages Among South Asian Immigrants', *Sociology and Social Research*, 73/4 (July 1989), 180–1.

[87] Some have argued that arranged marriages are not so different from dating via the Internet, newspaper ads, and introduction services, and that it is simply a more elaborate version of Western practices in which families make inquiries into the reputation and prospects of their children's prospective marriage partners.

task force represented women's rights groups that have actively opposed coerced marriages, such as the An-Nisa Society, Belgrave Baheno, and Southall Black Sisters. Although these representatives disagreed about the best way to combat the problem of forced marriages—and indeed the representative from Southall Black Sisters resigned in protest on the eve of the release of the Final Report—they were convinced of the political importance of their task. Far from rejecting their political role, the representatives of these women's groups used the Home Office's inquiry as an opportunity to complain that the British government was failing in its duties to cultural and community groups by withdrawing badly needed funding for community-run local services.[88]

Aside from these more manifestly political examples of individual and social responses to the practice of arranged marriage, there are subtler, but not insignificant, cultural shifts taking place in the perception and practices surrounding this custom in the Indian subcontinent and in diasporic communities. Many of these changes are discussed by sociologists and social and cultural anthropologists who address arranged marriage. Fiction writers provide another vista into the myriad ways in which men and women resist and revise the cultural frameworks they have in some sense received. In her collection of short stories entitled *Arranged Marriage*, US-based author Chitra Banerjee Divakaruni portrays Indian heroines as responding in a wide range of ways to the custom of arranged marriage: in 'The Word Love', an Indian student living in Berkeley moves in with her American lover only to have her mother disown her, prompting her to face the incommensurability of her life choices with those of her mother; in 'Affair', Abha resolves to leave a loveless marriage after seeing her friend Meena choose an unconventional love, sending ripples of both scandal and possibility through their close-knit community; and in 'Clothes,' Sumita agrees to an arranged marriage in India and follows her husband to America, where she comes to love him quite against her own expectations.[89] These and other stories of Indian women revising their own cultural scripts and finding ways to confront social expectations and traditions without losing their own sense of self suggest that agency and self-definition is possible in even the most difficult of circumstances. These accounts furthermore illustrate how women's agency is often directed toward negotiating and transforming social and cultural practices through everyday actions, responses, and choices.

---

[88] For example, Najma Ibrahim of the Muslim Women's Helpline, a faith-based group, reports that her group lost two grants from the Home Office around this time.

[89] Chitra Divakaruni, *Arranged Marriage* (New York: Anchor Books, 1996).

The observation that cultural group members revise and remake their own traditions and customs is of course a general truism among social and cultural anthropologists. Sally Engle Merry articulates this (by now) noncontroversial observation:

Culture is now understood as historically produced rather than static; unbounded rather than bounded and integrated; contested rather than consensual; incorporated within structures of power such as the construction of hegemony; rooted in practices, symbols, habits, patterns of practical mastery and practical rationality within categories of meaning rather than any simple dichotomy between ideas and behaviour; and negotiated and constructed through human action rather than superorganic forces.[90]

Although this more fluid understanding of culture—which credits individuals with the ongoing revision of social practices, cultural meanings, and community arrangements—is not a new insight for anthropologists, it has only recently begun to impact discussions within political theory about controversial cultural practices in liberal democratic states.[91] As Gurpreet Mahajan has argued in the case of India, normative political theorists have construed tensions between liberal norms and cultural traditions as requiring that we opt for one of two possibilities: either the transcendence of community identities and their replacement with secular liberal democratic principles; or else the embrace of traditional cultural structures as a foundation to country-specific forms of democracy.[92] Ongoing efforts by cultural group members to adapt, resist, and revise aspects of their own social practices and arrangements appear to play no role in either of these two models. Yet these informal democratic activities are critical sources of cultural change; moreover, they can speak to the question of the legitimacy or illegitimacy of controversial cultural practices.

I have argued that cultural practices seemingly at odds with dominant liberal conceptions of autonomy are best approached not by showing that the custom falls short of an ideal of independence, but rather by asking about the shifting cultural contexts in which such practices appear and the resulting individual and social responses. Liberal norms of consent and choice cause both defenders and critics of contested practice to characterize contested customs as overly static: they are seen as either compatible with, or in violation of, core values of liberal society. Rather than seeking to discover whether specific social practices violate (or, contrarily, support) personal autonomy, we should instead ask about individual and social responses to

---

[90] Merry, 'Changing Rights, Changing Culture', pp. 41–42.

[91] Also see Scott, 'Culture in Political Theory'.

[92] Gurpreet Mahajan, *Identities and Rights: Aspects of Liberal Democracy in India* (Oxford and Delhi: Oxford University Press, 1998), pp. 14–15.

contested cultural practices, including the extent to which members can revise and transform customs in accordance with their own needs and values. Agency, construed more broadly than liberal conceptions of personal autonomy, remains important to discussions about the validity of contested cultural practices, but mainly insofar as it illuminates the evaluative and transformative activities of group members vis-à-vis social customs in flux.

Does such a contextualized approach both to autonomy and to questions about the validity of gendered cultural practices merely reflect one of many possible ' "cultural justifications" for violating women's human rights' that some have warned about?[93] I think not. The ways in which British South Asian girls and women respond to cultural practices in their communities through acts of revision, reinvention, and resistance is inextricably bound up with the validity of those customs. More generally, how women affected by controversial customs evaluate and propose to reform their own cultural arrangements is critical to a democratic resolution of disputes surrounding these practices.

[93] Okin, 'Feminism, Women's Human Rights, and Cultural Differences', p. 45.

7

Gender and Cultural Justice in South Africa

The controversy over the status of African customary law in postapartheid South Africa illuminates some of the main tensions between cultural group accommodation and individual sex equality protections. As an instance of a state's attempting to balance constitutional recognition for both liberal and traditional, or customary, systems of law, this may prove to be a particularly instructive case for other culturally plural, democratic societies. South Africa's 1996 Constitution, widely hailed as the most liberal in the world, recognizes African customary law—with its patrilineal systems of inheritance and political rule, and patriarchal customs of family law—and yet paradoxically offers extensive protection for individual rights and equality, including sex equality. The legal and constitutional tensions created by these seemingly contradictory protections have given rise to recent court cases in which black women have cited sex discrimination as a result of applying customary law. These legal challenges, and the surrounding robust political debate over the future status of customary law in a liberal and democratic South Africa, provide an occasion for thinking about how such dilemmas of cultural accommodation might justly be resolved.

The South African debate over the status of customary law illustrates my claim that constitutional and legislative tensions between cultural rights and sex equality protections should be understood as primarily *political* tensions, rather than as entrenched conflicts over moral values. The controversy over customary law's future constitutional status, in which African traditionalists went head-to-head with liberal equality advocates, is a particularly good example of the strategic character of cultural disputes. More of a political than a moral or metaphysical dilemma—in Rawls' sense of the distinction[1]—the customary law dispute shows how misleading it is to view tensions between traditional cultures and liberal constitutional norms as strictly a struggle between opposing normative frameworks. In South Africa, this misconception has led to an unfortunate and deeply unhelpful framing of

---

[1] John Rawls, 'Justice as Fairness: Political not Metaphysical', *Philosophy and Public Affairs*, 14 (1985), 223–51 and *Political Liberalism* (New York: Columbia University Press, 1993).

the customary law debate as a choice 'between culture and equality'.[2] When understood instead as primarily political conflicts—or as conflicts of power and interests—tensions between cultural recognition and equality (especially sex equality) may emerge as more amenable to resolution, with effective conflict-negotiation processes in place.

The South African case shows why neither judicial decisions alone, nor bald appeals to liberal norms and principles as trumps, can provide a feasible resolution to cultural conflicts. Instead, where traditional systems of law and constitutional guarantees of individual rights are at odds, a strategy of negotiating disagreements democratically by means of practical deliberation among stakeholders is normatively preferable. But legal and legislative processes for settling rights conflicts can also be made more deliberative, and indeed, rights may sometimes include deliberative dimensions. In South Africa, I argue, the constitutional debate and subsequent efforts to reform customary marriage through legislative means exemplify certain aspects of the deliberative approach to cultural conflicts developed in the last chapter.

CUSTOMARY LAW AND SEX EQUALITY IN SOUTH AFRICA

South Africa's 1996 Constitution promises more extensive legal protection of individual rights than probably any other contemporary liberal state. Especially notable is its inclusion of racial and sex equality, as well as protection from discrimination on the basis of sexual orientation. Section 1 (b) of chapter one proclaims a commitment to 'nonracialism and non-sexism', and the Bill of Rights embedded in the constitution includes a section on equality stating that neither the state nor individuals may 'unfairly discriminate directly or indirectly against anyone on one or more grounds, including race, gender, sex, pregnancy, marital status, ethnic or social origin, colour, sexual orientation, age, disability, religion, conscience, belief, culture, language, and birth'. The Constitution is also far-reaching in its protection of cultural rights, in recognition of the country's deep social diversity: With respect to culture, section 31 (1a, 1b) of the Bill of Rights states that 'persons belonging to a cultural, religious or linguistic community may not be denied the right, with other members of their community, to (a) enjoy their culture, practice their religion, and use their language; and (b) form, join and maintain cultural, religious and linguistic associations and other organs of civil

---

[2] W. Van Der Meide, 'Gender Equality v. Right to Culture', *South African Law Journal*, 116 (1999), 100–12, p. 112.

society'.[3] The juxtaposition of these individual equality rights and cultural group protections has, however, proven predictably problematic.

Protection for culture has been interpreted in the South African context as including formal recognition of African customary law as it has developed and been codified over the years. The precise degree of recognition customary law would enjoy, however, was a subject of much heated debate during the constitution building process, as I discuss shortly. Briefly, traditional leaders sought to establish 'customary law and general South African law [as] parallel legal systems, neither empowered to interfere with the other', as in nearby Zimbabwe.[4] Traditional leaders were keen to establish the independent authority of customary law at this time because aspects of customary law stand in conflict with the provisions in the new Bill of Rights. Chiefs worried that customary restrictions on women's ability to hold and inherit property and traditional leaders' own patrilineal system of leadership and succession might be struck down or ruled unconstitutional.

In the constitutional process leading up to adoption of the 1993 Interim Constitution, traditional leaders sought, but ultimately failed, to ensure that customary law would in no respect be limited by the Bill of Rights. Women's rights activists, by contrast, wanted the equality clauses in the Bill of Rights to supersede the authority of customary law, especially in cases of conflicting principles and protections. Facing pressure and seemingly irreconcilable demands from African traditional leaders, legal reform groups, and women's rights advocates, the drafters opted to recognize customary law alongside individual equality rights, leaving the precise relationship between the two indeterminate. By contrast, the final 1996 Constitution recognizes the legitimacy of customary law but indicates quite clearly that specific applications are limited by the fundamental rights guaranteed in the document.[5] Additionally, in the list of nonderogable rights cited in the Bill of Rights, the right to equality is listed—'with respect to race and sex only'—along with human dignity, life, and several others, but not culture.

Despite this affirmation of the equal rights of South African citizens, it remains unclear 'whether the Bill of Rights should apply directly or indirectly to common law and to customary law'.[6] Effectively, this leaves open the question of how conflicts between constitutional provisions and practices

---

[3] *Constitution of the Republic of South Africa* (1996), ch. 2 (Bill of Rights), section 9 (3).

[4] Ian Currie, 'The Future of Customary Law: Lessons from the *Lobolo* Debate', in *Gender and the New South African Legal Order*, ed. C. Murray (Kenwyn, South Africa: Juta, 1994), p. 149.

[5] *Constitution of the Republic of South Africa* (1996), ch. 2, section 39 [2, 3].

[6] Chuma Himonga and Craig Bosch, 'The Application of African Customary Law Under the Constitution of South Africa: Problems Solved or Just Beginning?', *South African Law Journal*, 117 (2000), 306–41, p. 316.

associated with customary law will be treated in future. Indeed, some South African courts have interpreted the sections pertaining to culture in the Constitution as reaffirming the relative autonomy—and authority—of customary law in matters of family law and inheritance rights, despite protest from women's equality proponents. In June 2000, for example, the South African Supreme Court of Appeal upheld protection for the custom of male primogeniture (or male-line inheritance) against a constitutional challenge, arguing that 'women, if married under African customary law, are bereft of all rights under a matrimonial property regime'.[7] Yet four years later, three important cases posing a similar challenge to primogeniture[8] resulted in the striking down of the sexually discriminatory provisions of the Black Administration Act of 1927 as regards succession. The legal void left when customs are deemed invalid, and the difficulty of fully implementing reforms through the courts, means there is still clearly a pressing need for legislative reform of many aspects of customary law, and deliberations about the validity of contested social and cultural practices more generally.

Despite recent court decisions, then, which increasingly uphold the Constitution's emphasis on equality rights, important tensions persist between traditional practices and certain individual rights enshrined in the Bill of Rights. This is particularly so in such areas as family law, property law, inheritance, and succession. Human rights advocates and women's rights lobbyists have mounted legal challenges in order to draw attention to these conflicts. In this chapter, I focus on efforts to reform customary marriage practices in South Africa so as to bring certain traditions in line with the Constitution.

SOURCES OF CONFLICT

In order to understand the nature and depth of the tensions between customary law and sex equality in South Africa, it is helpful to know how this system of law has developed in the modern era. The version of customary

---

[7] Khadija Magardie, 'Customary Law Undermines Constitutional Rights', *Mail and Guardian*, June 22, 2000, p. 1. In the case in question, a widow challenged her father-in-law's right to inherit the property of her deceased husband, claiming that the law of male primogeniture 'was unconstitutional because it violated her right to gender equality'. The father-in-law claimed that 'no customary union in fact existed because her family had only paid a part installment towards her lobola (bridewealth)', an argument that the court accepted in ruling against the appellant.

[8] Under primogeniture, the property of men who die intestate goes to their male heirs, and if they have none, goes to the eldest (near) male relative.

law recognized by the Constitution is known as the 'official code of customary law', which colonial courts and administrators formalized in the nineteenth and first half of the twentieth centuries; according to customary law specialist T.W. Bennett, this official version is widely believed to have 'exaggerated the subordinate status of women,' and even contributed to a 'decline in [women's] overall status'.[9] A parallel development that further entrenched African women's subordination was the spread of capitalism, for although it 'forced women to play roles never expected of them by traditional society, its long-term effect was to downgrade or marginalize women in both the family and market place'.[10]

A still more sinister side to the development of customary law in South Africa lies in the history of manipulation and cooptation of traditional leaders by colonial and Apartheid administrators. Under Apartheid, administrators strategically reinforced the cultural differences of African groups to facilitate the organization of separate tribal 'homelands'. These homelands notoriously made possible the monitoring and control of blacks, and reflected the Apartheid ideology of 'separate development' of the races. Traditional African leaders were wooed by Apartheid administrators, who shored up and underwrote the chiefs' power and authority in return for guarantees of loyalty. These chiefs had added incentive to cooperate when customary law, finally recorded and formalized, secured their authority still further. Indeed, 'it was a law of the "white" parliament, the Black Administration Act of 1927, that reinstated customary law'.[11] Unsurprisingly, the formal code of customary law has frequently been described as forging an 'alliance between the colonial authorities and African male elders', whose superior status within African society was thereby entrenched.[12]

Which aspects of the official code of customary law have been most criticized by women's rights activists, legal reformers, and human rights proponents? Women's lack of authority and power under customary law stands out as exceedingly problematic—women may not seek or hold political office—as does their general marginalization in local political decision-making. But perhaps most troubling is women's status as perpetual minors under customary law, unable to enter contracts in their own name or to hold,

---

[9] T. W. Bennett, *Human Rights and Customary Law Under the South African Constitution* (Kenwyn, UK: Juta, 1999), p. 84.

[10] Ibid.

[11] Carolyn White, *Gender on the Agenda: Will Women Gain Equality in the New South Africa?* (Johannesburg: Centre for Policy Studies, 1995), p. 23.

[12] Thandabantu Nhlapo, 'African Customary Law in the Interim Constitution', in *The Constitution of South Africa from a Gender Perspective*, ed. S. Liebenberg (Belleville, South Africa: Community Law Centre, University of the Western Cape, 1995), p. 161.

inherit, or dispense of property. At the heart of the official code of customary law lies the institution of primogeniture, whereby the senior-most male relative in an extended family inherits the property and the responsibilities of his deceased male kin. Ironically, it is women who have mounted constitutional challenges to the authority of customary law, the very system that denies their *locus standi in judicio*, or power 'to bring actions in their own names' without a husband's (or father's, etc.) legal guardianship and assistance.[13] Until very recently, women married under customary law, as most rural and many urban black South African women are, passed from their father's to their husband's realm of authority and remained under their guardianship, or that of the nearest male relative, for their entire lives. Since women's proprietary capacity was not recognized, a woman married under customary law could not hold property separately from her husband. Aside from the question of land, 'any movable property accumulated in the course of the marriage is not hers either: when a husband dies his kin may remove everything from the joint homestead and leave his wife destitute, unless her own family or children are prepared to take care of her'.[14] Moreover, because of a woman's minor status, she could not '(directly at least) negotiate her marriage, terminate it, or claim custody of her children'.[15] These aspects of customary law—inheritance, succession, and family law—clearly conflict sharply with women's individual equality and property rights as stipulated in the Constitution, and very possibly with their political rights.

Whether the system of customary law is permitted to operate without significant limitations by the Constitution and the Bill or Rights, or whether it will be subject to extensive reforms, will depend in part on whether its defenders can establish that women's status under customary law does not reflect *unfair* discrimination. The Constitution permits differentiation and discrimination when used to redress historical unfairness—the classic example being affirmative action. It directs courts to ask about the grounds for differentiation, determine whether a discrimination has been made, and finally, whether unfair discrimination has occurred—that is, whether given treatment violates 'equal dignity and respect', a rather difficult effect to demonstrate.[16] As Venter argues, even if it is recognized that customary law discriminates, '[c]ustomary law adherents may ... claim that their legal system

---

[13] Bennett, *Human Rights*, p. 89.
[14] White, *Gender on the Agenda*, p. 22.
[15] Bennett, *Human Rights*, p. 80.
[16] Pierre de Vos, 'Equality for all? A Critical Analysis of The Equality Jurisprudence of the Constitutional Court', *THRHR*, 63 (2000), 62–75, p. 73.

does not unfairly discriminate against women, because it is not predicated on the individual but on the community. Since it is the community or group that is important and not the individual, the fact that women do not bear the rights on behalf of the group [may be deemed] more incidental and not "unfair".[17] Finally, even if the Constitutional Court were to rule that customary law does indeed perpetuate unfair sex discrimination, questions surrounding the relationship of the Bill of Rights to the system of customary law are by no means resolved, because of the Constitution's recognition of the right of culture and the legal authority of customary law.

Protections for affirmative action in the new Constitution, and related considerations that must be factored into the interpretation of rights set out in the Bill of Rights, may further complicate the resolution of the relationship between customary law and equality rights. As noted, the use of the term 'unfair discrimination' in the Bill of Rights is specifically intended to ensure that affirmative action schemes are not prohibited. In addition to employing this term, section 9 (5) of the Bill states that 'Discrimination on one or more of the grounds listed in subsection (3) is unfair unless it is established that the discrimination is fair'. As legal scholar Mark Kende observes, 'By comparison [to the United States Supreme Court's constitutional jurisprudence] South African equality guarantees are remedial and presume correctly that the Apartheid regime oppressed certain groups. The societal baseline is presumed to be nonneutral. Affirmative measures are therefore equalizing, not preferential'.[18] Proponents of sex equality in South Africa argue that whereas affirmative action policies that aim to ameliorate the status of disadvantaged groups in South Africa do not risk violating the Constitution's prohibition on 'unfair discrimination', practices and arrangements under customary law that systematically restrict and disadvantage women do. But the legal and political context surrounding the issue of discrimination in South Africa may make it possible, as noted above, to deny the charge that customary law unfairly discriminates against women. Moreover, this context also makes possible the argument that recognition and accommodation of customary law constitutes a legitimate and necessary form of affirmative action for an oppressed group, namely, black, and especially black rural, South Africans—and the claim that this recognition trumps concerns for sex equality.

[17] Christine M. Venter, 'The New South African Constitution: Facing the Challenges of Women's Rights and Cultural Rights in Post-Apartheid South Africa', *Journal of Legislation*, 21/1 (1995), 1–22, p. 17.

[18] Mark Kende, 'Stereotypes in South African and American Constitutional Law: Achieving Gender Equality and Transformation', *Southern California Review of Law and Women's Studies*, 10/1 (2000), 3–33, p. 26.

THE POLITICAL CONTEXT OF THE CUSTOMARY
LAW DEBATE

The framers of the postapartheid Constitution found it difficult simultaneously to accommodate sex equality and recognition of culture not only
because of the tensions mentioned above, but because of the intense political
pressure exerted from all sides. In the multiparty negotiations leading up to
the drafting of the 1993 interim Constitution—the Convention for a Democratic South Africa (CODESA) talks—the traditional African leaders' lobby
fought hard to establish protection for customary law as a parallel system of
law not subject to the Bill of Rights. If customary law was to be limited by the
fundamental rights set out in the Constitution, including the equality provisions, the scope of power of customary law and the authority of leaders
themselves would be severely curtailed. Of equal, if not greater, concern to
traditional leaders was the fact that the anticipated equality clause in the Bill
of Rights, with its protection for gender equality, effectively 'placed a question
mark over the custom of patrilineal succession to the chieftaincy'.[19] Traditionalists managed to secure several concessions in the Interim Constitution,
such as mention of customary law as a legitimate system of informal law, but
did not win the entrenched cultural rights they sought. Due to the efforts of a
strong feminist lobby as well as the African National Congress's (ANC) fear
that customary law could undercut a democratic bill of rights, the constitutional framers were careful to include a limiting clause.

That customary law received formal recognition in the Interim Constitution at all was in large part the result of strong pressure from traditional
leaders and the Inkatha Freedom Party (IFP, or Inkatha), whose leadership
threatened to boycott the first national election if this key concession were
denied. It was widely understood that the ANC was bowing to pressure from
the IFP and other groups for its own pragmatic political reasons. Specifically,
the ANC did not want to risk a boycott of the elections by the IFP, or to lose
the slim support it enjoyed among African traditionalists to the IFP, or to the
Pan African Congress (PAC).[20] Indeed, according to Fishbayn, 'the ANC was
also implicated in putting forth arguments in defence of the integrity of

---

[19] Currie, 'The Future of Customary Law', p. 149.

[20] The ANC still considers the traditional leaders' lobby to be a potentially derailing force: 'as
the 1999 elections drew nearer, the ANC politicians seemed more and more hesitant to take a
stance against traditional leadership, as this could cause traditional leaders, and their subjects, to
break ranks and join the IFP or the new United Democratic Movement (UDM)'. Barbara
Oomen, 'Group Rights in Post-Apartheid South Africa: The Case of the Traditional Leaders',
Journal of Legal Pluralism and Unofficial Law, 44 (1999), 73–103, p. 88.

culture. It had assisted in the formation of the Congress of Traditional Leaders of South Africa (CONTRALESA) to act as a moderate voice in the Constitutional negotiations. However, CONTRALESA joined with Inkatha to argue explicitly for the inclusion of a right to culture which would protect discriminatory practices rooted in patriarchal customary law and patriarchal forms of traditional leadership.[21] As if this political backfire were not enough, the executive of the ANC had to fend off internal opposition from women within the ANC in order to strike a compromise with the traditional leaders' lobby: not surprisingly, the ANC Women's League opposed the entrenchment of customary law in the Constitution on the grounds that it would weaken the sex equality provisions in the Bill of Rights. Until the constitutional negotiations, the ANC generally seemed to endorse this egalitarian line, but then changed its position for purely strategic reasons. As one scholar recounts:

In May 1990, the National Executive Committee of the ANC said that any '[l]aws, customs, traditions and practices which discriminate against women shall be held to be unconstitutional'. This appeared to be confirmed in their draft constitution called 'A Bill of Rights for a New South Africa'.... Unfortunately, this provision was not incorporated into the interim constitution.[22]

Meanwhile, women's rights groups mounted their own lobby efforts to try to prevent the entrenchment of customary law in the Constitution, and to guarantee that any constitutional protection for traditional law (which looked likely) would be subject to limitations by a Bill of Rights. As Constitutional Court Justice Yvonne Mokgoro comments, '[f]ighting this rearguard battle, the feminist lobby aimed to prevent an outright traditionalists victory'.[23] As far as the Interim Constitution of 1993 was concerned, their efforts met with only limited success: in the end, it was tentatively decided that the extensive list of rights in the Bill of Rights would not bind citizens *horizontally*—that is, it would not apply to citizens in their private relationships—either in matters of customary law or common law. This was most decidedly a compromise, for liberal reformers (especially feminists) sought to have constitutional rights apply not only vertically in the state's relationship to citizens, but also horizontally, in relations between citizens.[24] The issue of the Constitution's ambit of application subsequently became the focus of intense political and

---

[21] Lisa Fishbayn, 'Litigating the Right to Culture: Family Law in the New South Africa', *International Journal of Law, Policy and the Family*, 13 (1999), 147–73, p. 157.

[22] Jaqueline Krikorian, 'A Different Form of Apartheid? The Legal Status of Married Women in South Africa', *Queen's Law Journal*, 21 (1995), 221–60, p. 249.

[23] Yvonne Mokgoro, 'The Customary Law Question in the South African Constitution', *Saint Louis University Law Journal*, 41 (1997), 1279–89, p. 1284.

[24] Halton Cheadle and Dennis Davis, 'The Application of the 1996 Constitution in the Private Sphere', *South African Journal on Human Rights*, 13 (1997), 44–66, p. 45.

legal debate, with the effect that the final Constitution allows for horizontal application of selected 'relevant' individual rights, including the right of equality.[25]

While women's rights advocates were effectively marginalized from many aspects of the constitutional process, one area in which their voices were heard was on the issue of customary law, particularly on whether customary law should be subject to the provisions contained in the Bill of Rights.[26] There is little doubt that without pressure from women's groups, the issue of the implications of customary law protections for sex equality rights would not have received such direct attention. The controversy over the status of customary law in the Bill of Rights was formidable, and was estimated to have 'delayed the constitutional discussions by four or five weeks'.[27] The political lobbying efforts of women activists were particularly intense around the CODESA talks leading up to the draft of the Interim Constitution. Women's rights proponents who intervened in the negotiations—foremost among them, African women—warned that without limitation by the Bill of Rights, constitutional recognition of customary law would entrench African women's oppression.[28] The ANC's Women's League and the Federation of African Women were foremost among those advancing this argument.[29] Nor were women's activists convinced that the recognition of cultural rights was entirely necessary in the new South Africa, taking a more guarded view of these demands. Given the political alliance struck between traditional leaders and colonial administrators under Apartheid, there was cause to be suspicious of claims about the autonomous authority of traditional law and culture. As Oomen explains:

[I]t can be said that many 'traditional' structures have continued to exist for other reasons than merely the constitutional dedication to multiculturality. The absence of viable alternatives is one of those reasons, as [is] the political clout of traditional leaders.... The recognition of traditional leadership and customary law, presented as a prime example of South Africa's multiculturality, thus strongly resembles the recognition of these institutions under, and as a constituting element in, Apartheid.[30]

[25] See T. W. Bennett, 'The Equality Clause and Customary Law', *South African Journal on Human Rights*, 10 (1994), 122–30.

[26] Cathy Albertyn, 'Women and the Transition to Democracy in South Africa', in *Gender and the New South African Legal Order*, ed. C. Murray (Kenwyn, South Africa: Juta, 1994), p. 57.

[27] Krikorian, 'A Different Form of Apartheid?', p. 250.

[28] F. Kaganas and C. Murray, 'Law and Women's Rights in South Africa: An Overview', in *Gender and the New South African Legal Order*, ed. C. Murray (Kenwyn, South Africa: Juta, 1994), p. 20.

[29] Venter, 'The New South African Constitution', p. 7.

[30] Oomen, 'Group Rights', p. 92.

Armed with their misgivings about the motives of traditional leaders and tribal chieftains who sought extensive protection for patriarchal customs and arrangements in the name of 'culture', women's groups stood united in their demand that the individual equality provisions in the Bill of Rights should take precedence. In April 1992, they formed the Women's National Coalition (WNC)—composed of representatives from all political parties—during the multiparty negotiation process in order to counter their exclusion from the political negotiations. The opposition on the part of the WNC, the ANC's Women's League, and the African Women's Federation to the entrenchment of customary law was heard loud and clear. As a concession to the standoff between traditional leaders and women's rights activists, a committee of legal experts was appointed to devise a compromise that could assuage both sides. Despite much internal disagreement among the panel members, they managed to come up with a draft clause—clause 32—which would have qualified the recognition of customary law somewhat by establishing that in the event that aspects of customary law were found to 'conflict with the principle of equality contained in the constitution', [a] court 'could determine, to the extent that its jurisdiction allows, conditions on and a time within such rules and practices shall be brought in conformity with [the equality clause].'[31] The so-called compromise solution suited no one, and was ultimately abandoned. Once again, the decisive factor was the threat by traditional leaders to withdraw from the process entirely, to demand wider, unfettered protection for their cultural rights, and so to grind the constitutional talks to a halt.

The ANC Women's League—who thought clause 32 was insufficient to protect women's equality rights—also rallied to have the clause removed.[32] In the end, customary law was not specifically subjected to the Bill of Rights in the Interim Constitution; instead, a weaker and rather circular stipulation was included in the 'Interpretation' section of the document. This was subsequently replaced by a much stronger limiting clause in the final 1996 Constitution. But the partial success of women's groups in the period surrounding the Interim Constitution is itself remarkable. Women's groups were essentially united in their call for limitations to the recognition of customary law, in itself no small accomplishment: since white women are not subject to customary law, and enjoy protections under South African common law, it was by no means a forgone conclusion that white feminist activists would lobby alongside black women on this cause. Albertyn recounts the political mood of women's solidarity:

---

[31] Currie, 'The Future of Customary Law', p. 150.
[32] Albertyn, 'Women and the Transition', p. 60.

The claim made by all women's organizations was a simple one. It stated that equality was indivisible. All women should be able to claim equality through the Bill of Rights. To exclude customary law from the Bill of Rights was to exclude the most oppressed and marginalized groups, namely rural women. Thus not only should equality apply to all women but also it should trump claims to culture and custom that justified discrimination against women. The practical demand was for the removal of clause 32 and the insertion of an equality trump.[33]

The mobilization of women's groups during 1990–3 was focused, then, on the issue of how best to protect the equality rights of all South African women under the new Constitution, particularly in light of proposed recognition for customary law. As in the case of Native women in constitutional negotiations in Canada, women were very poorly represented in the multiparty CODESA negotiations beginning in 1990, much to the frustration of women's activists. In 1991, in response to protests at this exclusion, a Gender Advisory Group was established to ensure that the CODESA talks did not overlook gender issues altogether. This group was instrumental in making sure that sex equality and prohibition on sex-based discrimination were in fact included in the interim constitution.[34] However, women's groups did not demobilize once these partial concessions were won: at work on a Women's Charter in the negotiations period, the Women's National Council completed and released the document in 1994, and so were able to highlight the various problems of the interim constitution from the point of view of concerns about gender equality.[35] Moreover, Article 119 of the Interim Constitution established a Commission on Gender Equality (CGE), a national governmental advisory commission with regional offices, whose work is ongoing.

THE CURRENT CONSTITUTIONAL DILEMMA

The 1996 Constitution addresses the subject of the relationship between equality rights and cultural rights more clearly than the Interim Constitution. Equality heads the list of 'nonderogable rights' appended to the Bill of Rights, and only with regards to sexual and racial equality. The interpretative section [s. 39] at the end of the Bill of Rights accords priority to individual rights (including sex equality); section 39 (2) states that 'When interpreting any

[33] Ibid., p. 59.
[34] A. K. Wing and E. P. de Carvalho, 'Black South African Women: Toward Equal Rights', *Harvard Human Rights Journal*, 8 (1995), 57–100, p. 77.
[35] This was the second Women's Charter in South African history. The first Women's Charter was drawn up in 1954, a year before the ANC's 1955 Freedom Charter.

legislation, and when developing the common law or customary law, every court, tribunal or forum must promote the spirit, purport, and objects of the Bill of Rights'. Additionally, the clause that acknowledges the validity of customary law states that such recognition is limited 'to the extent that [these other systems of law] are consistent with the Bill', thereby inviting limitation by the equality clause (section 9). And finally, section 39 (1) states that 'When interpreting the Bill of Rights, a court, tribunal or forum' (b) 'must consider international law'. Importantly, South Africa is a recent signator to the CEDAW.[36] Pointedly, however, South Africa is also signator to the Banjul Charter (1986), which does 'not incorporate CEDAW's provisions about eliminating customary practices which discriminate against women'.[37]

The consensus of legal scholars writing on this issue is that the 1996 Constitution clearly attributes greater weight to equality provisions than to the right to culture, or stipulates that the latter is limited by the former.[38] This has been confirmed by recent judgments, such as those concerning primogeniture decided by the Constitutional Court in 2004. But early interpretations by the courts in the postapartheid period were mixed. In *Mthembu* v. *Letsela and Another,*[39] a widow challenged the custom of male-only inheritance, and sought a ruling against this practice. Her argument—essentially a challenge against primogeniture—was unsuccessful, and the custom of male-only inheritance was upheld. The judge claimed that this particular case hinged upon determining whether the appellant and her deceased husband were actually married according to customary law, and argued that if they were, she would be protected as a widow by receiving the treatment due to her under this system of customary law. His judgment took no account, however, of the failure of families today to carry out this duty toward widows.[40]

In a different case concerning Muslim family law, in *Rylands* v. *Edros*, the appellant unsuccessfully sought to claim retrospective maintenance support from her ex-husband, who had left her without resources.[41] While not directly

---

[36] South Africa signed CEWAW on January 29, 1993 and ratified it on December 15, 1995. Source: http://www.un.org/womenwatch/daw/cedaw/states.htm

[37] Venter, 'The New South African Constitution', p. 18.

[38] See for instance, aforementioned works by Fishbayn (esp. pp. 157–8) and Mokgoro (esp. p. 1287). A recent government discussion paper on customary law also claims that the equality provisions in the Constitution trump the protection of cultural rights. Traditional leaders, the paper states, invoke their cultural rights as protected by sections 30 and 31 of the Constitution in order to justify the exclusion of women from leadership positions; but they do so without warrant, for 'it is clear that the provisos to sections 30 and 31 make the right to culture subject to the equality clause which suggests that the exclusion of women from membership of traditional courts is unconstitutional'. See *The Harmonisation of the Common Law and Indigenous Law* (1999), p. 5.

[39] 1997 (2) SA 936 (CC), cited in Mokgoro, p. 1286.

[40] Fishbayn, 'Litigating the Right to Culture', p. 164.   [41] Ibid., pp. 160–3.

relevant to the issue of customary law, the judge's ruling in this case was significant, for he 'interpreted the right to equality as the right of a cultural group to govern itself in accordance with its own system of private law without discrimination by the State'.[42] The view that the right to enjoy one's culture is an absolute good, one not to be qualified or limited by equality provisions, could set the tone for subsequent court challenges. Moreover, there is some indication that the constitutional recognition of customary law and the right to culture could contribute to courts' assumption that unless specifically married under civil law, black Africans are taken to be bound willy-nilly by the customs and rules of customary law. Without clear evidence of a civil marriage, according to one government discussion paper, 'a court may apply the law that is consonant with [the appellant's] cultural orientation (as indicated by their lifestyles and other relevant factors) and with the rites and customs governing their marriage'.[43]

In striking contrast to the *Mthembu* and *Rylands* cases, the Cape High Court ruled on October 1, 2003 in favor of two daughters seeking to inherit from their deceased father's estate, in contravention to the succession customs of primogeniture. The *Bhe* case, as it is known, involved two girls from Khayelitsha (a township outside Cape Town), ages 9 and 12, who were denied inheritance rights under customary law. In ruling in favor of the girls' claim, and against their grandfather's claim that he should inherit, the High Court justices argued that the only obstacle to their inheriting—namely, the law of primogeniture—was in fact unconstitutional. The Women's Legal Centre, which had successfully filed the case on behalf of the girls, along with the South African Human Rights Commission, subsequently took the case to the Constitutional Court of South Africa, seeking to have sex discriminatory succession rules based on primogeniture (in cases of intestate succession) ruled 'unconstitutional and invalid'.[44] The subsequent ruling against these discriminatory rules, along with those of two other primogeniture challenge cases heard in the Constitutional Court, will now require tremendous overhaul of the customary law of succession.[45]

---

[42] Ibid., p. 161. As Fishbayn goes on to note, the judge 'never took the further step, explicitly contemplated by the constitutional provisions permitting the recognition of systems of personal law, of determining that such recognition is consistent with the other rights in the Constitution, including the rights of women to equality under family law'.

[43] Oomen, 'Group Rights in post-Apartheid South Africa', p. 96. Oomen cites a discussion paper by the South African Law Commission, whose findings were subsequently incorporated in the *Recognition of Customary Marriages Bill 110/1998*.

[44] *Bhe and Others* v. *The Magistrate, Khayelitsha and Others*, case #CCT 49/03.

[45] The three cases effectively challenging the constitutionality of primogeniture were decided in the Constitutional Court of South Africa on October 15, 2004. In addition to *Bhe*, there was *Shibi* v. *Sithole and Others* [case #CCT 69/03] and *South African Human Rights Commission and Another* v. *President of South Africa and Another* [case #CCT 50/03]. The third of these cases was 'brought in the public interest [by the South African Human Rights Commission and the

Since it is the role of the Constitutional Court and the High Courts to hear challenges against practices or laws that stand in tension with the Constitution, as well as to determine the appropriate interpretation of any ambiguous sections of the Constitution, these early cases are not insignificant. The courts play close attention to the claims and concerns of traditional groups, dissenters within those communities, and the legal opinions of South African constitutional experts. However, there is no doubt that judicial interpretations thus far have tended to reify the culture/equality dichotomy by framing the cases in terms of the friction between cultural traditions (including customary law) and individual equality rights. This is regrettable, for to treat culture and equality as fixed categories that signify irreducibly different or incommensurable goods misconstrues both entities: it is the contextual *interpretation* of rights and culture alike that will determine their compatibility, to a large extent. For example, in the case of the customary law of succession that prevents women from inheriting in intestate cases, it will be important to know how communities are responding to changed family conditions. Fieldwork by Mbatha suggests that customary 'practices are intended to avoid conflict and .... inheritance is compensatory and directed toward protecting the needy members of the family. Communities that lead a customary life have no problems with allowing a woman to inherit property'.[46] At the same time, however, Mbatha cautions that it would make little sense to simply replace the customary law of succession (primogeniture) with a rule requiring that widows inherit all of their deceased husbands' property, 'since this would unfairly allow customary wives to benefit from inheritance rights at the expense of other family members'.[47]

While the courts will continue to try to make sense of the new Constitution in light of the tensions between customary law and individual rights and equality, especially sex equality, a parallel political process is clearly needed. A more thorough and far-reaching resolution to constitutional tensions between cultural recognition and sex equality must come from further legislative reform efforts, incorporating political negotiation and compromise among different stakeholders, as well as grassroots political and community initiatives. Constitutional challenges will play an important role in this process, but should not, I argue, supplant it. In addition to the important work

Women's Legal Trust], and as a class action on behalf of all women and children prevented from inheriting by reason of the impugned provisions and the rule of male primogeniture'. See 'Media Summary' (Constitutional Court of South Africa)of the three cases decided on October 15, 2004.

[46] Likhapha Mbatha, 'Reforming the Customary Law of Succession', *South African Journal on Human Rights*, 18/2 (2002), 259–86, p. 283.

[47] Ibid., p. 282.

being done by a range of NGOs advocating issues from women's rights to land reform and antipoverty legislation, there are other developments that signal the possibility of broader political change. There is, for example, the CGE. While it has met with mixed success—and chronic underfunding has crippled some of its initiatives—the CGE has at least been able to identify a number of women's issues requiring government action, such as poverty, sexual violence, unemployment, discrimination in laws of succession, and HIV prevention and treatment.[48] At its best, the CGE has also served as a bridge between government policymakers and politically disenfranchised women. There is also the recent development of the 'Equality Courts,' established by the Promotion of Equality and Prevention of Unfair Discrimination Act 4 of 2000, and which should shortly be operational. One scholar suggests that these courts 'could, when dealing with customary law gender discrimination cases in particular, serve as a forum for hearing the different voices of marginalised people affected by customary law practices', using narrative and storytelling techniques to maximize the inclusion of these court processes.[49]

INTERPRETING CULTURE AND RIGHTS IN POLITICAL CONTEXT

The importance of including diverse voices in debates about the status and possible reform of customary law and practices, as well as the interpretation and application of sexual equality, cannot be overstated. In South Africa, both customary law and gender equality norms have been profoundly shaped by social and political processes in which the strategic interests of different groups and actors have never been far from view. To view disagreements between African traditionalists and gender equality proponents as reflecting opposing commitments to deeply incommensurable moral principles and goods is to ignore the way that interests and power have shaped the debate to date. And as noted earlier, the official code of customary law that was recorded by colonial administrators in the nineteenth and twentieth centuries reflected an especially patriarchal interpretation of local customs and arrangements. Such an interpretation was perhaps inevitable given that European

[48] For a discussion of the work of the CGE, including its challenges and failures, see Gay Seidman, 'Institutional Dilemmas: Representation Versus Mobilization in the South African Gender Commission', *Feminist Studies*, 29/3 (2003), 541–63.

[49] Narnia Bohler, 'Equality Courts: Introducing the Possibility of Listening to Different Voices in South Africa?', *THRHR*, 63 (2000), 288–94, p. 288 and pp. 290–1.

officials desired to establish clear authorities in African communities to facilitate their own political and administrative ends, and so put a patriarchal slant on authority and leadership. As it happens, such an interpretation suited tribal leaders very well: particularly in the twentieth century under the Apartheid regime, local headmen and chiefs clung tenaciously to their positions of authority, which in many cases were created through colonial bureaucracy.[50] Nor did traditional leaders see colonial and Apartheid power-sharing structures as a means of forging radical political transformation; rather, 'traditional leaders in the "homelands" saw the delegation of power over African people to them as a means of retaining authority which was being eroded by the migration of the young from the rural areas to the cities'.[51]

The prospect that customary law and traditional leadership might not be formally recognized in the new South African Constitution mobilized tribal leaders and their political supporters—the IFP and CONTRALESA—in the constitutional negotiations of 1990–1 and subsequently. Both CONTRALESA and the IFP, closely linked with traditional leaders based in rural areas, pressed hard in negotiations to secure explicit recognition of cultural rights and respect for traditional forms of power. Once it was clear that the interim Constitution would protect customary law and practices, these same groups led the fight to prevent the equality provisions in the Bill of Rights from limiting either the application of customary law or the scope of traditional leaders' power. The chiefs' desire to protect their own authority and power seemed to fuel these lobbying efforts much more than any belief in the inviolability of cultural autonomy or the sanctity of (putatively) African norms of patriarchy and community. Their particular opposition to constitutional rights that could challenge the custom of patrilineal succession of leaders and the traditional (local) court system—used to settle disputes about land and inheritance as well as areas of family law—spoke volumes about their self-serving priorities. Throughout the transition to democratic rule, it was these bread-and-butter issues of power and interests that were of greatest concern to traditional rulers. If customary law were viewed as subject to the equality provisions in the Bill of Rights, the patrilineal line of political succession of chiefs would be threatened. Opening up traditional leadership positions to election would have entirely changed the power base and authority of headmen and chiefs in ways unacceptable to traditional leaders. The issue of resources also loomed large: Who would remunerate the chiefs if customary law and traditional leadership were not given formal, constitutional recognition? (Previously, resources were transferred from the

---

[50] Oomen, 'Group Rights in post-Apartheid South Africa', p. 92.
[51] Fishbayn, 'Litigating the Right to Culture', p. 154.

Apartheid government.) And how would chiefs maintain their control of land resources, the key component to their power?[52]

Women's lobby groups, by contrast, tried to make sure that their comparatively marginalized perspectives were heard in the constitutional process. Their interests lay, in the first instance, in securing a political voice for women, who were all but excluded from the Kempton Park talks and the subsequent multiparty constitutional negotiations.[53] This is why an ad hoc Gender Advisory Group was formed in 1991—namely to furnish the all-party CODESA talks with policy guidance on issues of gender justice. It was also clearly the impetus behind the formation of the WNC in April 1992. A second explicit goal of the women's lobby, as noted, was to block the attempts by traditional leaders to entrench customary law (with constitutional immunity) in the Bill of Rights. The official version of customary law, they argued, reinforced patriarchal norms and deepened women's subordination and mistreatment by rendering 'the existing separation between the public and private spheres of life ... more rigid'.[54] Women's groups demanded that the new South African Constitution recognize the inextricable links between the public and private spheres in matters of justice and injustice, vulnerability and oppression. Women's interests, they insisted, lay in the political and constitutional recognition of the interrelatedness of formal law and private subjugation (at the center of which lay the vexed issue of customary law).[55]

This challenge to the separation of public and private spheres of course met with predictable resistance in the South African constitutional debate. Cultural practices and arrangements in the private and domestic sphere typically play a role in shoring up political relationships in the public realm, where vested interests and power once again prevail. Especially in traditional communities, the social and family relations of power in the private sphere are reconfigured and potentially destabilized by the introduction of changes in civil and common law and 'new' rights. Accordingly, 'the attempt to homogenize the status of women has thus encountered deeper resistance

---

[52] As Oomen notes ('Group Rights', p. 89), 'By far the largest part of the land in the former homelands, which in themselves cover about thirteen percent of the South African territory, is communal property. Traditional leaders are still responsible for the allocation of this land.... [O]pponents point out how easy it is for chiefs to abuse this function.'

[53] Kempton Park was the site of the initial round of constitutional talks to establish the transition to a post-Apartheid government.

[54] Nhlapo, 'African Customary Law', p. 162.

[55] See Celina Romay, 'Black Women and Gender Equality in a New South Africa: Human Rights Law and the Intersection of Race and Gender', *Brooklyn Journal of International Law*, 21 (1996), 857–98, esp. pp. 870–6.

than the attempt to universalize gender-free rights'.[56] Such resistance should not, however, lead us to conclude that there is no prospect of reconciling the conflicting claims of cultural traditionalists and proponents of gender equality. However, the reconciliation aimed for must be, I suggest, *a practical one*, negotiated at the level of local practices. Below, I discuss the process surrounding the recent reform of customary marriage in South Africa, which rightly emphasized consultation and deliberation, as well as the virtues of compromise and political bargaining.

THE REFORM OF CUSTOMARY MARRIAGE

In late 1998, the South African legislature passed into law the *Customary Marriages Act*, for the first time granting traditional or customary African marriage equal status with civil (usually Christian) marriage. That the Act recognizes and sets out national guidelines and laws governing customary marriage for the *first* time is surprising given that at least half of the country's 80 percent black majority marries under some form of customary arrangement. Finally put into effect in November 2000, the Act was the culmination of deliberative and consultative hearings sponsored by the South African Law Commission, whose aim was to solicit views about the practice of customary marriage and to draft proposals for its reform. For this reason, it is an instructive example for exploring how deliberative solutions to cultural conflicts might work in practice.

Customary marriage was understandably at the top of the list of cultural practices to be brought in line with the 1996 Constitution. Nowhere are the tensions between constitutional protections of the right to culture and the right to sex equality seen to clash more than in practices governing marriage, divorce, and family law (including inheritance) in black South African communities. Under the system of customary law that most black South Africans adhere to in their family affairs, women were until recently accorded the legal status of a minor—unable to inherit land, enter into contracts, or indeed to initiate their own divorces. Payment for the bride—known as bridewealth, or *lobolo*, traditionally paid in cattle but nowadays more commonly in cash—passes from the prospective groom to the father of the bride (or a male guardian in the event of his death) and without it,

---

[56] Andrew Nathan, 'Universalism: A Particularistic Account', in *Negotiating Culture and Human Rights*, eds. L. Bell, A. Nathan, and I. Peleg (New York: Columbia University Press, 2001), p. 256.

marriages are deemed invalid. If a woman subsequently seeks to leave her marriage, the bride's family is expected to return the lobolo to the groom or the groom's family—a requirement widely blamed for keeping women, fearful of impoverishing not only herself but her family, trapped in abusive marriages. Finally, custody of children is automatically awarded to fathers (or the father's family) under customary law, as required by the principle of primogeniture.

In light of these features of customary marriage, the South African Law Commission sponsored a series of consultations and hearings on the reform of this custom in 1998, as part of a long-term project on the *Harmonisation of the Common law and the Indigenous Law.* These meetings included a cross section of the community, including representatives of legal reform groups and women's associations; chiefs from CONTRALESA; and scholars of constitutional law and customary law. CONTRALESA representatives, in keeping with their position during constitutional negotiations, argued that the government should simply recognize marriage under customary law as it is currently practiced, including those aspects that subordinate women. A customary law specialist at the University of the Witswatersrand, Likhapa Mbatha, reports that in the meetings she attended traditional leaders kept hiding behind the word 'culture' when making their case against proposed reforms, and steadfastly resisted suggestions that women should enjoy greater decision-making roles in African society.[57] More generally, she notes an increase in opportunistic claims by individual men now that cultural rights and customary law are constitutionally recognized:

Many heirs ... have realised that their individual claims are enforceable if phrased or based on the codified customary law. This situation has resulted in the widespread exploitation of property rights by heir. For example, where there is no male issue, the property is contested by senior men such as fathers, siblings, uncles, and even their sons (the list is endless). In consequence, women are often forced to leave their homes. The inheritance claims made by male family members, especially where there is no son, are often selfish and negate women's property rights under customary law. These men view themselves as successors not only to the status of the deceased but also to the ownership of the property. This is a complete distortion of the values and purposes underlying customary law and indicates a need for redefining customary entitlements.[58]

On the other side, women's equality and legal reform advocates voiced tremendous opposition to women's status as minors (in marriage) under

---

[57] Interview with Likhapa Mbatha of the Centre for Applied Legal Studies (CALS) at the University of the Witswatersrand (Johannesburg) January 25, 2002.
[58] Mbatha, 'Reforming the Customary Law of Succession', p. 267.

customary law, and to the systems of primogeniture more generally. Proponents of more radical reform advocated the institution of a single civil marriage code that would protect the rights of all women, irrespective of their race, culture, or religion. Interestingly, this option was unpopular with many involved in the consultations, and could not generate enough support to go forward.[59]

By including participants who represent different interests in African communities—traditional leaders, customary law scholars, rural women's advocates, etc.—as well as members of legal reform and women's groups, the Commission made it possible for a range of views on the merits and disadvantages of different aspects of traditions surrounding customary marriage to be heard. This deliberative process also ensured that no single, canonical (and likely false) account of customary marriage was taken at face value. Instead, discussion focused on marriage under the actual or 'living' customary law and the changing gender roles and practices that it reflects. Mbatha and others pointed out to traditional leaders in the Law Commission meetings that women's roles have in fact *already* changed in African communities, and that chiefs misrepresent reality by conjuring up romantic ideals of separate spheres and men's leadership. For example, under the 'living' (as opposed to codified) customary law, women negotiate and receive bridewealth or lobolo (contrary to official custom) and often act on behalf of their sons and daughters in negotiating the precise terms of marriages.[60] Another widespread but false belief identified in the course of discussions was the view that wives have no economic responsibilities in marriage and that they are provided for both by their husbands, or by their husband's families if they are widowed. In reality, married black South African women must often support themselves and their children financially, and when widowed, assistance from their deceased husband's relatives is now the exception rather than the rule.[61]

The reasonably broad representation of participants in deliberations about the future of customary marriage made possible not only a more accurate description of the specific practices surrounding this institution, but a frankly political style of debate. Indeed, the process of deliberation initiated by the

---

[59] Cathy Albertyn, director of CALS, reports that her organization recommended a single, civil marriage status which could have ceremonial aspects if the participants so desired, but that this proposal was politically unviable as it was seen as a demotion of customary marriage and customary law more generally. Interview, January 24, 2002, Johannesburg.

[60] Mbatha, aforementioned interview.

[61] See also Chuma Himonga, 'Law and Gender in Southern Africa: Human Rights and Family Law', in *The Changing Family: International Perspectives*, eds. J. Eekelaar and T. Nhlapo (Oxford: Hart Publishing, 1998), p. 289; and Fishbayn, 'Litigating the Right to Culture', p. 165.

Law Commission can best be characterized as putting into motion a politics of negotiation and compromise in which the focus was on practical interests, prospective policies and their potential consequences. This frankness accounts for the easy exposure of some of the more pernicious interests and motivations on the table, particularly those of the chiefs who were concerned that their own positions of power might be endangered if they were no longer permitted to adjudicate matters of divorce, custody, and inheritance in their local traditional courts. The openness and political tone of deliberations also account for the relative ease with which compromises were ultimately reached regarding specific reforms and policies. Crucially, traditional leaders were eventually persuaded that it was in their best interests, and those of their constituents, to agree to moderate reforms of customary marriage that would preserve the essence of the institution, albeit in modified form.

As in the debate on the status of customary law in Constitutional negotiations, a political compromise was struck in the debate on customary marriage. On the side of reform, women's contractual and proprietary capacities are now fully affirmed and wives have (formally) equal status. In monogamous marriages, both spouses are deemed to be married in community of property[62] as the default arrangement, consistent with the wide popularity of the principle of shared or joint property among black South African women.[63] Women are now equally entitled to initiate divorce proceedings, and married parents have equal guardianship and custody rights with respect to their children. On the issue of family law jurisdiction, it was decided that in future only family courts may handle divorce, maintenance, and custody matters, taking this power away from local chiefs (who still retain their right to try to mediate relationship disputes).

Equally, the South African Law Commission deliberations yielded a number of concessions for chiefs or traditional leaders. Chiefs were relieved that lobolo is to keep its status, although it is no longer required to prove a marriage's validity. Initially the Law Commission thought lobolo might be

---

[62] The community of property reform was viewed as especially important by women's legal reform groups, which view women's financial destitution (both as the result of desertion and divorce) as probably the gravest problem facing rural black women. Interview with Coriaan de Villiers of the Women's Legal Centre, Cape Town, January 18, 2002.

[63] A study of attitudes of women in the Western Cape and Eastern Cape Provinces conducted by the National Association of Democratic Lawyers found that 82% of women supported joint ownership and control of property in monogamous marriages. This number dropped to 69% among women in polygamous marriages (some women feared conflict with other wives resulting from joint property). Prakashnee Govender, *The Status of Women Married in Terms of African Customary Law: A Study of Women's Experiences in the Eastern Cape and Western Cape Provinces* [Research Report No. 13] (Cape Town: National Association of Democratic Lawyers, 2000), pp. 26–8.

eliminated on the grounds that it is offensive to women's dignity, but the widespread support for the custom voiced in consultations made this impossible.[64] An important reform of the practice, however, now leaves it open to either parent to assume the function of negotiating and receiving bride-wealth.[65]

Another custom that the Commission originally expected to be abolished is that of polygyny, but again, most participants in deliberations felt that this would be a mistake—both because the practice is deemed by many to be an important (though comparatively rare) variation of customary marriage, and because merely abolishing it in law would be ineffectual, leaving women in polygynous marriages essentially unprotected.[66] An agreement was eventually reached whereby polygyny will continue to be permitted, but a man intending to marry another wife must 'apply to court to approve a proposed contract which will regulate the future matrimonial property system of his marriage'.[67] This application requires the participation of both the existing wife and the proposed wife. In this way, the new legislation aims to protect the financial interests of wives in a multiple marriage, by establishing an 'equitable distribution of property' (including a man's pension) for wives and other family members in the event of divorce or death. These protections will not, of course, extend to the many informal multiple-partner relationships among black South Africans, which historically have been particularly prevalent among migrant male workers.[68]

The explicitly political nature of the consultation process surrounding the recognition and reform of customary marriage in South Africa, I argue, rendered the power relationships and interests at stake much more visible, but also, at least on some level, more open to contestation. Reforms that might not have been thought necessary were proposed, and other reforms were dismissed

---

[64] As Govender (Ibid.) notes, 'abolishing it would merely have meant passing a law which would be consistently disregarded'; her study found that women overwhelmingly (85%) supported the custom of lobolo.

[65] As Likhapha Mbatha discusses, the case of *Mabena* v. *Letsoalo* (1998 [2] SA 1068 [T]) has set precedent in this regard, confirming that the father or male guardian of the bride need *not* necessarily participate in the *lobolo* exchange in order to render it legitimate, contrary to (historically) codified customary law. In making this decision the court recognized the changing nature of the 'lived' customary law. See Mbatha's 'Reforming the Customary Law', pp. 278–9.

[66] Even the influential Women's Legal Centre in Cape Town, which takes on precedent-setting legal cases in furtherance of women's equality, did not want to oppose polygamy in consultations on the grounds that this would merely penalize women in existing polygamous marriages. (Interview with Coriaan de Villiers.)

[67] I. P. Maithufi and J. C. Bekker, 'The Recognition Of The Customary Marriages Act of 1998 and its Impact on Family Law in South Africa', *Comparative and International Law Journal of Southern Africa*, 35/1 (2002), 182–97, p. 190.

[68] J. C. Bekker, 'Human Rights and Customary Law', *The Human Rights and Constitutional Law Journal of Southern Africa*, 1/4 (1997), 21–3, pp. 22–3.

or amended as a response to political pressures. The relative transparency of the political process clarified just what the most forceful complaints were. The denial of women's proprietary and contractual capacities was seen as the most odious aspect of customary law, and proposals to eliminate these were not especially contested.[69] Similarly, it was only through consultation and deliberation that the Law Commission was able to discover which practices were widely thought to be valuable and worth keeping.

This example of customary marriage law reform illustrates that a deliberative approach to resolving disputes about contested cultural practices, one that emphasizes strategies of negotiation and compromise, can produce fair and equitable solutions. The outcome of deliberations, namely the draft proposals that became the *Customary Marriages Act*, did not please all of the participants. Traditional leaders would have much preferred to retain their role in adjudicating divorce and custody disputes, largely because of the power that it represents. Some women's groups, including the government-initiated CGE, were unhappy with the retention of polygyny.[70] But the compromises that the hearings eventually produced were nonetheless seen by most as a fair outcome of deliberation and negotiation. As such, the consultation process lent legitimacy to the reforms that they would not otherwise have enjoyed. To sustain this legitimacy, following up the new legislation with government spending on programs and training to implement the reforms will be important.[71]

This case also shows that deliberation may yield outcomes with *nonliberal* features—in this case, the preservation of African customs of polygyny and bride-wealth payment—that are consistent with norms of political equality and democratic legitimacy. The revisability of the outcome of deliberations (through future amendments to the *Act*) will help to ensure that any unjust or unfeasible aspects of the new laws that come to light can be revisited and changed. For instance, one problematic aspect of the new *Act* is that it has only very limited applicability to customary marriages entered into before

[69] Likhapa Mbatha (afore mentioned interview). Also, Govender's study found that a mere 2% of women in polygamous and monogamous marriages supported the principle of primogeniture (p. 27).

[70] The Commission for Gender Equality (CGE), in a brief addressing the Recognition of Customary Marriages Bill, stated that by retaining polygyny, 'the Bill therefore perpetuates gender inequality by continuing an institution which benefits men at the expense of women, in the name of culture.... The CGE therefore rejects the practice of polygamy and regards such practice as discriminatory'. CGE, *Submission to the Justice Portfolio Committee* (September 30, 1998), p. 7.

[71] In particular, local magistrates need to be trained to apply the new laws, and it must be made easier for rural women to register their customary marriages. Interview with Johanna Kehler, director, National Association of Democratic Lawyers, Cape Town, January 18, 2002.

it came into effect. In part this provision reflects the difficulty of amending marriage contracts retrospectively, but also signals a concession to traditional leaders. Already there are calls from women's equality groups and legal reform groups to reform this aspect of the *Act*, and it seems almost certain that new legislation will need to be drafted to ensure greater equity for those whose customary marriages predate the *Act*. Similarly, at some point the new laws governing polygyny may well need to be changed to reflect changing attitudes and practices in black South African communities.

Finally, these deliberations about the status and necessary reform of customary marriage, much like the broader constitutional debate surrounding customary law, revealed a struggle over concrete needs and interests, and power, much more than a deep conflict of values. This struggle was partly over the definition and meaning of cultural practices, involving contested interests as much as contested norms. But the dispute was also fundamentally about who can speak for whom, and who can decide what for whom, in the new South Africa. These contests of interests and legitimacy show why the debate over tensions between culture rights and gender equality does not end with the finalizing of the Constitution, nor should it end there. The Constitution does charge the courts with helping to 'develop' (or reform) customary law in keeping with protections enshrined in the Bill of Rights, so they will play a critical role. But as I have argued, the courts alone should not be left to decide the fate of customary law. What is needed is a parallel political process much like that described here, in which members of affected cultural communities and representatives from NGOs and government can reassess, debate, evaluate, and where necessary, propose reforms of many of the practices and arrangements that exist under customary law.

DELIBERATION, NEGOTIATION AND COMPROMISE IN THE SOUTH AFRICAN CONTEXT

To claim that some cultural conflicts should be understood primarily as conflicts of political interests and power is not to dismiss the role of moral- and value-based disagreement altogether. Rather than focusing on contrasting norms and values to account for the conflict between traditionalists and women's rights advocates in South Africa, however, I would argue that we should instead aim to identify norms that enjoy wide acceptance across the communities in question for the purpose of structuring a practical dialogue. To a large extent this is what occurred in the process surrounding the reform of customary marriage. An obvious contender for a norm that enjoys asymmetrical but overlapping support in South Africa is that of equality, but as the earlier discussion of constitutional conflict showed, equality is too widely and variously interpreted in this society to be of much strategic use. Instead, another norm, that of political inclusion or political participation, was arguably used as the starting point for a negotiated compromise solution to the customary marriage reform question. Political inclusion as both an ideal and a guide for political practice has particular resonance for South Africans: its importance is reflected at all levels of political life, as evinced, for example, by demands for inclusion by different communities and lobby groups during the constitutional negotiations of the 1990s. By including and giving political voice to some of the different constituencies with a stake in the customary marriage/gender equality dispute—although admittedly inclusion could and should have been even wider, according to critics—and permitting these deliberations to impact policy formation, the broad outlines of a solution emerged. The outcome of this particular policy challenge was legislation that reflected an imperfect but viable compromise, one that can and probably should be renegotiated in the future, as social needs, interests, and political commitments evolve.

If the struggle between traditionalists and women's groups over the future status of customary law in South Africa is primarily a political one, reflecting different vested interests and forms and degrees of power, then future gender/customary law policy disputes should proceed as a dialogue between parties with competing and legitimate claims and interests. The kind of dialogue suggested by the antifoundationalist, pragmatist perspective argued for here is directed toward securing concessions for parties whose interests may be deeply at odds. The ground rules of such a dialogue are not metaphysically grounded—they are not universalizable norms that rational agents could or would agree to, in Rawls' or Habermas' sense. Rather, they reflect more minimal requirements, designed to prevent the conversation from digressing into a contest of raw power and influence. Of use here is John Dryzek's idea of a 'discursive design' which is inclusive and informal, free of 'hierarchy and formal rules', but shaped by conversational conventions. This model emphasizes the maximum inclusivity (no interested parties are excluded) and insists that 'the focus of deliberations should include, but not be limited to, the individual or collective interests of the individuals involved'.[72] As argued in Chapter 4, however, it is critical that the relative vulnerability and power of agents be recognized and fully articulated as part of any deliberations. In the South African context, for example, this would mean that debates about primogeniture under customary law acknowledge that it is especially vulnerable

---

[72] Dryzek, *Discursive Democracy*, p. 43.

women and children who are most harmed by the practice, as this rule 'effectively upholds the right of an already empowered person to make countless others destitute'.[73]

On the view advanced here, dialogue between dissenting parties begins from overlapping norms but *is not directed toward identifying shared norms* or toward achieving an overall normative consensus on values or even policy issues. This marks a key difference between a deliberative democratic approach of the sort sketched here and models of public dialogue proposed by discourse ethicists and many proponents of deliberative democracy. The actual agreement of participants is needed in order to ratify those norms that provide the starting point, so to speak, but participants need not (and probably will not) share identical understandings of norms nor value them for precisely the same reasons. Political inclusion is a widely shared norm in South Africa, for instance, but traditional leaders understand this differently than liberal sex equality advocates. However, both groups share overlapping understandings of the norm of inclusion, and this agreement provides a starting point for discussion. Similarly, participants need not agree on the actual application of the norm in question, in terms of procedures that are to guide deliberations. Once the initial norms and procedures are selected, a conversation directed toward compromise can proceed.

Such a negotiation model for resolving constitutional-level conflicts between cultural practices and liberal constitutional norms might make use of an arbitrator—or arbitrators—who can help determine which overlapping norms should anchor the deliberation process. For example, in South Africa's 'equality courts', judges trained in equality jurisprudence but also well versed in African customary law and international human rights law could serve as arbitrators in this forum. Arbitrators might also be representatives of a government or semigovernmental regulatory body—for instance, a member of the South African Law Commission, as in the hearings on customary marriage reform. Alternatively, an arbitrator could be a community or public figure who commands the respect of dissenting parties—a political figure, respected journalist, or even a religious leader with a reputation for neutrality. The role of the arbitrator would vary depending on the dispute, but would minimally include the following:

(a) help to determine which norms enjoy overlapping (but likely asymmetrical) understanding and support in the diverse communities participating in negotiations;

---

[73] Kristina Bentley, 'Whose Right Is It Anyway? Equality, Culture and Conflicts of Rights in South Africa'. Cape Town: Human Sciences Research Council, Democracy and Governance Programme, *Occasional Paper* 4 (2003), p. 4.

(b) help to determine which practices and ground rules best reflect these overlapping norms, and work to implement these; and

(c) facilitate fair and open deliberation between the participants and guide them toward a fair, negotiated compromise solution.

The idea of a third party that facilitates and guides open deliberation among participants to the discussion is a feature of other discourse-based models of conflict resolution. Dryzek's idea of a discursive design, for instance, features a *mediator* who helps to construct a fair dialogue among participants and guides them toward some reasoned compromise. As he explains, 'the mediator can also take actions to reduce rigidities in the bargaining positions of adversaries, attempt to reconceptualize issues through reference to novel problem definitions or normative judgments, offer inducements to the parties involved, and oversee subsequent compliance with any agreements reached'.[74]

As made clear in Chapter 4, this approach to democratic conflict resolution differs from other available models of public dialogue in its practical focus on the *concrete interests* of the participants. Compromise, not consensus, is the goal of the approach developed here. Rather than guiding citizens to discover shared public norms, as Habermas's discourse ethics proposes,[75] I propose that we begin from asymmetrical but overlapping understandings of norms valued by the participants but move toward securing workable compromises and negotiated solutions to concrete policy problems. Although my approach eschews direct reliance on formal norms of rationality and public reason, and does not explicitly endorse liberal norms as trumps, it by no means assumes a position of moral relativism. Rather, it entails a procedural and pluralist account of justice, wherein justice follows from the observance of fair procedures that enjoy legitimacy among the diverse participants to the practical dialogue—procedures that reflect moral and political norms.

What would it mean to apply the model of negotiation and compromise to conflicts between African customary law and constitutional law, and to future disputes between traditional leaders and sex equality advocates in South Africa? I have argued that one norm stands out as readily accepted by all dissenting parties in the customary law debate, namely, that of *political inclusion*. This norm has special currency in the South African context given the history of systematic exclusion under apartheid and the lack of inclusive democratic structures. Traditional leaders and women's rights lobby groups alike agree that political inclusion is a critical norm in the new, democratic South Africa. Negotiation and compromise are two other norms that have

[74] Dryzek, *Discursive Democracy*, p. 445.

[75] Jürgen Habermas, *Moral Consciousness and Communicative Action*, trans. C. Lenhardt and S. W. Nicholsen (Cambridge, MA: MIT Press, 1993) and *Between Facts and Norms*.

real currency in contemporary South African politics, as the political, ethnic, and religious pluralism of the country has required that these norms take precedent at every stage of the transition to democratic rule. While neither the traditional leaders' lobby nor women's groups were entirely satisfied with the particular resolution reached in the debate over the constitutional status of customary law or the legislation surrounding the reform of customary marriage, they did agree to adhere to the norms of negotiation and compromise which underpinned this process. In the end, both the constitutional debate and customary marriage legislation yielded important concessions for reformers and traditionalists. These kinds of negotiated political compromises, I argue, will enable fair accommodation of both demands for cultural justice and protection for gender equality.

8

Conclusion: Legitimizing Democracy and Democratizing Legitimacy

In this final chapter, I want to revisit two of the most important challenges that greet proposals for a more democratic approach to resolving disputes about contested minority cultural practices and arrangements. The first objection suggests that it is not at all clear why the principle of democratic legitimacy should be widely acceptable in a culturally and morally diverse society. Why should a *democratic* conception of legitimacy prevail over other understandings of legitimacy, such as those that appeal to religious authorities? I call this the problem of *legitimizing democracy*. A second challenge is one that I have addressed in passing throughout the book, but warrants more focused attention here: if we democratize decision-making about contested cultural practices and arrangements, and foreground the deliberations of cultural group members themselves, how is it possible to protect and empower vulnerable individuals, such as women? If greater decision-making power is accorded to communities that are sexist and hierarchical, will this not leave women even less protected than before? These risks notwithstanding, I have argued that a deliberative democratic approach to mediating conflicts of culture makes it possible for women to contest and shape social practices through both formal and informal political means. In formal spaces of political debate, principles of nondomination, political inclusion, and revisability help to ensure that vulnerable group members can openly challenge practices and customs. Outside of such political deliberation, women can and do also contest and revise their cultural arrangements. To better support them in this, and to enable us to see the political and normative character of such interventions, it is important to expand our understanding of the basis of political legitimacy. Specifically, informal democratic expressions and activities should also be seen as bearing on the validity of social and cultural practices. I call this part of the project the challenge of *democratizing legitimacy*.

LEGITIMIZING DEMOCRACY

How should we define democratic legitimacy in culturally diverse societies? What makes a particular political process, or a particular outcome, valid from the standpoint of democratic legitimacy? There is of course a range of possible responses to these questions within political theory. Classical liberals, such as social contract theorists, locate legitimacy in the liberty-protecting state institutions to which citizens give their consent. Contemporary political liberals like John Rawls interpret the contractarian argument somewhat differently: Rawls locates legitimacy in the rationality and reasonableness of principles of justice as fairness, as well as in the claim that liberal principles and institutions resonate with citizens' normative intuitions about fairness and justice. Republicans such as Rousseau locate legitimacy in the expression of popular sovereignty. By contrast, some contemporary neorepublicans deny that democratic legitimacy is established by gauging the popular will; Phillip Pettit, for example, argues that democratic legitimacy requires instead that political processes be free from relations of domination, and that policies, laws, and institutions be democratically contestable.[1]

Taken alone, none of these accounts of democratic legitimacy seems adequate to the demands of culturally plural, liberal democracies. In Chapter 4, I argued that deliberative democracy theory comes closer to these other conceptions in imagining a robust and egalitarian account of democratic political legitimacy. But although proponents of deliberative democracy agree on a general ideal of political conflicts as best mediated through normative argumentation, they do not have a uniform understanding of democratic legitimacy. As we saw earlier, these thinkers alternately point to both the procedures and the outcomes of deliberative rationality in accounting for democratic legitimacy. We can in fact identify two main conceptions of legitimacy at work here, thick and thin. The thick account of democratic legitimacy is very demanding indeed, insofar as it holds both the procedures and the outcomes of deliberation to a number of conditions of normative validity. For reasons discussed earlier, in Chapter 4, this conception is not one that can be expected to have broad appeal among cultural minorities, most especially, nonliberal minorities. By contrast, the thin conception of democratic legitimacy focuses on the procedures, not the outcome, of deliberation. But even this thinner account needs to be amended if it is to enjoy wide normative appeal, and also

---

[1] Phillip Pettit, *Republicanism: A Theory of Freedom and Government* (Oxford and New York: Oxford University Press, 1997).

if it is to reflect the diverse *sources* of democratic legitimacy in private and social life.

Let me briefly recap the thick and thin conceptions of legitimacy set out first in Chapter 4:

(a) *Thick:* Proponents of the thick view, such as Benhabib and Cohen, begin from the idea that free and reasoned deliberation is the basis of democratic legitimacy. However, they conceptualize deliberation as bound by strong normative constraints of egalitarian reciprocity, publicity, and reasonableness. Moreover, they argue that the outcomes that issue from deliberation should be subjected to a further test of legitimacy: outcomes are said to be legitimate if they are the product of deliberative communication constrained by norms of rationality and publicity, and if the agreements that participants reach *also* reflect these norms. For some proponents of the thick conception, deliberation should also aim to yield consensus on pivotal norms, which communicative agents must be able to endorse for the same, shared (normative) reasons.[2]

(b) *Thin:* On the thin account, a political procedure is democratically legitimate if all affected individuals are freely included in reasoned deliberation aimed at establishing *which* political principles or policies they and others should be bound by. Bohman argues that we should locate democratic legitimacy in the process of striving to reach free agreement through dialogical activity, and rejects strong constraints on deliberative outcomes, such as consensus.[3] Young also endorses a version of the thin conception of legitimacy, emphasizing the requirement of political inclusion.[4]

The project of legitimizing democracy, I argue, depends in part on rejecting the thick conception of democratic legitimacy. Only the *procedures* of political deliberation should be held to a test of democratic legitimacy, and a minimalist one at that; we must also ensure that the thin conception of democratic legitimacy does not smuggle in any strenuous and unnecessary normative constraints. At the same time, it is necessary to expand the thinner conception to include an account of how informal democratic activity and contestation by cultural group members affects the validity of social practices and arrangements. From South African women changing the customs surrounding lobolo and customary marriage, to Muslim women protesting the banning

---

[2] According to Jürgen Habermas, 'a rationally motivated (*Einverständnis*) consensus rests on reasons that convince all parties *in the same way*'. See his *Between Facts and Norms*, p. 166.

[3] Bohman, *Public Deliberation*, p. 34.

[4] Young, *Inclusion and Democracy*, p. 52.

of headscarves in French schools, and British South Asian women's activism around the issue of forced marriage, informal democratic activity can speak volumes about the legitimacy or illegitimacy of roles and customs. Formal political processes can and should incorporate evidence of citizens' democratic activity in deliberations about contested social practices.

The reconceived conception of deliberative legitimacy I have developed in this book aims to incorporate these neglected spheres and aspects of democratic activity. It also eschews strong norms of moral consensus and universalizability in public reason-giving, and rejects an idealized conception of moral discourse. My approach to mediating conflicts of culture emphasizes open deliberation, and proposes negotiation and compromise as tools for reaching resolutions. As such, the account of democratic legitimacy I am reaching for here cannot guarantee liberal outcomes: participants to deliberation may ultimately choose to preserve customs that are nonliberal in some regard (such as the decision not to prohibit polygamy in South Africa). Just as holding deliberative outcomes to a test of democratic legitimacy is intended to eliminate agreements that are not recognizably liberal, so are the normative constraints employed by most deliberative democrats expected to yield liberal results. Yet as I have argued, in plural societies with democratic constitutional frameworks, arguably there may exist policies that challenge liberal values but which are nonetheless valid outcomes of deliberation. For instance, we might imagine deliberation leading to policies in which certain substantive equality protections are deemed to take a back seat to collective Aboriginal rights and sovereignty. It seems unjust from the standpoint of democratic legitimacy to rule out *these* kinds of agreements a priori.

Idealized forms of deliberation, I argued in Chapter 4, are normatively problematic in the potential exclusions that they effect, and so are also of limited use in mediating conflicts in culturally plural societies. Such idealized accounts of deliberation pose similar difficulties when it comes to the task of *justifying* the principle of democratic legitimacy in diverse societies. A thin, procedural conception of democratic legitimacy seems more likely than the thick conception to meet with the provisional agreement of members of diverse communities. Although it surely will not win the allegiance of *all*, this account certainly expresses a widely held belief—by no means limited to liberal democratic societies—that people should have a say in establishing which practices, principles, and arrangements they are to be bound by. By contrast, a thick notion of deliberative legitimacy employs a sustantive ideal of communicative rationality, which requires that participants discuss disagreements in a process of moral argumentation. As we saw earlier, this view presupposes normative commitments to universalizability and public reason, and may also hold out moral consensus as the goal of deliberation. Yet even proponents of deliberative democracy who reject idealized forms of deliberation claim, problematically, that certain substantive liberal principles must be taken as nonnegotiables in democratic discourse, or as normatively prior to deliberation. For instance, Amy Gutmann, who espouses an ideal of democratic constitutionalism, argues that liberal democracies should insist on core democratic principles of civic equality, equal freedom, and basic opportunity.

As the discussion of Native women in Canada and the reform of customary law in South Africa illustrated, however the stipulation of norms of reason-ableness, egalitarian reciprocity (Benhabib), and publicity in advance of deliberation can make it difficult to reframe gender justice in terms other than liberal individual equality. Idealized versions of deliberative democracy stipulate that no reasons can be given, and no norms appealed to, which are not fully in keeping with the ideal of individual equality. Sometimes this requirement is construed merely as the recognition of interlocutors' equal worth and dig-nity—a norm of reciprocity, in other words. But from here, more substantive conceptions of equality quickly find their way into the formulation of delib-erative democracy, thus opening up the possibility of incommensurability. For example, as we saw in Chapter 5, some Aboriginal peoples consider values such as social harmony as much more central to their way of life than individual equality. Legal scholar Mary Ellen Turpel writes that for many First Nations communities, '[e]quality is not an important political or social concept'.[5] In devising formal procedures for political deliberation about contested cultural practices, it seems both normatively unjust and counter-productive to begin by asserting *as background norms* ideals that are either controversial or open to widely conflicting interpretations. If a substantive ideal of equality is taken as an a priori norm of rational political discourse, it may place beyond the ambit of valid deliberation and decision-making those conflicts in which equality is precisely what is contested. Disputes about gender roles and arrangements, as well as about membership rules, funda-mentally concern the social relationships of different individuals within the group, their relative positions of power, and so forth. Some of the arguments and reasons offered by factions within traditional cultural and religious communities are in effect claims about who matters most, and whose voice counts in political life; group members may justly reject the imposition of an a priori norm of equality on the terms and outcome of political debate. Consider, for example, the US Supreme Court's decision to uphold the Pueblo Indians' discriminatory membership rules disenfranchising women (but not men) who marry outside the band. Those who opposed the decision argued that

---

[5] Turpel, 'Patriarchy and Paternalism,' p. 179.

the state thereby perpetuated the unequal status of all Pueblo women.[6] By contrast, those who supported the decision claimed that it affirmed the cultural equality and sovereignty of the Pueblo nation. Yet had individual and sexuality equality been thematized more sharply as contested norms in more democratic deliberations about the issue of membership, perhaps the more controversial justifications for excluding women would have come to light.

Deliberative democrats and political liberals might say, in response to this point, that arguments by Native leaders in Canada and the United States aimed at excluding certain individuals from the benefits of membership rightly fail the tests of publicity and reasonableness. Claims that imply or assert women's inequality are unreasonable and so should be excluded from democratic deliberation. Yet if these beliefs, interests, and motives are crucial factors in the dispute, then they need to be put on the table where they can be discussed, evaluated, and contested. The belief that vulnerable group members, such as women, are best protected by always seeking to prevent the introduction of normatively unreasonable or unjust claims in political dialogue gambles that these ostensibly unjust reasons will cease to influence debate and decisions in important ways. Instead of insisting that arguments made in the course of deliberation must cohere with a particular conception of individual equality, then, it could be instructive and worthwhile to permit such beliefs to be presented and contested in political deliberation. As Dryzek notes, '[o]ne cannot abolish prejudice, racism, sectarianism, and rational egoism by forbidding their proponents from public speaking. A model of deliberative democracy that stresses the contestation of discourses in the public sphere allows for challenge of sectarian positions, as it allows for challenge of all kinds of oppressive discourses'.[7]

* * *

So far I have been concerned with what democratic legitimacy should *not* require. But what does it take to make deliberative procedures democratically *legitimate*? To recap the argument from Chapter 4, such processes must firstly ensure nondomination, by not violating the basic rights and freedoms of individuals, including the right to expression and the right to participate in political life free from intimidation or coercion. Second, democratic legitimacy requires that formal decision-making procedures meaningfully include all individual stakeholders who wish to debate and to try to impact particular proposals. Those who stand to be impacted more than others, and those who

---

[6] This case—*Santa Clara Pueblo* v. *Martinez* 436 U.S. 49 (1978)—is widely discussed in the literature on internal minorities. See for example Carla Christofferson, 'Tribal Courts' Failure to Protect Native American Women: A Reevaluation of the Indian Civil Rights Act,' *Yale Law Journal*, 101/1 (1991), 169–85.

[7] Dryzek, *Deliberative Democracy and Beyond*, pp. 168–9.

have in-depth experience of a particular practice, may have an even greater right to be heard and to influence decisions, as Ian Shapiro has argued.[8] The precise means through which members might make their political voices heard will vary depending on the kinds of lives they lead and the positions they occupy within their communities. Political participation and activity may also be informal, in democracy's expanded sites.

The third criterion for the democratic legitimacy of political processes requires that deliberative outcomes be revisable: political institutions and forms of governance decisions must always be open to discursive challenge, and ultimately, to revision. To some extent, of course, genuine political inclusion already depends on the possibility of such contestation; but where such inclusion is achieved, publicly articulated ideals, laws, institutions must be seen to be genuinely open to revision. In conceiving of the criterion of contestability, I borrow from Phillip Pettit's work on republicanism: Pettit argues that individuals must be free from relations of domination in both their public and private lives, where domination is understood as vulnerability to arbitrary interference and exploitation by the state or other individuals. But rather than arguing that nondomination depends on minimalist negative liberties as we might expect, Pettit claims that 'what is required for non-arbitrariness in the exercise of a certain power is ... the permanent possibility of effectively contesting it'.[9] This criterion of contestability is thus in some ways the true mark of democratically legitimate decision-making procedures.

Similarly, I have argued that the legitimacy of controversial cultural practices is thus at least partly bound up with their contestability and revisability. Cultural group members must also be free to publicly criticize their customs and arrangements without fear of reprisals from the traditional leaders in their communities. A person cannot be said to readily accept or consent to an arrangement unless one could also reject it, as we saw in the discussion of O'Neill's thesis on 'possible consent', in Chapter 4.

Having whittled down the idea of democratic legitimacy to a more minimalist conception, the problem of justifying democratic legitimacy is somewhat simplified. Let me finally turn to the question, why democratic legitimacy? Why should the principle of democratic legitimacy, and decision-making processes based on this principle, be persuasive to members of communities with nonliberal and possibly deeply hierarchical social traditions within plural liberal states? I argued in Chapter 4 that the political inclusion mandated by the principle of democratic legitimacy is a normative requirement of genuinely democratic processes of decision-making. But there

---

[8] Ian Shapiro, *Democratic Justice* (New Haven, CT: Yale University Press, 1999), pp. 37–8.
[9] Pettit, *Republicanism*, p. 63.

is also a formal reason why even members of traditional or nonliberal cultural communities should agree to democratic legitimacy as a principle shaping political deliberation and decision-making. Appeals to the validity of cultural and religious forms of life, and to the importance of cultural self-determination, presuppose that group members have capacities for reason and autonomy. Cultural members are, after all, valuing agents, capable of forming judgments, and of understanding and arguing about the value of their cultural practices. There is no good reason to limit these capacities strictly to *non*political evaluative activity; political agency is a central part of what it is to have rational (nonidealized) autonomous agency.

As argued earlier, even nonliberal cultural minorities have cause to accept the principle of democratic legitimacy as broadly applicable to deliberation and decision-making for it will ultimately enable them to maintain a degree of self-determination as regards cultural reforms. Even within the most traditional cultural communities, there are competing interpretations of customs and variations on their practice; usually these differences are unremarkable and not a source of strife. But sometimes these differences manifest as disagreements with very concrete social and political consequences for group members. Attempts simply to suppress these disagreements within communities cannot really be in the interests of the group as a whole (or, arguably, the self-interest of leaders) over the long term. The cultural practices of traditional communities residing within liberal democratic states will continue to evolve, with or without the support of prevailing authorities. If cultural groups want to retain as much say as possible over the evaluation and reform of their own practices then democratizing their internal processes and agreeing to hold their social arrangements to a test of democratic legitimacy may actually be the best options available.

Habermas has remarked that 'When a culture has become reflexive, the only traditions and forms of life that can sustain themselves are those that *bind* their members, while at the same time allowing members to subject the traditions to critical examination and leaving later generations the *option* of learning from other traditions.'[10] There is ample evidence that nonliberal cultural groups ensconced within liberal democratic states frequently face formidable demands from within their own communities for reform, including more democratic methods of resolving disputes. In refusing to let their members adapt cultural practices to better fit their lives, or in refusing to let individuals opt out of

---

[10] Jürgen Habermas, 'Struggles for Recognition in the Democratic State', in *The Inclusion of the Other: Studies in Political Theory*, eds. Ciarin Cronin and Pablo De Greiff (Cambridge, MA: MIT Press, 2001), p. 222.

certain practices (such as arranged marriage), traditional leaders risk eroding their own bases of support and splintering their communities. Dissenting members may increasingly choose to exercise their right of exit in particularly confining contexts.

Religious groups pose a particular challenge to this argument for democratic legitimacy, since nondemocratic forms of decision-making and authority are often constitutive of their identity (e.g. the Roman Catholic Church and Orthodox Judaism) and central to the power of religious leaders. But even in these cases, it is possible for the liberal state to encourage more democratic means of settling disputes about the status and possible reform of contested cultural practices. When cultural rules, practices, or exclusions are protested by individual members as unjust, or else push against liberal norms and rights protections, it will usually be more fruitful to let those communities proceed with internal processes of reform, where these exist (provided they adhere to the principles of nondomination, political inclusion, and revisability). Where such internal processes are nonexistent or thin on the ground, the liberal state can and should encourage the development of other inclusive processes of debate, evaluation, and reform, and foster specifically *democratic* resolution of such conflicts. These processes will oftentimes include stakeholders from groups committed to, for example, legal reform and advocacy of women's rights, and may even include representatives from governmental and semigovernmental bodies.

Democratic processes for evaluating, and if necessary, reforming traditions from within, will require that those in positions of power in cultural communities not block their members' efforts to democratically negotiate and shape the terms of their own relationships to social practices and arrangements. Admittedly, this is a tall order—especially in the case of religious groups—and not easily brought about. Traditional cultural authorities may resist efforts at reform and resent any interference in the running of their communities. They may also try to marginalize internal critics by associating them with ideological agendas of those outside the group. Some liberal political theorists have at this juncture proposed that the state needs to reinforce opportunities for exit for group members who face discrimination or persecution. I agree. But perhaps more importantly, the liberal democratic state can and should support internal group processes for the reevaluation and reform of contested customs and arrangements, particularly for women. It can do so by reinforcing existing democratic expressions and resistance, and requiring that all stakeholders, including marginalized persons, be included in consultation processes regarding contested practices. Or, as Spinner-Halev has argued, where a largely autonomous ethnic or religious group is charged with reforming its own personal laws, the state can 'insist that these laws be established by democratically accountable representatives, not just the traditional male religious leaders'.[11]

DEMOCRATIZING LEGITIMACY

Moving to more democratic methods of settling disputes about contested cultural practices, particularly those concerning sex roles and arrangements, raises questions about the internal power dynamics of cultural groups, as we have seen. Are not vulnerable members of nonliberal national, ethnic, and religious groups open to manipulation and harm in a more democratic setting—especially women? Moreover, might not women in highly constrained circumstances merely capitulate to the social roles that are most familiar to them, and which may offer them a modicum of protection? These two concerns, raised by such thinkers as Okin, O'Neill, and Nussbaum, do not in my view vindicate a liberal over a democratic approach to mediating conflicts about women's roles and arrangements. Okin and O'Neill are right to assert that coercion and manipulation undercut agents' freedom and capacity to resist and revise social practices, but both are overly pessimistic about the prospect for developing (and reforming) forums for democratic deliberation in minority communities. They also underestimate the extent to which women can and do contest and shape their roles and arrangements. Similarly, while Nussbaum's concerns about the adaptive preferences of women in traditional settings are warranted, this challenge, as argued earlier, is not best met by introducing a ranked (and controversial) list of necessary human capabilities as a means of determining which social practices to support and which to prohibit. Rather, by recognizing and supporting—both morally and materially— women's existing ways of shaping their cultural practices and arrangements, and by helping to empower women in both formal and informal democratic life, it becomes more possible to view women's stated preferences as valid.

These concerns raised by Okin, O'Neill, Nussbaum, and other liberals make it all the more necessary, however, to specify which cultural conflicts and decisions are good candidates for democratization, and which are not. In addition to cultural practices that are already prohibited by criminal laws (such as honor killings), sanctions can and usually ought to be applied in cases where members claim mistreatment or discrimination at the hands of their group. So, for example, this would suggest that in states where religious institutions are legally exempt from equality and nondiscrimination statutes

---

[11] Spinner-Halev, 'Feminism, Multiculturalism, Oppression', p. 108.

(such as the United States, Canada, and Israel), it may be just to withdraw tax exempt status and other benefits where a religious group has consistently refused to redress claims of sexual or race-based discrimination. The backup protection that such a legal approach can offer vulnerable group members is not inconsiderable. However, such a strategy is by no means mutually exclusive with the more deliberative democratic approach that I argue it is still to be preferred, both within cultural communities and in groups' dealings with the liberal state. Whatever deliberative procedures are adopted, it is important to protect the rights of all group members to participate in the political process, advancing their own accounts, for example, of how particular customs do and ought to function, and how they might be reformed. Those who are most impacted by a custom, and those most likely to be silenced by power dynamics within the community, might even be given a more prominent role in deliberation where the process involves state institutions. Nor can this right to have a say in the customs and arrangements that one is to be bound by be permanently surrendered (except through exit, in some circumstances).

Aside from these protections, legitimizing democracy will ultimately require that we think a little differently about the concept of democratic legitimacy itself. In particular, we have seen that it requires that we expand our understanding of the *basis* of democratic legitimacy in culturally plural, liberal democracies, and to take a broader view of what makes a practice valid or invalid. Liberal and deliberative democratic accounts of legitimacy claim that particular political procedures and/or norms establish the legitimacy of decisions about contested policies or practices. Political procedures indeed play a central role in securing the legitimacy of a contested norm or practice, and writers such as Benhabib are right to try to conceive of ways to open up and democratize spaces of public deliberation.[12] However, I have also tried to show that such procedures do not exhaust the sources of democratic legitimacy in plural democratic states. As we have seen in the cases of South Africa, Canada, and Britain, *informal* kinds of democratic activity in private and social life may also be understood as speaking to the issue of a custom's legitimacy, or lack thereof. Democratic legitimacy, on this view, requires that debate and decision-making processes acknowledge the multiple sources of validity within cultural communities, the many points of contestation, and the undeniable fluidity of cultural practices.

Not all controversial cultural practices will become the subject of formal political debate and decision-making, let alone legislation. Nor should they: there are ways short of formal political procedures to help communities determine the democratic validity of customs. For example, one might ask

---

[12] Benhabib, *The Claims of Culture*.

whether group members seem to strongly identify with specific customs, and whether these are, by their account, central components of their lives. To what extent have group members tried to modify certain practices to better meet their own changing needs and circumstances, or to reflect the shifting or evolving shared understandings in their community? And finally, to what extent are practices and arrangements contested, and contestable, on the ground? Group members' responses to social practices may range from subtle subversions of customs, to the retrieval of forgotten but empowering social arrangements, to outright refusal of a tradition that some members find restrictive or demeaning. These responses can and do also occur even within very restrictive and traditional social contexts; indeed, in such contexts, informal resistance and ad hoc revision of practices may be all that is possible. Yet as I have argued, there are good reasons to view these individual and collective social responses as contributing to an assessment of the legitimacy or illegitimacy of customs, either taken alone, or used to inform more structured political deliberations on contested customs discussed earlier. Rather than viewing cultural change and contestation as signs that a custom lacks validity, then (as some argue), we might consider these as precisely markers of a vibrant and dynamic culture.[13]

Democratic theorists who endorse public deliberation as a means of mediating cultural conflicts have tended to ignore informal democratic activity as a source of normative validity. Benhabib argues in *The Claims of Culture* that we need to conceive of democratic forms of intercultural dialogue, but she conceives of these along the broad outlines of formal public deliberation.[14] Spinner-Halev also favors democratic decision-making procedures, but again, limits his discussion to institutionalized political processes. Both of these thinkers are surely right about the importance of fostering democratically inclusive, formal political deliberation and decision-making in trying to resolve conflicts of culture. However, as I have argued, it is also important to conceive of the sources of democratic expression much more broadly than do either Benhabib or Spinner-Halev.

Some deliberative democrats have urged the expansion of *formal* sites of political dialogue in contemporary democratic polities. For example, Bohman argues that a dialogical approach to deliberation requires the 'expanding (of) opportunities and access to deliberative arenas ...'.[15] My own recommendation that democratic legitimacy should be seen as including informal

---

[13] As Alison Renteln writes, 'The denial of the existence of cultural traditions on the grounds of a lack of unanimitiy is manifestly absurd'. See *The Cultural Defense*, p. 12.

[14] Benhabib, *The Claims of Culture*, p. ix.

[15] Bohman, *Public Deliberation*, p. 36.

democratic activity is compatible with this general idea. Concretely, expanding sites of political dialogue might mean developing mechanisms to make sure that less powerful cultural group members can contribute to deliberations where contested practices are under discussion. Individuals whose voices are not readily heard within their groups' own political processes are still possessed of agency. It may also be possible to create new spaces for political debate that can help to empower such individuals, like special legislative advisory bodies, organized forums for immigrant youth, and so forth. But other forums can and should develop from cultural group's own structures for decision-making (e.g., in the case of Native peoples and some religious groups).

Deliberative democracy theorists should be thinking about ways to *expand* the ability and opportunities of less powerful citizens to influence decisions about contested social practices and arrangements outside formal political deliberation.[16] The liberal state can also help to amplify and give political clout to this informal democratic activity in numerous ways: the example of the British inquiry into arranged marriage shows how government consultations can help underscore the authority of community groups that are aiming to support cultural dissenters. It is most helpful, as I have argued, if these consultative processes focus on the practical needs and interests of group members, for a variety of reasons, not least because a practical focus invites cultural group members to talk about the ways in which social customs are evolving, or have already changed. Although legislation governing cultural practices and arrangements can also take account of the fluidity of traditions, it cannot do so without the input of community members who have local knowledge of those customs—or a 'lived experience' of practices.[17]

The deliberative democratic approach to cultural conflicts advanced in this book does not purport to guarantee liberal solutions, nor does it promise that deliberative outcomes will always be the most fair or just from the point of view of all concerned. But the procedures for evaluating and, if necessary, reforming contested cultural customs outlined here are democratic and practically grounded; as such, they can generate proposals that are both democratically legitimate and politically viable in their reflection of cultural

[16] Excluding coercive, violent, and outright manipulative forms of influence, of course.

[17] The liberal state can support formal and informal democratic activity in other ways. Better funding for cultural community and grassroots groups is one way to extend support, for example. Trusted arbitrators could be supplied to help foster fair decision-making within cultural groups when disagreement is acute. Legislative and judicial bodies in the broader society can also be made more open to democratic processes. In particular, courts could be made more receptive to culturally distinctive forms of argumentation and evidence-giving. See discussions by Iris Young and Angie Means, both of whom have advanced compelling arguments in favor of expanding democratic legal and political norms to acknowledge the authority of alternative cultural narratives.

practices and communities in flux. I have argued that a democratic, politically focused approach to resolving disputes about contested cultural practices is to be preferred over liberal juridical and toleration approaches as well as unmodified deliberative democratic approaches. This argument is grounded in a defense of the principle of democratic legitimacy, which I have said requires the meaningful political inclusion in decision-making of all those whose lives will be affected by deliberative outcomes. Legitimizing democracy in culturally diverse societies therefore requires that we take a much broader view of both legitimacy and democracy. It follows from this that any formal processes for determining the status of contested customs should acknowledge the diverse sources of democratic legitimacy; thus, the everyday ways in which cultural group members contest, revise, and shape their own cultural traditions and roles should move from the periphery to the foreground of debates about disputed customs. In recognizing the internally contested nature of so many cultural practices, we acknowledge that cultures evolve and change through individual and collective imagination, initiative, and agency.

Bibliography

Abraham, Margaret, *Speaking the Unspeakable: Marital Violence Against South Asian Immigrants in the United States* (Rutgers, NJ: Rutgers University Press, 2000).

Ackerly, Brooke, 'Women's Human Rights Activists as Cross-Cultural Theorists', *International Journal of Feminist Politics*, 3/3 (2001), 1–36.

Afary, Janet, 'The War Against Feminism in the Name of the Almighty: Making Sense of Gender and Muslim Fundamentalism', *New Left Review*, 224 (1997), 89–110.

Albertyn, Cathy, 'Women and the Transition to Democracy in South Africa', in C. Murray (ed.), *Gender and the New South African Legal Order* (Kenwyn, South Africa: Juta, 1994).

Alfred, Taiaiake, *Peace, Power, and Righteousness: An Indigenous Manifesto* (Oxford: Oxford University Press, 1999).

Ali, Shaheen Sardar, 'Women's Rights, CEDAW and International Human Rights Debates: Towards Empowerment?', in Jane Parpart, Shirin Rai, and Kathleen Staudt (eds.), *Rethinking Empowerment: Gender and Development in a Global/Local World* (London and New York: Routledge, 2002).

Alibhai-Brown, Yasmin, 'After Multiculturalism', *The Political Quarterly*, special issue (2001), 47–56.

An-Na'im, Abdullahi Ahmed, 'Problems of Universal Cultural Legitimacy for Human Rights', in Abdullahi Ahmed An-Na'im and Francis Deng (eds.), *Human Rights in Africa: Cross-Cultural Perspectives* (Washington, DC: The Brookings Institution, 1990).

—— ,'Towards a Cross-Cultural Approach to Defining International Standards of Human Rights', in Abdullahi Ahmed An-Na'im (ed.), *Human Rights in Cross-Cultural Perspectives: A Quest for Consensus* (Philadelphia, PA: University of Pennsylvania Press, 1992).

—— and Francis Deng, 'Introduction', in Abdullahi Ahmed Na'im and Francis Deng (eds.), *Human Rights in Africa: Cross Cultural Perspectives* (Washington, DC: The Brookings Institution, 1990).

Arneil, Barbara, 'Sexual Equality and Cultural Protections' (unpublished manuscript, 2003).

—— 'Cultural Protections vs. Cultural Justice', in Barbara Arneil, Rita Dhamoon, Monique Deveaux, and Avigail Eisenberg (eds.), *Sexual Justice/Cultural Justice: Critical Perspectives in Theory and Practice* (forthcoming 2006, Routledge).

—— Monique Deveaux, Rita Dhamoon, and Avigail Eisenberg (eds.), *Sexual Justice/ Cultural Justice: Critical Perspectives in Theory and Practice* (forthcoming 2006, Routledge).

Askin, Kelly and Dorean Koenig (eds.), *Women and International Human Rights Law*, Vol. 1 (Ardsley, NY: Transnational Publishers, Inc., 1999).

Bader, Veit, 'Culture and Identity: Contesting Constructivism', *Ethnicities*, 1/2 (2001), 251–73.

Baker, Judith, (ed.), *Group Rights* (Toronto: University of Toronto Press, 1994).

Barclay, Linda, 'Autonomy and the Social Self', in Catriona Mackenzie and Natalie Stoljar (eds.), *Relational Autonomy: Feminist Perspectives on Autonomy, Agency, and the Social Self* (Oxford: Oxford University Press, 2000).

Barry, Brian, *Culture and Equality* (Cambridge, MA: Harvard University Press, 2001).

—— *Justice as Impartiality* (Cambridge, MA: Harvard University Press, 1995).

—— *Theories of Justice* (Cambridge, MA: Harvard University Press, 1989).

Barsh, Russel L., 'Indigenous Peoples and the Idea of Individual Human Rights', *Native Studies Review*, 10/2 (1995), 35–55.

Beitz, Charles, 'Human Rights as a Common Concern', *American Political Science Review*, 95/2 (2001), 269–82.

Bekker, J. C., 'Human Rights and Customary Law', *The Human Rights and Constitutional Law Journal of Southern Africa*, 1/4 (1997), 21–3.

Bell, Catherine and David Kahane, *Intercultural Dispute Resolution in Aboriginal Contexts* (Vancouver and Toronto: University of British Columbia Press, 2004).

Bellamy, Richard, *Liberalism and Pluralism: Towards a Politics of Compromise* (London and New York: Routledge, 1999).

Benhabib, Seyla, 'Deliberative Rationality and Models of Democratic Legitimacy', *Constellations*, 1 (1994), 26–52.

—— *The Claims of Culture: Equality and Diversity in the Global Era* (Princeton, NJ: Princeton University Press, 2002).

Benn, S. I., 'Individuality, Autonomy, and Community', in Eugene Kamenka (ed.), *Community as a Social Ideal* (London: Edward Arnold, 1982).

Bennett, T. W., *Human Rights and Customary Law Under the South African Constitution* (Kenwyn, South Africa: Juta, 1999).

—— 'The Equality Clause and Customary Law', *South African Journal on Human Rights*, 10 (1994), 122–30.

Bentley, Kristina, 'Whose Right is it Anyway? Equality, Culture and Conflicts of Rights in South Africa', *Occasional Paper* 4 (Cape Town: Human Sciences Research Council, Democracy and Governance Programme, 2003).

Bohler, Narnia, 'Equality Courts: Introducing the Possibility of Listening to Different Voices in South Africa?', *THRHR*, 63 (2000), 288–94.

Bohman, James, 'Public Reason and Cultural Pluralism', *Political Theory*, 23 (1995), 253–79.

—— 'Deliberative Democracy and Effective Social Freedom: Capabilities, Resources, and Opportunities', in James Bohman and William Rehg (eds.), *Deliberative Democracy: Essays on Reason and Politics* (Cambridge, MA and London: MIT Press, 1997/9).

—— 'The Coming of Age of Deliberative Democracy', *The Journal of Political Philosophy*, 6/4 (1998), 400–25.

—— *Public Deliberation: Pluralism, Complexity, and Democracy* (Cambridge, MA: MIT Press, 2000).

—— and William Rehg (eds.), *Deliberative Democracy: Essays on Reason and Politics* (Cambridge, MA and London: MIT Press, 1997/9).

Bronstein, Victoria, 'Reconceptualizing the Customary Law Debate in South Africa', *South African Journal on Human Rights*, 14 (1998), 388–410.

Carens, Joseph, *Culture, Citizenship and Community: A Contextual Exploration of Justice as Evenhandedness* (Oxford: Oxford University Press, 2000).

—— and Melissa Williams, 'Muslim Minorities in Liberal Democracies: The Politics of Misrecognition', in Rainer Bauböck, Agnes Heller, and Aristide Zolberg (eds.), *The Challenge of Diversity: Integration and Pluralism in Societies of Immigration* (Aldershot, UK: Avebury, 1996).

Cerna, Christina and Jennifer Wallace, 'Women and Culture', in Kelly Askin and Dorean Koenig (eds.), *Women and International Human Rights Law,* Vol. 1 (Ardsley, NY: Transnational Publishers, Inc., 1999).

Chambers, Simone, 'Discourse and Democratic Practices', in Stephen White (ed.), *The Cambridge Companion to Habermas* (Cambridge: Cambridge University Press, 1995).

—— *Reasonable Democracy: Jürgen Habermas and the Politics of Discourse* (Ithaca, NY: Cornell University Press, 1996).

—— 'Democracy, Popular Sovereignty, and Constitutional Legitimacy', *Constellations,* 11/2 (2004), 153–73.

Chanock, Martin, ' "Culture" and Human Rights: Orientalising, Occidentalising and Authenticity', in Mahmood Mamdani (ed.), *Beyond Rights Talk and Culture Talk* (New York: St. Martin's Press, 2000).

Charlesworth, Hilary, 'The Challenges of Human Rights Law for Religious Traditions', in Mark Janis and Carolyn Evans (eds.), *Religion and International Law* (Boston, London, and The Hague: Martinus Nijhoff Publishers, 1999).

Cheadle, H. and D. Davis, 'The Application of the 1996 Constitution in the Private Sphere', *South African Journal on Human Rights,* 13 (1997), 44–66.

Chinkin, Christine, 'Cultural Relativism and International Law', in Courtney Howland (ed.), *Religious Fundamentalisms and the Human Rights of Women* (New York: St. Martin's Press, 1999).

Chiste, Katherine Beaty, 'Aboriginal Women and Self-Government: Challenging Leviathan', *American Indian Culture and Research Journal,* 18/3 (1994), 19–43.

Christman, John (ed.), *The Inner Citadel: Essays on Individual Autonomy* (New York and Oxford: Oxford University Press, 1989).

Christofferson, Carla, 'Tribal Courts' Failure to Protect Native American Women: A Reevaluation of the Indian Civil Rights Act', *Yale Law Journal,* 101/1 (1991), 169–85.

Clark, Belinda, 'The Vienna Convention Reservations Regime and the Convention on the Discrimination Against Women', *The American Journal of International Law,* 85/2 (1991), 281–321.

Cohen, Joshua, 'Deliberation and Democratic Legitimacy', in James Bohman and William Rehg (eds.), *Deliberative Democracy: Essays on Reason and Politics* (Cambridge, MA, and London: MIT Press, 1997/9).

—— 'Procedure and Substance in Deliberative Democracy', in James Bohman and William Rehg (eds.), *Deliberative Democracy: Essays on Reason and Politics* (Cambridge, MA, and London: MIT Press, 1997/9).

Cohen, Joshua, Matthew Howard, and Martha Nussbaum, *Is Multiculturalism Bad for Women?* (Princeton, NJ: Princeton University Press, 1999).

Constitution of the Republic of South Africa (1996).

Coomaraswamy, Radhika, 'Reinventing International Law: Women's Rights as Human Rights in the International Community', in Peter Van Ness (ed.), *Debating Human Rights: Critical Essays from the United States and Asia* (London and New York: Routledge, 1999).

Currie, Ian, 'The Future of Customary Law: Lessons from the Lobolo Debate', in C. Murray (ed.), *Gender and the New South African Legal Order* (Kenwyn, South Africa: Juta, 1994).

Delacourt, Susan, 'Natives Divided Over Charter: Women Will Not Accept Self-Government Without Guarantees', *The Globe and Mail*, March 14, 1992.

—— 'Text Being Altered, Native Women Say', *The Globe and Mail*, September 19, 1992.

Deveaux, Monique, *Cultural Pluralism and Dilemmas of Justice* (Ithaca, NY: Cornell University Press, 2000).

—— 'Conflicting Equalities? Cultural Group Rights and Sex Equality', *Political Studies*, 48/3 (2000), 522–39.

—— 'Political Morality and Culture: What Difference Do Differences Make?', *Social Theory and Practice*, 28/3 (2002), 503–18.

—— 'A Deliberative Approach to Conflicts of Culture', *Political Theory*, 31/6 (2003), 780–807.

——, Barbara Arneil, Rita Dhamoon, and Avigail Eisenberg, eds., *Sexual Justice/Cultural Justice: Critical Perspectives in Theory and Practice* (forthcoming 2006, Routledge).

de Vos, Pierre, 'Equality for All? A Critical Analysis of the Equality Jurisprudence of the Constitutional Court', *THRHR*, 63 (2000), 62–75.

Dhamoon, Rita, 'Shifting from Culture to Cultural: Critical Theorizing of Identity/Difference Politics', forthcoming, *Constellations*, 13/3 (2006).

Dick, Caroline, 'The Politics of Intragroup Difference: First Nations' Women and the *Sawbridge* Dispute', *Canadian Journal of Political Science*, 39/1 (2006), 95–116.

Donnelly, Rachel, 'Arranged Marriages on Cultural Heritage But Man-Made Law', *The Irish Times*, June 3, 1999.

Dryzek, John, *Deliberative Democracy and Beyond: Liberals, Critics, Contestations* (Oxford: Oxford University Press, 2000).

—— 'Deliberative Democracy in Divided Societies', *Political Theory*, 33/2 (2005), 218–42.

Dworkin, Gerald, *The Theory and Practice of Autonomy* (Cambridge: Cambridge University Press, 1988).

Eisenberg, Avigail, 'The Politics of Individual and Group Difference in Canadian Jurisprudence', *Canadian Journal of Political Science*, 27/1 (1994), 3–21.

—— 'Context, Cultural Difference, Sex and Social Justice', *Canadian Journal of Political Science*, 35/3 (2002), 613–28.

—— 'Diversity and Equality: Three Approaches to Cultural and Sexual Difference', *Journal of Political Philosophy*, 11/1 (2003), 41–64.

—— 'Public Institutions and the Assessment of Cultural Identity', *unpublished manuscript* (2004).

—— 'Identity and Liberal Politics: The Problem of Minorities Within Minorities', in Avigail Eisenberg and Jeff Spinner-Halev (eds.), *Minorities Within Minorities: Equality, Rights, and Diversity* (Cambridge: Cambridge University Press, 2005).

—— and Jeff Spinner-Halev, eds., *Minorities within Minorities: Equality, Rights, and Diversity* (Cambridge: Cambridge University Press, 2005).

Ewing, Katherine, 'Legislating Religious Freedom: Muslim Challenges to the Relationship between "Church" and "State" in Germany and France', *Daedalus*, 129/4 (2000), 31–54.

Favell, Adrian, 'Multicultural Race Relations in Britain', in Christian Joppke (ed.), *Challenge to the Nation State: Immigration in Western Europe and the United States* (Oxford: Oxford University Press, 1998).

Feinberg, Joel, 'Autonomy', in John Christman (ed.), *The Inner Citadel: Essays on Individual Autonomy* (New York and Oxford: Oxford University Press, 1989).

Ferejohn, John, 'Instituting Deliberative Democracy', in Ian Shapiro and Stephen Macedo (eds.), *Nomos XLII: Designing Democratic Institutions* (New York: New York University Press, 2000).

Fishbayn, Lisa, 'Litigating the Right to Culture: Family Law in the New South Africa', *International Journal of Law, Policy and the Family*, 13 (1999), 147–73.

Fleischacker, Samuel, *Integrity and Moral Relativism* (Leiden, The Netherlands: E. J. Brill, 1992).

Foucault, Michel, *Power/Knowledge: Selected Interviews and Other Writings 1972–1977*, ed. Colin Gordon (The Harvester Press,1980)

—— 'Afterward: the Subject and Power', in Hubert Dreyfus and Paul Rabinow (eds.), *Michel Foucault: Beyond Structuralism and Hermeneutics* (Chicago: University of Chicago Press, 1982).

Frankfurt, Harry, 'Freedom of the Will and the Concept of a Person', in John Christman (ed.), *The Inner Citadel: Essays on Individual Autonomy* (New York and Oxford: Oxford University Press, 1989).

Fraser, Nancy, 'From Redistribution to Recognition? Dilemmas of Justice in a "Postsocialist" Age', in *Justice Interruptus: Critical Reflections on the 'Postsocialist' Condition* (New York and London: Routledge, 1997).

—— 'Rethinking Recognition: Overcoming Displacement and Reification in Cultural Politics', in Barbara Hobson (ed.), *Recognition Struggles and Social Movements: Contested Identities, Agency, and Power* (Cambridge: Cambridge University Press, 2003).

Friedman, Elisabeth, 'Women's Human Rights: The Emergence of a Movement', in Julie Peters and Andrea Wolper (eds.), *Women's Rights, Human Rights: International Feminist Perspectives* (New York and London: Routledge, 1995).

Friedman, Marilyn, *Autonomy, Gender, and Politics* (Oxford: Oxford University Press, 2003).

Fullerton, Madeleine, 'A Sikh Girl's Bridal Path', *New Society*, 64 (June 16, 1983), 428–9.

Galeotti, Anna Elisabetta, 'Citizenship and Equality: The Place for Toleration', *Political Theory*, 21/4 (1993), 585–605.

Gauthier, David, *Morals by Agreement* (Oxford and New York: Oxford University Press, 1986).

Geertz, Clifford, *Available Light: Anthropological Reflections on Philosophical Topics* (Princeton, NJ: Princeton University Press, 2000).

Gewirth, Alan, 'Common Morality and the Community of Rights', in Gene Outka and John Reeder (eds.), *Prospects for a Common Morality* (Princeton, NJ: Princeton University Press, 1993).

Goodin, Robert, *Reflective Democracy* (Oxford: Oxford University Press, 2003).

—— 'Liberal Multiculturalism: Protective and Polygot', *Political Theory*, 34/2 (2006), 289–303.

Govender, Prakashnee, *The Status of Women Married in Terms of African Customary Law: A Study of Women's Experiences in the Eastern Cape and Western Cape Provinces* [Research Report No. 13] (Cape Town: National Association of Democratic Lawyers, 2000).

Government of Canada, *Consensus Report on the Constitution* (Charlottetown Accord), 1992.

Green, Joyce, 'Constitutionalising the Patriarchy: Aboriginal Women and Aboriginal Government', *Constitutional Forum*, 4/4 (1993), 110–20.

—— 'Canaries in the Mines of Citizenship: Indian Women in Canada', *Canadian Journal of Political Science*, 34/4 (2001), 715–38.

Green, Leslie, 'Internal Minorities and their Rights', in Judith Baker (ed.), *Group Rights* (Toronto: University of Toronto Press, 1994).

—— 'Rights of Exit', *Legal Theory*, 4/2 (1998), 168–85.

Griffin, Christopher, 'Debate: Democracy as a Non-Instrumentally Just Procedure', *The Journal of Political Philosophy*, 11/1 (2003), 111–21.

Grimshaw, Patricia, Katie Holmes, and Marilyn Lake, *Women's Rights and Human Rights: International Historical Perspectives* (New York: Palgrave MacMillan, 2001).

Guerrero, M. A. Jaimes, 'Exemplars of Indigenism: Native North American Women for De/ Colonization and Liberation', in C. Cohen, K. Jones, and J. Tronto (eds.), *Women Transforming Politics* (New York: New York University Press, 1997).

Gutmann, Amy, *Identity in Democracy* (Princeton, NJ: Princeton University Press, 2003).

—— and Dennis Thompson, *Democracy and Disagreement* (Cambridge, MA: Harvard University Press, 1996).

Habermas, Jürgen, 'Discourse Ethics: Notes on a Program of Philosophical Justification', in Fred Dallmayr and Seyla Benhabib (eds.), *The Communicative Ethics Controversy* (Cambridge, MA: MIT Press, 1990).

—— *Moral Consciousness and Communicative Action*, trans. C. Lenhardt and S. W. Nicholsen (Cambridge, MA: MIT Press, 1993).

—— *Between Facts and Norms*, trans. William Rehg (Cambridge, MA: MIT Press, 1996).

—— 'Struggles for Recognition in the Democratic State', in Ciarin Cronin and Pablo De Greiff (eds.), *The Inclusion of the Other: Studies in Political Theory* (Cambridge, MA: MIT Press, 2001).

'Headscarf Ban Sparks New Protests', BBC News world (web) edition, January 17, 2004.

Hernández-Truyol, Berta, Esperanza, 'Human Rights Through a Gendered Lens: Emergence, Evolution, Revolution', in Kelly Askin and Dorean Koenig (eds.), *Women and International Human Rights Law*, Vol. 1 (Transnational Publishers Inc., 1999).

Higgins, Tracy, 'Anti-Essentialism, Relativism, and Human Rights', *Harvard Women's Law Journal*, 19 (1996), reprinted in Henry Steiner and Philip Alston (eds.), *International Human Rights in Context: Law, Politics, Morals* (New York and Oxford: Oxford University Press, 2000).

Hill Jr., Thomas, *Autonomy and Self-Respect* (Cambridge: Cambridge University Press, 1991).

Hill, Sharon Bishop, 'Self-Determination and Autonomy', in R. Wasserstrom (ed.), *Today's Moral Problems* (New York: Macmillan, 1979).

Himonga, Chuma, 'Law and Gender in Southern Africa: Human Rights and Family Law', in J. Eekelaar and T. Nhlapo (eds.), *The Changing Family: International Perspectives* (Oxford: Hart publications, 1998).

—— and Craig Bosch, 'The Application of African Customary Law under the Constitution of South Africa: Problems Solved or Just Beginning?', *South African Law Journal*, 117 (2000), 306–41.

Hirst, Paul, *Associative Democracy* (Amherst, MA: University of Massachusetts Press, 1994), first published by Polity Press, 1994.

—— and Sunil Khilnani (eds.), *Reinventing Democracy* (Oxford: Blackwell, 1996).

Hogg, Peter and Mary Ellen Turpel, 'Implementing Aboriginal Self-Government: Constitutional and Jurisdictional Issues', *The Canadian Bar Review*, 74/2 (1995), 187–224.

Huntington, Samuel, 'The Clash of Civilizations', *Foreign Affairs* (Summer 1993), 22–49.

Ibhawoh, Bonny, 'Between Culture and Constitution: Evaluating the Cultural Legitimacy of Human Rights in the Africa State', *Human Rights Quarterly*, 22 (2000), 838–60.

Isaac, Thomas, 'The 1992 Charlottetown Accord and First Nations Peoples: Guiding the Future', *Native Studies Review*, 8/2 (1992), 109–14.

—— and Mary Sue Maloughney, 'Dually Disadvantaged and Historically Forgotten?: Aboriginal Women and the Inherent Right of Aboriginal Self-Government', *Manitoba Law Journal*, 21/3 (1992), 453–75.

James, Michael Rabinder, 'Communicative Action, Strategic Action, and Inter-Group Dialogue', *European Journal of Political Theory*, 2/2 (2003), 157–82.

Johnson, James, 'Arguing for Deliberation: Some Skeptical Considerations', in Jon Elster (ed.), *Deliberative Democracy* (Cambridge: Cambridge University Press, 1998).

—— 'Liberalism and the Politics of Cultural Authenticity', *Politics, Philosophy, and Economics*, 1/2 (2002), 213–36.

—— 'Why Respect Culture?', *American Journal of Political Science*, 44/3 (2000), 405–18.

Kaganas, F. and C. Murray, 'Law and Women's Rights in South Africa: An Overview', in C. Murray (ed.), *Gender and the New South African Legal Order* (Kenwyn, South Africa: Juta, 1994).

Kahane, David, and Catherine Bell (eds.), *Intercultural Dispute Resolution in Aboriginal Contexts* (Vancouver and Toronto: University of British Columbia Press, 2005).

—— 'What is Culture?: Generalizing About Aboriginal and Newcomer Perspectives', in Catherine Bell and David Kahane (eds.), *Intercultural Dispute Resolution in Aboriginal Contexts* (Vancouver and Toronto: University of British Columbia Press, 2005).

Kaplan, Temma, 'Women's Rights as Human Rights: Grassroots Women Redefine Citizenship in a Global Context', in Patricia Grimshaw, Katie Holmes, and Marilyn Lake (eds.), *Women's Rights and Human Rights: International Historical Perspectives* (Palgrave, 2001).

Kende, Mark, 'Stereotypes in South African and American Constitutional Law: Achieving Gender Equality and Transformation', *Southern California Review of Law and Women's Studies*, 10/1 (2000), 3–33.

Kibria, Nazli, 'The Construction of "Asian American": Reflections on Intermarriage and Ethnic Identity Among Second-Generation Chinese and Korean Americans', *Ethnic and Racial Studies*, 20/3 (1997), 523–44.

Knight, Jack and James Johnson, 'What Sort of Political Equality Does Deliberative Democracy Require?', in James Bohman and William Rehg (eds.), *Deliberative Democracy: Essays on Reason and Politics* (Cambridge, MA, and London: MIT Press, 1997/9).

Koshan, Jennifer, 'Aboriginal Women, Justice, and the Charter: Bridging the Divide?', *University of British Columbia Law Review*, 32/1 (1998), 23–54.

Krikorian, J., 'A Different Form of Apartheid? The Legal Status of Married Women in South Africa', *Queen's Law Journal*, 21 (1995), 221–60.

Krosenbrink-Gelissen, L. E., *Sexual Equality as an Aboriginal Right: The Native Women's Association of Canada and the Constitutional Process on Aboriginal Matters, 1982–1987* (Saarbrücken, Germany: Verlag breitenback, 1991).

Kukathas, Chandran, 'Are There Any Cultural Rights?' *Political Theory*, 20 (1995), 105–39.

—— *The Liberal Archipelago: A Theory of Diversity and Freedom* (Oxford: Oxford University Press, 2003).

Kymlicka, Will, *Liberalism, Community and Culture* (Oxford: Clarendon Press, 1989).

—— 'Two Models of Pluralism and Tolerance', *Analyse & Kritik*, 13 (1992).

—— 'Reply to Modood', *Analyse & Kritik*, 15 (1993), 92–6.

—— *Multicultural Citizenship: A Liberal Theory of Minority Rights* (Oxford: Oxford University Press, 1995).

—— 'Do We Need a Liberal Theory of Minority Rights?: Reply to Carens, Young, Parekh and Forst', *Constellations*, 4/1 (1997).

—— 'Liberal Complacencies', in Joshua Cohen, Matthew Howard, and Martha Nussbaum (eds.), *Is Multiculturalism Bad for Women?* (Princeton, NJ: Princeton University Press, 1999).

—— *Politics in the Vernacular: Nationalism, Multiculturalism, and Citizenship* (Oxford: Oxford University Press, 2001).

LaDuke, Winona, *All Our Relations: All Our Struggles for Land and Life* (Cambridge, MA and Minneapolis, MN: South End Press, 1999).

Larmore, Charles, *Patterns of Moral Complexity* (Cambridge: Cambridge University Press, 1987).

LeBaron, Michelle, 'Learning New Dances: Finding Effective Ways to Address Intercultural Disputes', in Catherine Bell and David Kahane (eds.), *Intercultural Dispute Resolution in Aboriginal Contexts* (Vancouver and Toronto: University of British Columbia Press, 2005).

Levy, Jacob, *The Multiculturalism of Fear* (Oxford: Oxford University Press, 2000).

—— 'Sexual Orientation, Exit and Refuge', in Avigail Eisenberg and Jeff Spinner-Halev (eds.), *Minorities Within Minorities: Equality, Rights, and Diversity* (Cambridge: Cambridge University Press, 2005).

Mackenzie, Catriona, 'Imagining Oneself Otherwise', in Catriona Mackenzie and Natalie Stoljar (eds.), *Relational Autonomy: Feminist Perspectives on Autonomy, Agency, and the Social Self* (Oxford: Oxford University Press, 2000).

—— and Natalie Stoljar (eds.), *Relational Autonomy: Feminist Perspectives on Autonomy, Agency, and the Social Self* (Oxford: Oxford University Press, 2000).

Magardie, K., 'Customary Law Undermines Constitutional Rights', *Daily Mail and Guardian*, June 22, 2000.

Mahajan, Gurpreet, *Identities and Rights: Aspects of Liberal Democracy in India* (Oxford: Oxford University Press, 1998).

Maithufi, I. P. and J. C. Bekker, 'The Recognition of the Customary Marriages Act of 1998 and its Impact on Family Law in South Africa', *Comparative and International Law Journal of Southern Africa*, 35/1 (2002), 182–97.

Mayer, Ann Elizabeth, 'A "Benign" Apartheid: How Gender Apartheid Has Been Rationalized', *UCLA Journal of International Law and Foreign Affairs*, 5 (2000), 237–338.

—— 'Current Muslim Thinking on Human Rights', in Abdullahi An Na'im and Francis Deng (eds.), *Human Rights in Africa: Cross-Cultural Perspectives* (Washington, DC: The Brookings Institution, 1990).

Mbatha, Likhapha, 'Reforming the Customary Law of Succession', *South African Journal on Human Rights*, 18/2 (2002), 259–86.

Means, Angelia, 'Intercultural Law: Justifying Rights to Others', unpublished manuscript (2004).

—— 'Narrative Argumentation: Arguing with Natives,' *Constellations* 9/2 (2002), 221–245.

Menon, Ramdas, 'Arranged Marriages Among South Asian Immigrants', *Sociology and Social Research*, 75/4 (July 1989), 180–1.

Menon, Usha, 'Does Feminism Have Universal Relevance? The Challenges Posed by Oriya Hindu Family Practices', *Daedalus* (Fall 2000), 77–99.

Mercredi, Ovide, *Public Hearings, Rounds I–IV*, Royal Commission on Aboriginal Peoples (June 26, 1992).

—— and Mary Ellen Turpel, *In the Rapids: Navigating the Future of First Nations* (Toronto: Viking/Penguin, 1993).

Merry, Sally Engle, 'Changing Rights, Changing Culture', in J. K. Cowan, M. B. Dembour, and R. Wilson (eds.), *Culture and Rights: Anthropological Perspectives* (Cambridge: Cambridge University Press, 2001).

—— and Rachel Stern, 'The Female Inheritance Movement in Hong Kong: Theorizing the Local/Global Interface', *Current Anthropology*, 46/3 (2005), 387–409.

Meyers, Diana, *Self, Society, and Personal Choice* (New York: Columbia University Press, 1989).

—— 'The Rush to Motherhood—Pronatalist Discourse and Women's Autonomy', *Signs*, 26/3 (2001), 735–73.

Mill, John Stuart, *On Liberty* (Indianapolis, IN and Cambridge: Hackett Publishing Co., 1978).

Modood, Tariq, 'Anti-Essentialism, Multiculturalism, and the "Recognition" of Religious Groups', *The Journal of Political Philosophy*, 6/4 (1998).

Mokgoro, Yvonne, 'The Customary Law Question in the South African Constitution', *Saint Louis University Law Journal*, 41 (1997), 1270–89.

Molyneux, Maxine and Shahra Razavi, 'Gender, Justice, Development and Rights', *Report of the United Nations Research Institute for Social Development Workshop* (2000).

Monture-Okanee, Patricia, 'Reclaiming Justice: Aboriginal Women and Justice Initiatives in the 1990's', in *Aboriginal Peoples and the Justice System* (Ottawa: Royal Commission on Aboriginal Peoples, 1993).

—— and Mary Ellen Turpel, 'Aboriginal Peoples and Canadian Criminal Law: Rethinking Justice', *University of British Columbia Law Review*, special issue (1992).

Moore, Erin, *Gender, Law, and Resistance in India* (Tucson, AZ: University of Arizona Press, 1998).

Murray, Christina (ed.), *Gender and the New South African Legal Order* (Kenwyn, UK: Juta, 1994).

Narayan, Uma, 'Essence of Culture and A Sense of History', *Hypatia*, 13/2 (1998), 80–100.

—— 'Minds of Their Own: Choices, Autonomy, Cultural Practices, and Other Women', in Louise Antony and Charlotte Witt (eds.), *A Mind of One's Own: Feminist Essays on Reason and Objectivity* (Boulder, CO: Westview Press, 2002 [2001]).

Nathan, Andrew, 'Universalism: A Particularistic Account', in L. Bell, A. Nathan, and I. Peleg (eds.), *Negotiating Culture and Human Rights* (New York: Columbia University Press, 2001).

Nedelsky, Jennifer, 'Reconceiving Autonomy: Sources, Thoughts and Possibilities', in Leslie Green and A. Hutchinson (eds.), *Law and the Community: The End of Individualism?* (Toronto: Carswell, 1989).

Newham Asian Women's Project, 'Growing Up Young, Asian and Female in Britain: A Report on Self-Harm and Suicide', Newham Asian Women's Project and Newham Innercity Multifund, 1998.

Nhlapo, Thandabantu, 'African Customary Law in the Interim Constitution', in S. Liebenberg (ed.), *The Constitution of South Africa from a Gendered Perspective*

(Belleville, South Africa: Community Law Centre, University of the Western Cape, 1995).

Norton, Anne, 'Review Essay on Euben, Okin and Nussbaum', *Political Theory*, 29/5 (2001), 736–49.

Nussbaum, Martha, *Sex and Social Justice* (Oxford: Oxford University Press, 1999).

—— *Women and Human Development: The Capabilities Approach* (Cambridge: Cambridge University Press, 2000).

—— 'On Hearing Women's Voices: A Reply to Susan Okin', *Philosophy and Public Affairs*, 32/2 (2004), 193–205.

—— and Jonathan Glover (eds.), *Women, Culture and Development: A Study of Human Capabilities* (Oxford: Oxford University Press, 1995).

O'Hare, Ursula, 'Realizing Human Rights for Women', *Human Rights Quarterly*, 21/2 (1999), 364–402.

Okin, Susan, 'Feminism and Multiculturalism: Some Tensions', *Ethics*, 108/4 (1998), 661–84.

—— 'Feminism, Women's Human Rights, and Cultural Differences', *Hypatia*, 13/2 (1998), 32–55.

—— *Justice, Gender and the Family* (New York: Basic Books, 1989).

—— 'Is Multiculturalism Bad for Women', in Joshua Cohen, Matthew Howard, and Martha Nussbaum (eds.), *Is Multiculturalism Bad for Women?* (Princeton, NJ: Princeton University Press, 1999).

—— 'Reply', in Joshua Cohen, Matthew Howard, and Martha Nussbaum (eds.), *Is Multiculturalism Bad for Women?* (Princeton, NJ: Princeton University Press, 1999).

—— ' "Mistresses of Their Own Destiny": Group Rights, Gender, and Realistic Rights of Exit', *Ethics*, 112 (2002), 205–30.

—— 'Poverty, Well-Being and Gender: What Counts, Who's Heard?', *Philosophy and Public Affairs*, 3/3 (2003), 281–316.

—— 'Multiculturalism and Feminism: No Simple Questions, No Simple Answers', in Avigail Eisenberg and Jeff Spinner-Halev (eds.), *Minorities Within Minorities: Equality, Rights, and Diversity* (Cambridge: Cambridge University Press, 2005).

O'Neill, Onora, *Constructions of Reason: Explorations of Kant's Practical Philosophy* (Cambridge: Cambridge University Press, 1989).

—— 'Practices of Toleration', in Judith Lichtenberg (ed.), *Democracy and the Mass Media* (Cambridge: Cambridge University Press, 1990).

—— 'Justice, Gender, and International Boundaries', in Martha Nussbaum and Amartya Sen (eds.), *The Quality of Life* (Oxford: Clarendon Press, 1992).

—— *Towards Justice and Virtue* (Cambridge: Cambridge University Press, 1996).

—— *Bounds of Justice* (Cambridge: Cambridge University Press, 2000).

Oomen, Barbara, 'Group Rights in Post-Apartheid South Africa: The Case of Traditional Leaders', *Journal of Legal Pluralism and Unofficial Law*, 44 (1998), 73–103.

Parekh, Bhikhu, 'Moral Philosophy and its Anti-Pluralist Bias', in David Archard (ed.), *Philosophy and Pluralism* (Cambridge: Cambridge University Press, 1996).

Parekh, Bhikhu, 'A Varied Moral World', in Joshua Cohen, Matthew Howard, and Martha Nussbaum (eds.), *Is Multiculturalism Bad for Women?* (Princeton, NJ: Princeton University Press, 1999).

—— *Rethinking Multiculturalism: Cultural Diversity and Political Theory* (Cambridge, MA: Harvard University Press, 2000).

Peach, Ceri and Günther Glebe, 'Muslim Minorities in Western Europe', *Ethnic and Racial Studies*, 18/1 (1995), 26–45.

Peach, Lucinda, *Legislating Morality: Pluralism and Religious Identity Lawmaking* (Oxford: Oxford University Press, 2002).

Peters, Julie and Andrea Wolper (eds.), *Women's Rights, Human Rights: International Feminist Perspectives* (New York and London: Routledge, 1995).

Pettit, Phillip, *Republicanism: A Theory of Freedom and Government* (Oxford and New York: Oxford University Press, 1997).

Phillips, Anne, 'Feminism and Liberalism Revisited: Has Martha Nussbaum Got it Right?', *Constellations*, 8/2 (2001), 249–66.

—— 'Multiculturalism, Universalism, and the Claims of Democracy', in Maxine Molyneux and Shahra Razavi (eds.), *Gender Justice, Development, and Rights* (Oxford: Oxford University Press, 2002).

—— and Moira Dustin, *U.K. Initiatives on Forced Marriage: Regulation, Dialogue and Exit*, Nuffield Foundation policy research paper, (2003).

Platiel, Rudy, 'Aboriginal Women Divide on Constitutional Protection', *The Globe and Mail*, January 20, 1992.

—— 'Gender Issue Sparks Native Disunity: Women's Group Charges Constitutional Proposals Will Undermine Female Equality', *The Globe and Mail*, July 20, 1992.

—— 'Native Women Fear Loss of Rights', *The Globe and Mail*, July 12, 1992.

Quebec Native Women's Association, *Presentation to Hearing on the First Nations Constitutional Circle* (Montreal: QNWA, February 5, 1992).

Quonq, Jonathan, 'Are Identity Claims Bad for Deliberative Democracy?', *Contemporary Political Theory*, 1/3 (2002), 307–28.

Ramaswami, Srikant, 'Marriages in Little India: Arranged Marriages, Union of Families', *Little India*, 5/7 (1995), 1–10.

Rao, Arati, 'The Politics of Gender and Culture in International Human Rights Discourse', in Julie Peters and Andrea Wolper (eds.), *Women's Rights, Human Rights: International Feminist Perspectives* (New York and London: Routledge, 1995).

Rawls, John, 'Justice as Fairness: Political not Metaphysical', *Philosophy and Public Affairs*, 14 (1985), 223–51.

—— *Political Liberalism* (New York: Columbia University Press, 1993).

Raz, Joseph, 'How Perfect Should One Be? And Whose Culture Is?', in Joshua Cohen, Matthew Howard, and Martha Nussbaum (eds.), *Is Multiculturalism Bad for Women?* (Princeton, NJ: Princeton University Press, 1999).

—— 'Multiculturalism: A Liberal Perspective', *Ethics in the Public Domain: Essays in the Morality of Law and Politics* (Oxford: Clarendon Press, 1994).

—— *Ethics in the Public Domain: Essays in the Morality of Law and Politics* (Oxford: Clarendon Press, 1994).

—— *The Morality of Freedom* (Oxford: Clarendon Press, 1986).

Reitman, Oonagh, 'On Exit', in Avigail Eisenberg and Jeff Spinner-Halev (eds.), *Minorities Within Minorities: Equality, Rights, and Diversity* (Cambridge: Cambridge University Press, 2005).

Renteln, Alison, *The Cultural Defense* (Oxford: Oxford University Press, 2004).

Romay, Celina, 'Black Women and Gender Equality in a New South Africa: Human Rights Law and the Intersection of Race and Gender', *Brooklyn Journal of International Law*, 21 (1996), 857–98.

Rorty, Amélie, 'The Hidden Politics of Cultural Identification', *Political Theory*, 22/1 (1994), 152–66.

Royal Commission on Aboriginal Peoples, *Public Hearings, Rounds I–IV* (Ottawa, 1992).

Royal Commission on Aboriginal Peoples, *Overview of the First Round* (Ottawa, 1992).

Royal Commission on Aboriginal Peoples, *Overview of the Third Round* (Ottawa, 1992).

Royal Commission on Aboriginal Peoples, *Aboriginal Peoples and the Justice System* (Ottawa, 1993).

Royal Commission on Aboriginal Peoples, *Final Report of the Royal Commission on Aboriginal Peoples* (Ottawa, 1996).

Saharso, Sawitri, 'Female Autonomy and Cultural Imperative: Two Hearts Beating Together', in Will Kymlicka and Wayne Norman (eds.), *Citizenship in Diverse Societies* (Oxford: Oxford University Press, 2000).

—— 'Is Freedom of the Will but a Western Illusion? Individual Autonomy, Gender and Multicultural Judgement', in Barbra Arneil, Monique Deveaux, Rita Dhamoon, and Avigail Eisenberg (eds), *Sexual Justice, Cultural Justice: Critical Perspectives in Political Theory and Practice* (forthcoming 2006, Routledge).

Sarat, Austin and Thomas Kearns, 'The Unsettled Status of Human Rights: An Introduction', in Austin Sarat and Thomas Kearns (eds.), *Human Rights: Concepts, Contests, and Contingencies* (Ann Arbor, MI: University of Michigan Press, 2001).

Scholte, Jan Aart, 'Globalization and (Un)Democracy', in *Globalization: A Critical Introduction* (New York: St. Martin's Press, 2000).

Scott, David, 'Culture in Political Theory', *Political Theory*, 31/1 (2003), 92–115.

Scott, James C., *Weapons of the Weak: Everyday Forms of Peasant Resistance* (New Haven, CT: Yale University Press, 1985).

Seidman, Gay, 'Institutional Dilemmas: Representation Versus Mobilization in the South African Gender Commission', *Feminist Studies*, 29/3 (2003), 541–63.

Sen, Amartya, *Development as Freedom* (New York: Random House, 1999).

—— 'How Does Culture Matter', in Vijayendra Rao and Michael Walton (eds.), *Culture and Public Action* (Stanford, CA: Stanford Social Sciences [Stanford University Press], 2004).

Shachar, Ayelet, 'On Citizenship and Multicultural Vulnerability', *Political Theory*, 28 (2000), 64–89.

Shachar, Ayelet, *Multicultural Jurisdictions: Cultural Differences and Women's Rights* (Cambridge: Cambridge University Press, 2001).

Shapiro, Ian, *Democratic Justice* (New Haven, CT: Yale University Press, 1999).

Shiva, Vandana, 'Food Rights, Free Trade, and Fascism', in Matthew Gibney (ed.), *Globalizing Rights: The Oxford Amnesty Lectures 1999* (Oxford: Oxford University Press, 2003).

Shweder, Richard, 'What About "Female Genital Mutilation"? And Why Understanding Culture Matters in the First Place', *Daedalus* (Fall 2000), 208–32.

Song, Sarah, 'Majority Norms, Multiculturalism, and Gender Equality', *American Political Science Review*, 99/4 (2005), 473–89.

South African Commission on Gender Equality, *Submission to the Justice Portfolio Committee* (September 30, 1998).

South African Law Commission, *The Harmonisation of the Common Law and Indigenous Law* (1999).

Spinner-Halev, Jeff, 'Difference and Diversity in an Egalitarian Democracy', *The Journal of Political Philosophy*, 3/3 (1995).

—— 'Feminism, Multiculturalism, Oppression, and the State', *Ethics*, 112 (2001), 84–113.

—— *Surviving Diversity: Religion and Democratic Citizenship* (Baltimore, MD: Johns Hopkins University Press, 1994).

Stacey-Moore, Gail, 'Aboriginal Women, Self-Government, the Canadian Charter of Rights and Freedoms, and the 1991 Canada Package on the Constitution', *Address to the Canadian Labour Congress* (Ottawa, December 3, 1991).

Stewart, John, 'Democracy and Local Government', in Paul Hirst and Sunil Khilnani (eds.), *Reinventing Democracy* (Oxford: Blackwell, 1996).

Sullivan, Donna, 'Gender Equality and Religious Freedom: Toward a Framework for Conflict Resolution', *New York Journal of International Law and Politics*, 24 (1992), 795–856.

Sunder, Madhavi, 'Piercing the Veil', *Yale Law Journal*, 112 (2003), 1399–472.

Taylor, Charles, 'The Politics of Recognition', in Amy Gutmann (ed.), *Multiculturalism and the 'Politics of Recognition'* (Princeton, NJ: Princeton University Press, 1992).

—— 'Conditions of an Unforced Consensus on Human Rights', in Joanne Bauer and Daniel Bell (eds.), *The East Asian Challenge for Human Rights* (Cambridge: Cambridge University Press, 1999).

Tully, James, 'The Crisis of Identification: The Case of Canada', *Political Studies*, 42 (1994), 77–96.

—— *Strange Multiplicity: Constitutionalism in an Age of Diversity* (Cambridge: Cambridge University Press, 1995).

Turpel, Mary Ellen, 'Patriarchy and Paternalism: The Legacy of the Canadian State for First Nations Women', *Canadian Journal of Women and the Law*, 6/1 (1993), 174–92.

—— and P. A. Monture, 'Ode to Elijah: Reflections of Two First Nations Women on the Rekindling of Spirit at the wake for the Meech Lake Accord', *Queen's Law Journal*, 15/2: 345–59.

United Kingdom Home Office, *A Choice By Right: Report of the Working Group on Forced Marriages* (London, 2000).

United Kingdom Home Office, *Forced Marriage Progress Report* (London: British Government Publication, 2001).

—— 'Forced Marriage Progress Report—Update on the Joint Action Plan and Package of Care', November 6, 2001.

United Kingdom Foreign and Commonwealth Office, *Forced Marriage—The Overseas Dimension*, Report of the Foreign and Commonwealth Office (2000).

United Nations General Assembly, *Convention on the Elimination of All Forms of Discrimination Against Women* (1979).

United Nations Research Institute for Social Development Workshop, *Gender, Justice, Development and Rights* (Geneva, 2003).

Valadez, Jorge, *Deliberative Democracy, Political Legitimacy, and Self-Determination in Multicultural Societies* (Boulder, CO: Westview Press, 2001).

Van Der Meide, W., 'Gender Equality v. Right to Culture', *South African Law Journal*, 116 (1999), 100–12.

Venter, Christine M., 'The New South African Constitution: Facing the Challenges of Women's Rights and Cultural Rights in Post-Apartheid South Africa', *Journal of Legislation*, 21/1 (1995), 1–22.

Voice, Paul, *Morality and Agreement: A Defense of Moral Contractarianism* (New York: Peter Lang, 2002).

Warren, Mark, 'A Second Transformation of Democracy?', in B. Cain, R. Dalton, and S. Scarrow (eds.), *Democracy Transformed? Expanding Political Opportunities in Advanced Industrial Democracies* (Oxford: Oxford University Press, 2003).

Weinstock, Daniel, 'Is "Identity" a Danger to Democracy?', in I. Primoratz and A. Pavkovic (eds.), *Identity, Self-Determination and Secession* (Aldershot: Ashgate Publishing, 2006).

White, Carolyn, *Gender on the Agenda: Will Women Gain Equality in the New South Africa?* (Johannesburg: Centre for Policy Studies, 1995).

Wikan, Unni, *Generous Betrayal: Politics of Culture in the New Europe* (Chicago and London: University of Chicago Press, 2002).

Williams, Melissa, 'Justice Towards Groups: Political Not Juridical', *Political Theory*, 23/1 (1995), 67–91.

—— *Voice, Trust, and Memory: Marginalized Groups and the Failings of Liberal Representation* (Princeton, NJ: Princeton University Press, 1998).

Wing, A. K. and E. P. de Carvalho, 'Black South African Women: Towards Equal Rights', *Harvard Human Rights Journal*, 8 (1995), 57–100.

Wing, Susanna, 'Questioning the State: Constitutionalism and the Malian *Éspace d'Interpellation Démocratique*', *Democratization*, 9/2 (2002), 121–47.

Working Group on Forced Marriage, *A Choice By Right: Report of the Working Group on Forced Marriages* (London: British Home Office Communications Directorate, 2000).

Young, Iris, *Inclusion and Democracy* (Oxford: Oxford University Press, 2000).

Young, Iris, 'Activist Challenges to Deliberative Democracy', in James Fishkin and Peter Laslett (eds.), *Debating Deliberative Democracy* (Blackwell, 2003).

Young, Robert, 'Autonomy and Socialization', *Mind*, 89 (1980), 565–76.

—— *Personal Autonomy: Beyond Negative and Positive Liberty* (New York: St. Martin's Press, 1986).

Court cases:

Canada:

Native Women's Association of Canada v. Canada (1992), 4 C.N.L.R. (Federal Court of Appeals).

U.S.

Santa Clara Pueblo v. Martinez 436 U.S. 49 (1978).

South Africa:

Bhe and Others v. The Magistrate, Khayelitsha and Others, case #CCT 49/03.

Mabena v. Letsoalo (1998 [2] SA 1068 [T])

Mthembu v. Letsela and Another, 1997 (2) SA 936 (Constitutional Court).

Shibi v. Sithole and Others, case #CCT 69/03.

South African Human Rights Commission and Another v. President of South Africa and Another, case #CCT 50/03.

Interviews:

Interview with Najma Ibrahim, Muslim Women's Helpline, London, June 12, 2001.

Interview with Likhapa Mbatha, Centre for Applied Legal Studies, University of the Witswaatersrand, Johannesburg, January 25, 2002.

Interview with Cathy Albertyn, Centre for Applied Legal Studies, University of the Witswaatersrand, Johannesburg, January 24, 2002.

Interview with Coriaan de Villiers, Women's Legal Centre, Cape Town, January 18, 2002.

Interview with Johanna Kehler, National Association of Democratic Lawyers, Cape Town, January 18, 2002.

Newspaper Articles

'Arranged Marriages Under the Spotlight', *Press Association Newsfile*, June 29, 2000.

'Native Women Lose Bid for Spot at Talks: Exclusion from Constitutional Negoti-ations Doesn't Violate Rights, Judge Rules', *The Globe and Mail*, April 1, 1992.

Index